More Than a Game

MORE THAN A GAME

A Classic Cricket Collection

Edited by

David Rayvern Allen

VICTOR GOLLANCZ
LONDON

First published in Great Britain 1995
by Victor Gollancz
An imprint of the Cassell Group
Wellington House, 125 Strand, London WC2R 0BB

This compilation © David Rayvern Allen 1995

A catalogue record for this book is
available from the British Library.

ISBN 0 575 06142 1

Typeset by Rowland Phototypesetting Ltd,
Bury St Edmunds, Suffolk
Printed in Great Britain by
St Edmundsbury Press Ltd,
Bury St Edmunds, Suffolk

Contents

Acknowledgements

The editor and publishers wish to thank the following for permission to include their work and for their kindness in equating a need with the clash of the coin: Alex Bannister; Scyld Berry; Henry Blofeld; Mihir Bose; Mike Brearley; David Frith; Kenneth Gregory; Eric Hill; Desmond H. Jackson; Martin Johnson; Simon Kuper; Tony Lewis; Robin Marlar; Christopher Martin-Jenkins; Hugh McIlvanney; Sam Mendes; Geoffrey Moorhouse; Mark Nicholas; Peter Roebuck; Paul Sheahan; E. W. 'Jim' Swanton; John J. Warr.

Appreciation is also due to the *Daily Telegraph* for the articles on 'Malcolm Marshall' and 'Shane Warne'; the *Sunday Telegraph* for 'Brave New World'; the *Guardian* for 'Pleasures of the Civilised Mind'; the *Independent* for 'Message from Oz'; the *Observer* for 'Sri Lanka' and 'Viv Richards'; the *Financial Times* for 'The Global Pavilion'; the *Sunday Times* for 'A Monument to Heart and Craft', 'Mike Brearley' and 'Master of the Universe'; *The Cricketer* for 'Return from Australia'; *Wisden Cricket Monthly* for 'The Shambles of Things to Come'; Leslie Frewin, Keith Lewis and The Lord's Taverners, Australia; B. T. Batsford Ltd, London; Pavilion Books Ltd; Pelham Books Ltd; The Peters Fraser & Dunlop Group Ltd for permission to reprint 'Sutcliffe and I'; David Higham Associates for 'Hutton's Match' (*Days Without Sunset* – Denzil Batchelor); Robert Anderson and Stanley Paul Ltd for 'A Sunday in the Country'; and Reed Consumer Books Ltd for 'Fred'.

Extensive efforts have been made to contact copyright holders; in a handful of cases this has proved impossible. The publishers would welcome hearing from the owners of such material.

Preface

Apart from anything else, an anthology is meant to entertain, inform and relive and hopefully this one meets those requirements. If any excuse is needed for another collection on cricket it is that, unlike some predecessors, here the balance is tilted away from the so-called Golden Age to the more immediate past.

Neville Cardus is generally thought to have opened the studded door to the best writing in the cricket library, and his contemporaries and successors have not been slow to stock the shelves. Most of the current crop who process words for national newspapers and books do so with insight and no little wit. Added to which, there would appear to be a growing number of front-rank players who forsake the playing area for a lap-top view and bring to their writing an on-field authority as well as a different dimension. In this book alone, around a quarter of the contributors have played at county, state or international level since the Second World War.

My choice started on the basis of what interests me might well interest others. It continued with a search for logical if stray connections. Borne in mind also was the need for comment globally and domestically. Therefore journalist Shiva Naipaul's pragmatic look at Sri Lanka's emergence was equally as compelling as commentator Henry Blofeld's impressions of his early cricketing days in Norfolk. Just as attractive was the chance of juxtaposing one-time Australian Test batsman Paul Sheahan's colonial view of social games in Hampshire, where the windows of adjoining houses were in constant danger of being broken, with Martin Johnson's *Independent* message from Oz where the only things to be broken were the bones of the England side.

The game worldwide is given a whistle-stop survey by Simon Kuper with separate studies of the Indian sub-continent and South

Africa. Writer Mihir Bose transmits an almost video-like quality
to his description of the urban environment of Bombay and cricket
played on a stone-chipped, coal-tarred track known as the gully
with a sewer at square-leg and the clamour of the city-centre
maidan with its matted grass criss-crossed by tiny canals. And the
same feeling of being on the spot is to be found in the recently
deceased broadcaster Marshall Lee's picture of Sacboc matches on
grassless wickets in 'corrugated iron sort of' places in the
Transvaal.

There is, as well, a sojourn in Pakistan and, in particular, the
Dharampura district of Lahore, the backdrop for a feature on
Pathan leg-spinner Abdul Qadir by Scyld Berry that is unusual
and appealing not only for its glimpses of Muslim etiquette but
also of the Byzantine intricacies that surround cricket in that part
of the world.

Different arenas and different observations. The former Middlesex and England fast-medium bowler John Warr transposes his
mastery of the after-dinner speech to words on the page with a
funny yarn about celebrity cricket in Sussex where recognizable
characters parade their egos in an attempt to disguise their shortcomings. And, staying close to the Downs, a tale of Tillingfold – in
reality the village of Storrington – by Hugh de Sélincourt originally
penned for the old *Cornhill Magazine*. De Sélincourt earned the
approbation of no less a luminary than J. M. Barrie, who declared
the former's fictional account of 'The Cricket Match' 'the best that
has ever been written about cricket or any other game'.

However, the Test match stage dominates: a retrospective from
Geoffrey Moorhouse on the encounters of one hundred years
between the old enemies England and Australia; an introspective
from Denzil Batchelor on the nearly immortal feat of Len Hutton
in what could have been an interminable game at the Oval in 1938;
and the extrovert, unequivocal opinions of Jack Fingleton on the
never-to-be-forgotten tie between Australia and the West Indies
at Brisbane in 1960.

But what makes the players who made the matches? Many have
tried to find out. The personality assessments are candid and

revealing but not unkind. Each writer finds his own approach to the truth. From the West Indies there is the conceptual analysis of Rohan Kanhai by Trinidadian philosopher C. L. R. James; a valuation of Barbadian Malcolm Marshall by his Hampshire county captain Mark Nicholas; and an appraisal of Antiguan Viv Richards by award-winning sports columnist Hugh McIlvanney. The Caribbean contingent is completed with Robin Marlar's words of wisdom for Brian Lara as he strives to carry on as a colossus.

The game in Australia is not forgotten. *Wisden Cricket Monthly* editor David Frith reminds us that he once held the same position with *The Cricketer* magazine, which first published his poignant piece on the Queensland Aboriginal fast bowler Eddie Gilbert. The description of his search to find a soul lost in his private world in a psychiatric ward is moving in the extreme and leaves a feeling of desolation. And the clear reasoning of Christopher Martin-Jenkins is put to good use as he discusses the wiles and match-winning performances of a product of the Adelaide Cricket Academy, Shane Warne.

A quorum of England captains also come under the spotlight. The fact that three of them opened the innings and one continues to do so means that they are all used to facing the salvoes, although these probes on paper are shafts of light rather than lethal blows. If sometime sports editor of the *Observer* Clifford Makins found Ted Dexter something of an enigma, theatre director Sam Mendes has had no doubts about his hero-worship of Mike Brearley, 'who arranged the field like a visual artist . . .' Brearley himself describes what it is like to face the hostile deliveries of Jeff Thomson and when doing so perhaps surprisingly preferred to provide his own soundtrack of the beginning of Beethoven's first Rasoumoffsky Quartet rather than the opening bars of the same composer's Fifth Symphony. At least it was a victory of a sort to be there at all.

With the other two it is a question of appreciation by their own kind. A pair of opening batsmen for Somerset albeit four decades apart, Eric Hill and Peter Roebuck, look at David Sheppard and Michael Atherton respectively. Hill focuses on a stroke that in his opinion changed the direction of a Test match and Roebuck hails the current England captain as the finest batting technician since Geoffrey Boycott.

Yorkshire refused to be ignored and two of their favourite sons receive superbly sculpted studies from that grand old man of English literature, J. B. Priestley, and the master commentator, John Arlott. Priestley relishes with tongue not entirely in cheek the similarities between Herbert Sutcliffe and himself and Arlott almost psychoanalyses Fred Trueman.

The writers themselves are not immune to comment: Arlott attracts an encomium from Cardus and Cardus in turn is the recipient of a tribute by Kenneth Gregory that was broadcast for his seventy-fifth birthday, in 1964. Another broadcast salute was for the fortieth anniversary of E. W. Swanton's first radio cricket commentary from the Oval in 1938. In this instance 'Jim' himself takes a reflective look at the highlights of that period. He is also the subject of a companion article by Tasmanian magistrate Desmond Jackson about his time as a prisoner of the Japanese in the jungle at Tarso on the Burma–Siam Railway. In those grim surroundings a form of escapism was provided by mounting weekly 'Radio Newsreel' programmes: 'Good evening. This is the Allied Broadcasting transmitting from Tarso and tonight "Radio Newsreel" brings you a cricketing feature about the world's greatest batsman . . .'

A rapt audience sitting around the horseshoe-shaped hill listened to Major Swanton outlining the feats of the boy from Bowral interspersed with simulated commentary and pauses for protocol to acknowledge passing Japanese guards. But enough, for the story is there to be told by a fellow POW who was present in the crowd.

Earlier and more pleasant times are brought to life by Sir Robert Menzies, and also Alex Bannister, with his re-enactment of W. G. Grace's venture to the Australian outback in 1873.

This tour invitation, however, is of a sedentary nature and is for voyeurs as well as voyageurs. It is brought suitably to a close with two pieces: one from former England captain Tony Lewis taking a look into a crystal ball in 1975, and then, in the early 1980s, that man of many parts, Dennis Castle, amusingly visualizing the state of the art in this very year, 1995. With hindsight, this droll benedictory – did I hear, epitaph? – makes one realize that fantasy and reality can be locked together.

Here then, is a book-full of views which help confirm the prejudice that the game of cricket is still, for so many, more a way of life.

The Doctor in the Bush

ALEX BANNISTER

From the uppermost tier of the stadium at Kipling's ancient Lahore you can look across the plain and down on the distant city – a city in the permanent choke of dust raised by millions of feet. I remember Ron Roberts, Leslie Smith of Reuters and myself standing there at the end of a Test Match between Pakistan and England and wondering how we were going to get back to the hotel, shower and change, and be at the airport in time to catch the plane for the next stage of MCC's tour.

The team coach had long since gone. Taxis belonged to another world. Camels were plentiful enough, but their low-speed gear hardly matched our needs. We wandered to ground level. Suddenly, as if conjured up by some Oriental magic, a horse and trap emerged from the dust and darkness. The driver's pointed whip invited us to take seats.

The passenger accommodation was a narrow, low-slung, uncushioned bench already tilted dangerously downwards. By the time we were aboard, complete with typewriters and briefcases, the outer rim scraped the road. At any moment it seemed inevitable that the seriously outweighted horse would be lifted high into the night.

Our backs were to the driver. Not that we had enjoyed any verbal contact from the start. We had not started long before we realised we had not told him where we wanted to go, but there was no time for lesser details – we were too busy holding on. Only by hunching knees firmly into chins, and assuming postures which excited attention even in the land of the yogi, were we able to retain our positions.

The horse maintained a steady trot. Then, halfway home, Ron suddenly remembered he had forgotten to write a much-needed article. After some extraordinary manipulations and contortions he managed to rest his typewriter on his hunched knees, where it rose and fell in sympathetic rhythm to the clip-clop of the horse. To help him hold his position we pressed hard on him from both sides and, firmly enclamped in his human vice, Ron tapped his tortuous way through the dimly lit outer suburbs of Lahore. At one stage the sight of three Englishmen, one endeavouring to type, perched on the back of a sloping seat, provoked a considerable following of curious and excited cyclists. The rumour was that we were advertising a film.

On reaching the hotel – no doubt we were favoured by some uncanny horse sense – the driver's first act was to kiss his trusty charge. Ron, always generous, was so touched that he gave the driver an extra tip of five rupees, whereupon another ample kiss was planted. Alas, this further demonstration of affection went unrewarded, as Leslie, temporarily blinded by dust, was unable to see, and I was suffering from severe cramp – which again provided much entertainment to a considerable number of bystanders.

Miraculously we caught our plane, and I began to think of the days when our little adventure would have been taken as part of the day's routine by touring cricketers. When Dr W. G. Grace went to Australia in 1873 it took 52 days – and that was an improvement on the two previous English sides which had gone there.

Grace left Southampton on 23 October and arrived at Melbourne on 13 December. There was a frightening storm in the Mediterranean and the ship, going on the wrong side of a buoy, was stuck in the mud of the Suez Canal for the best part of a day. At Alexandria angry words were passed with the British Consul, who had expected the team to go ashore and play a match, and the party had to change ships at Colombo. The second was smaller and not to the Doctor's liking. At King George's Sound there was a brief shore excursion to watch an exhibition of boomerang throwing.

The Doctor, trying his hand, missed decapitating J. A. Bush by inches, and was forced to reprimand some of the professionals who had laughed loud and long at the incident.

On arriving at Melbourne the party went to the South Melbourne cricket ground to watch a cup match and were told by an official that the Australians managed their crowds better than the English at home. Within 15 minutes an umpire's decision caused a riot, and the match was abandoned.

Humphrey, one of the leading players, became the first casualty when he was thrown out of a trap driving to a match and fell on a tree stump. Leaving Ballarat for a 74-mile journey to Stawell, the Doctor found the track quite undeserving the description of a road. Some of the team flatly refused to take their seats when they saw the condition of the coach. Eventually, after much coaxing by their captain, they did so.

We left at 8.30 a.m. [wrote the Doctor]. The first 15 miles were through cultivated country, and the roads were tolerably decent, but for the remaining 60 miles we endured agonies. The horses laboured along up to their hocks in white dust, with which we were literally cloaked, so that we looked all the world like so many millers as we sat on the jolting and rickety vehicle.

To break the monotony of the journey, two members of the team, who had guns with them, amused themselves, if not their comrades, by banging at the magpies and parrots as we went along.

The secretary of the Stawell Cricket Club, and a few other enthusiasts in the neighbourhood, came twenty miles from home to meet us at Ararat. Four miles off Stawell it seemed as if the whole town had turned out *en masse* to greet us. As we approached the crowd cheered wildly, and two brass bands struck up a welcoming strain.

The horses in one of the wagonettes at once took fright and overturned the vehicle. Luckily, though the trap was smashed to atoms, no one was injured.

After all that the state of the pitch was found to be so bad that cricket was farcical. One slow ball at the Doctor stuck in the dust and never reached him. A plague of flies sweeping across the field added to the discomforts and the local side won by 10 wickets.

As the fly-bitten players assembled to leave, presumably with no other emotion than relief, torrential rain began to fall – much to the joy of the local inhabitants who had suffered a long and severe drought. The team were unable to share their unbridled enthusiasm. Soon the wheels of the coaches sank almost to the level of the axles in thick, clogging mud. The track was reduced to a virtual river of mud. The unfortunate players became drenched to the skin, and in the driving, pitiless rain over 31 miles were covered in five hours.

After a short stay at a small township for dinner – a crude meal but nevertheless welcome, observed the Doctor – the party set off again. They came to a slight incline. The horses jibbed, and six players had no alternative but to return to the town. The rest eventually arrived at their destination nearing midnight after 19 hours on the road. They were drenched to the skin, and the luggage, including the cricket bags, was a soggy mess.

The Doctor had just retired to bed when there was a knocking at his door so loud that he jumped up in alarm and banged his head on the bed rail. The caller was a local newspaper reporter. 'I did not think that midnight was the right hour for a man who had been travelling all day in the rain to encounter an interviewer', Grace observed with commendable dignity. Later the intrepid reporter made the proud boast that no less than 15 years before he had predicted that the results of cricket matches in Australia would be sent to England by cable. A prophet indeed!

Another journey by Grace's team, whose results were being sent to England by cable, was made in a small coastal steamer hugging the Victorian coast. The ship was uncomfortable, and even the strong breezes could not defeat the stench of burning oil. If the cable had been used to send the comments of the sick and harassed travellers they might well have been more entertaining, if slightly less informative, than the scores of the cricket matches.

The entire party surrendered to the constant pitching and rolling of the small steamer in vicious seas. The smells persisted, and the Doctor gasped on landing, 'The worst 15 hours I have ever spent at sea.'

Two days were spent in recuperation at Melbourne, and then there was nothing for it but to press on. The seas from Melbourne to Sydney were no less inhospitable, and no sooner had the ship left the protection of the harbour than the sickness started all over again. Indeed, the bouts of sickness and depression (for there are few depressions worse than sea sickness) affected the players' form.

After another nightmarish voyage, which took 72 hours instead of the scheduled 48, there was – understandably – a flat refusal to return to the ship once it reached dry land. So the last 100 miles were travelled by coach. Unfortunately somewhere in the darkness of the bush the driver lost his way. Rain began to fall and it seemed a long, long time before the dawn broke and the rough track was rediscovered.

Another nerve-shattering experience was to come. To reach Bathurst, on the other side of the Blue Mountains, a train had to make what must have been a unique journey. The ascent began with the line twisting round one of the mountains, and continued with a zig-zag course up the slope of another. The curves were so sharp that the tail-end coaches had a clear view of the straining locomotive. At times the engine was unable to turn, so acute were the bends. The coaches were then pulled along one section of the line and shunted up the next.

The railway, though a considerable feat of engineering, aroused the admiration but not the confidence of the team, and at the steepest gradients the strongest fears were expressed. The players were warned not to look down, and they admitted to varying sensations – such as thinking what would happen if a coupling snapped. The outcome would seem to have been certain!

In addition to the freak railway, storms at sea and the discomforts of coach travel, there was the recklessness of Australian four-in-hand drivers, who delighted in galloping their horses downhill. In places where an English driver would have prudently used his brakes, the Australians were apt to let rip and proceed at breakneck pace. The passengers, including the cricketers, never failed to be terrorised, and though the Doctor was wont to protest in the strongest if squeaky terms, the drivers cracked their whips, laughed and urged the horses on at even greater speeds.

As the adventurous tour ended the Doctor was threatened with court proceedings because he would not exceed the agreed number of matches. Today, the great cricketer, confronted with jets and luxury hotels, might justifiably observe that modern touring is distinctly cushy.

The Cricketers' Bedside Book
1966

Sutcliffe and I

J. B. PRIESTLEY

Herbert Sutcliffe has had such streams of printer's ink, frequently of the vilest quality, poured over him of late that I am sure he will not be offended at the little cupful I propose to add to the torrent. I will, however, offer my apologies to this fine cricketer and fellow Yorkshireman, if only because under cover of his name, which will probably lure so many honest cricketers to this page, I am about to write a very egotistical essay. I have chosen him as my stalking-horse because he and I have many things in common. We are about the same age, come from the same part of the world (though we are not acquainted, I regret to say), and have not entirely dissimilar biographies. Thus, we both served in France, first in the ranks and afterwards as officers, and then, when the war was over, we both became professional entertainers of a rather curious kind. He earned his bread by hitting a ball hard with a shaped piece of willow. I decided to earn mine by setting down on paper various odd fancies and thoughts about men and books. Oddly enough, there are several friends of mine who tell me that they dislike his profession, that a man should not play a game for money, though they do not object to my method of earning a living. They do not seem to see that if it is ridiculous that a man should play cricket for money, it is still more ridiculous that a man should air his feelings for money, that a professional batsman is less absurd than a professional sonneteer. The fact is, of course, that these friends of mine are unjust to Sutcliffe and his fellow professionals because they have not grasped the simple fact that sport and art are similar activities, that none of us, whether we

are batsmen or poets, bowlers or essayists, work away in our fields
or our studies for the money itself. We bat or write because we
have a passion for batting or writing, and only take the money so
that the butcher and baker may be paid while we are so happily
engaged. 'Don't stop', the community says to us, and hands us a
cheque now and then so that we have not to quit the cricket pitch
or the writing desk in order to seek a livelihood. Indeed, it would
not be difficult to turn the tables on these objectors to professional
sport and to prove that it is the amateur who is in the weaker ethical
position, for while he is playing cricket from May to September it
is possible that he is neglecting the estate it is his duty to manage
or the business house from which he draws a salary as director.

Both of us, then, have chosen these odd but by no means dis-
reputable means of earning a living. On the score of money, I do
not suppose there is much difference between us. But here the
likeness ends. Millions bandy his name who have never heard of
me. He himself has probably never seen my name, whereas I know
all about him and read about him every day all through the summer. If he strains a muscle, the evening papers tell me all about it
in great headlines, but if I should die, probably the tiny paragraph
giving the news would never reach the eye of this contemporary
and fellow countryman of mine. Do not misunderstand me, however; there is here no touch of bitterness. Not only is his work
harder than mine, but he is a better performer. If I sit down, tired,
dispirited, to fill these pages, it does not very much matter for I
can muddle through somehow. No wickets are scattered in the
middle of the second paragraph; no howl of disappointment goes
from a vast crowd, to be echoed all over England the next morning;
there is, for me, no melancholy walk back to the pavilion. If
Sutcliffe were to fumble as badly at the wicket as I have fumbled
many a time down a column of writing, his reputation would be
sent flying with the bails. I can mistime my strokes and drop
catches in page after page, but no one is any the wiser. I have only
to tell myself that I will try to do better next time, and have not
to show a shamed face to all England and half the Antipodes. Not
only must he work under conditions far more trying to the nerves

and temper, but he is, as I have said, the better performer. Not for long years, if ever at all, shall I achieve in this prose the grace, the lovely ease, that shines through innings after innings of his. I may pull off a little trick or two before I have done, but such mastery of the medium as he shows is to me only something gleaming on the far horizon, and long before I arrive there, before that distant gleam becomes a full flood of light, I shall probably be a crazy dodderer or dead and forgotten.

Yet these are facts with a double edge. There may be something nerve-racking in the conditions under which he works, but there is something heartening too. If I send a sentence flying to the boundary, no shout goes up to tell me that twenty thousand of my fellow men have followed the glorious stroke. When I take up my pen, there are for me no friendly slaps on the back, no cries of 'Good luck, old man'. I work alone, in silence, and often when all is done I cannot say whether it has been well or badly performed. It is true that no howl greets me if I fumble, but then no cheers come my way if I am on top of the bowling; nothing but silence, broken from time to time by little whispers of stilted praise or disapproval. How curious it would be if our conditions of work were changed about! Sutcliffe would have to go on batting, week after week, without a word, let alone a cheer, reaching his ears, until at last, after he had been slogging away for about two years, a little notice would appear in some newspaper saying: 'Undoubtedly Sutcliffe is proving himself to be one of the younger batsmen to be reckoned with', or 'With these 2500 runs, Sutcliffe is establishing himself as one of our younger cricketers'. And these, it must be understood, would be the complimentary notices, and there would be others. Already he probably imagines that nothing could be more nonsensical than some of the criticisms passed upon him, but if this change were brought about, he would soon realize that there are no limits to solemn nonsense. Thus, I remember once bringing out a book of strictly personal essays, in which it was avowedly my intention to write about myself, yet one newspaper chided me for being egotistical and having so many I's to the page. That newspaper would complain that Sutcliffe used a bat too much

during his innings: 'We should like Mr. Sutcliffe better as a batsman if he did not make such unnecessary use of the bat'. He would
also find himself confronted by a crazy difference of opinion. One
half of the papers would tell him that he did not hit hard enough,
the other half that he hits too hard, until at last, like the sensible
fellow he is, he would decide to laugh at the whole crew of them.

Meanwhile my own position would be so much more exhilarating that it would be embarrassing. I should wake up one morning
and find the country placarded with 'Priestley Disappoints' or
'Wonderful Essay by Priestley'. Now and then the evening papers
would come out with special editions: 'Priestley's Essay Begun.
Latest Reports. Some Good Phrases.' Retired essayists, writing
long reports every other day or so, would analyse every paragraph,
contrast this week's essay with that of a fortnight ago, and comment at length on every change of mood and style. If anything
went wrong with me, all the country would be told about it, just
as it was when Sutcliffe strained a muscle a short time ago. I can
see the placards and headlines: 'Priestley Out of Humour. Says in
No Mood for Work. May Not Write Essay this Week', and there
would probably follow then a long interview with the local wine
merchant, who would tell the reporters that I had just bought a
bottle of Chambertin so that there was still some chance of my
writing after all. There would be warm discussions all over the
country, in newspapers, clubs, bar parlours, on the subject of my
possible inclusion in the England Essay Team. Everybody would
send in lists: Belloc, Lynd, Chesterton, Beerbohm, Lucas, Tomlin-
son and so forth. In the end I should probably be selected as
twelfth man, to wait in the library. Messrs. Belloc and Lynd would
probably be sent in first. But I have no intention of discussing the
composition of this team: all that I wish to point out is that it
would beat Australia in any kind of weather. This is a fact worth
remembering, for after all there are other things in the world
besides games, and England is not ruined just because sinewy
brown men from a distant colony sometimes hit a ball further and
oftener than our men do. And I am sure that Sutcliffe, to whom,
after such a picture of a life passed in the full glare of public

interest, I offer my sympathy, will agree with me, though I hope, for his sake and mine, he will go on gracefully stealing runs, hitting the manful boundary, with more and more power to his elbow.

Open House
1927

Hutton's Match

DENZIL BATCHELOR

Between the first Test at Nottingham, with its brilliant first and second acts and feeble curtain, and the final game at the Oval, our last full pre-war summer drifted irresolute across a vast chequerboard of sunlit and clouded fields. There was the crowded battle-scene at Lord's: a match made glorious by imperial Hammond seen at his proudest, when a desperate early crisis had descended upon his team. More august straight driving, more majestic strokes to carry the covers could not be envisaged even by the morphia-ridden imaginations of those who had watched the colossus Mac-Laren bestriding the whirlwinds of Surrey in the twilight of the Golden Age. Yet for all of Hammond's predominance, for all the trustiness of Paynter, we were not to pass through this game without peril of defeat. The long and lustrous double century of Billy Brown, almost inhumanly perfect if lacking the colours and contours of any very strong personality, was responsible for this. Compton's coolness under fire was needed to save the day for us.

Then came the great blank at Manchester. It was not an interlude I personally regretted. I could never bring myself to hope that the rain would drain off the Old Trafford wicket so that I should have to quit the company of Hanson Carter and J. O'Connor of the Australian teams of long ago, and, above all, of the reminiscential MacLaren. It is arguable whether the best of cricket is not better remembered and talked over than seen. It is imaginable that it is better to listen to great cricketers reliving their royal prime than to watch their puny descendants display their shortcomings.

I should have seen nothing at Manchester to match the story

MacLaren told me of his experience in Philadelphia forty years back. 'There, outside the ground, was a row of houses. Far away, of course – but I'd the eye of an eagle in those days, and I noticed them at once. Not only noticed them – on the red roof of one, high up near the chimney stack, I spotted one blue tile. Just one! Why was it there? They told me in hushed voices. It seemed that years ago, George Bonnor had played on that ground, and that marvellous straight drive of his had carried the little pavilion on the boundary, and the row of elms beyond, and pitched high on the roof of that house outside the ground. It had broken a tile. They had reverently replaced it with that blue tile to mark the spot for evermore.

'"Pooh!" I said when they told me. "That's nothing! I'll break the next one to it."'

The old proconsul pulled himself up from his armchair and thumped his walking-stick fiercely on the ground. 'But my eye was dead out! I missed by several tiles.'

Finally, there was Leeds. There, on a ground traditionally unlucky to England, Australia beat us in the gloaming under equal conditions on a wicket friendly to spin. Bradman's century and Barnett's 57 in the low-scoring first innings sealed the match for them. The wicket-keeper had been put in high above his rightful place in the batting order to hold the fort on Saturday evening. I had sat next to him at dinner that night and asked him how many he expected to make. With unruffled confidence he indicated that he hoped his stamina would not let him down while he ran up his second century: this in a match in which a dozen wickets had already fallen with but one man surpassing thirty. There you have the Australian character in microcosm.

At the game's end we had streamed out into the dusky streets to hear the paper boys crying like curlews: 'Bad news from the Oval! Bad news from the Oval!' The crowds who had watched England defeated in the Test Match with perfect equanimity hurried out of the ground to form long anxious queues to buy the bad news about the county side at Kennington. You could hear cheerful clapping on one side of the fence, and weeping and lamentation on the other. And there you have the Yorkshire character in microcosm.

And so at last to the Oval, and the final Test Match. And so at last to the final weeks of the last full summer of peace: the final carefree days, sunlit and undarkened by the shadow of imminent war, the Indian summer of the pre-atomic age.

Those were, one supposes, the days. The newspaper advertisements urged you to get away from dusty London that August to take a 2,730-mile tour of the Italian Lakes, Milan, Florence, Venice, Rome, Naples and Capri for an inclusive charge of 23 guineas. You were begged, before selecting your new car, to consider the merits of a four-year-old 14.9 horse-power Ford saloon, perfect as to condition and tyres, for £15. If you were looking for a house, why be satisfied with London? In the heart of Surrey, yet within a comfortable distance of Waterloo, you could buy an old mansion in mint condition, with pleasure gardens and park-like grounds extending to three-quarters of an acre, four bedrooms, inglenooks in all three reception rooms, labour-saving kitchen and tiled bathroom for £995; or easy terms arranged.

There was a split in the French Cabinet. Messieurs Ramadier and Frossard (both of whom had left town to climb Mont Blanc) had fomented a Marseilles dock strike in favour of the 40-hour week which Daladier said France could not afford. The Czechoslovak Loan, paying a 7½ per cent dividend, was steady enough in the stock market. Austrian 4½ per cents were up. Captain Eyston had skied up the land speed record from 312 to 347 m.p.h. at Bonneville Salt Flats. A young composer named Benjamin Britten had played his first piano concerto at the Proms. The *Evening Standard* said of him that he was a 'composer who begins by laughing cynically at life and may end by sentimental nostalgia . . . Perhaps in twenty years we shall find him writing ballads swollen with a tearful nostalgia.' The advertisements shouted at us: 'Close of Play means opening "White Label"'; and old men were dolefully reminding us that they remembered the days when the twelve-and-sixpenny elixir could be got for 2s. 9d. a bottle: the same old men who today still dolefully remind us that they remember the days when our thirty-six bobs' worth of drink could – operative word – be got for two and ninepence. No doubt in their time these greybeards laughed cynically at life. Now they are ending, swollen with a tearful, sentimental nostalgia.

And so to the press box at the Oval for the end of an epoch. Fittingly enough, I found myself sitting beside no mere hack dealing in trundlers who despatch the leather or batsmen who defend their castles, but the great A. J. ('Ringside') Hopfinger himself. You will remember Hopfinger. He is the man you all read. His prose has the purity and refinement of Walter Pater moved to chilly ecstasy by the pale gold of the eyelids of a Boltraffio masterpiece. You love Hopfinger because, on top of this, he is ubiquitous. World upheavals have not stopped him, nor the passing of the years. He was there shedding the lustre of his prose's urbanity upon the occasion when Craganour was disqualified after heading Aboyeur home in the Derby of 1913 – the race when the King's horse was brought down in the straight by Miss Emily Davison, that passionate martyr to the Suffragette cause. As a matter of fact (though his description of the race is in two anthologies and has been chosen as an English Unseen for Russian children sitting for the Moscow Matric.) Hopfinger saw neither of these incidents. An uncontrollable sneeze unsighted him as the woman hurled herself at the horse; and a small fly got into his eye at the precise moment that Craganour committed his offence.

Perhaps you're not old enough to remember that Derby of 1913, when women wore hobble skirts and cartwheel hats, and noblemen bought ninepenny glasses of champagne at the bar in the Members' Stand and lit sixpenny cigars with unshaking fingers to show they weren't the worse for wear with the favourite down and a hundred to one shot top of the frame. But you certainly remember the account of Carpentier's victory over Beckett, the grandest roughcast essay on the subject since Hazlitt's coronach on The Gasman. It is true that Hopfinger missed the decisive (indeed the only) blow of the contest, as he was unfortunately lighting a cigarette at that moment.

Then again you will have read, and never forgotten, Hopfinger on the immortal New Zealand *v.* Wales Rugby match of 1906. His seat was precisely over the line at the spot where the New Zealander player did or did not score the try which would have preserved intact for his country her unbeaten record. His judgment on this point is therefore of historic importance; and he has always regretted that – while this in no way impairs his masterly summary of the incident – due to a heated conversation with a friend he happened to be looking in the opposite direction at the critical moment.

If you have handy – and who has not? – the charming little anthology his publishers offered last Christmas, you'll be able to check the long, unwinding Roman road of Hopfinger's career. The ball with which J. G. W. Davies bowled Bradman for a duck at Cambridge (he was having a quick one in the bar); the sixty seconds' defeat of Peter Kane by Jackie Paterson (he was bending down to tie up his shoelace); the triple dead-heat at Windsor twenty years back (he was returning the wave of an old friend who subsequently turned out to be a tic-tac man); the wonderful day at Eastbourne when MacLaren's team of lilywhites beat Australia (he misunderstood the editor's instructions and attended, in error, a Beauty Competition on Brighton Pier). The chapters these events have given us are lapidary things. The rearing waves of time shall not wash away a word of them till the seas are dried up on the Day of Judgment.

Hopfinger was, of course, at Hutton's match. He arrived a little late, having gone to Lord's through a momentary lapse of memory such as any great artiste, hard at work on the second column of his commentary, might be forgiven for suffering. However, an hour or two's steady scrutiny – he is nothing if not conscientious – of the batting of the Club Cricket Conference led him to an examination of the free score card provided by the management, and by lunch-time the well-loved figure was in his traditional place at the Oval, testily demanding mustard to soften the impact of veal and ham pie.

It was a game which took a good deal out of him. While the English second wicket was adding 382 runs the great stylist amused

himself with the composition of a prose poem on Hutton's technique. The fact that he depicted him as a bottle-shouldered left-
hander put a harassed sub-editor upon the horns of a dilemma. In
the early editions he crossed out Hutton and substituted Leyland;
later, when the former survived to make his record score, he sent
the copy through again for the Late Night Final with Hutton
reinstated as the hero and left-hander changed to right. That sub-
editor is still puzzled by the actual events of that historic occasion
– you see, he has Hopfinger's copy on the one hand, and on
the contradictious other, a miserable document claiming to be the
official score card. The sub-editor's own game is dominoes, and
the problem still gives him nightmares.

There are those who think that this monumental occasion
evoked something less than his majestic best from 'Ringside'
Hopfinger. In confidence, he admitted to me that he was disappointed with his own performance for once. 'The fact is,' he
said, 'I suffered from insomnia. *Nothing* would send me off. I
tried *The Times* cross-word puzzle. No good. The reference to
the Christian name of Palestrina's music-master's uncle was, of
course, child's play to me. I solved the clue which involved knowing the value of n to the tenth decimal place. The only thing that
bluffed me was 24 Down (five letters): *He hints blue (Browning)*.
Unfortunately Neville Cardus interferingly leaned over and pencilled in *Hobbs*. I shall never forgive him for that.

'Yes, Hutton had banished sleep. I sat on and on staring at him.
I was hypnotised. Really, you know, when you saw him at work,
there was nothing to say. All that happened was that O'Reilly
wheeled up and sent down a perfect length ball, and Hutton poked
it away for one. It happened over and over again. It always
happened.'

Such were the difficulties confronting poor Hopfinger on that
August evening ten years ago. Fortunately things have improved
since then. I met my friend last Christmas and exchanged with
him memories of what he has aptly named 'the unforgettable
match.' He was vague as to Hutton's actual performance. 'The
Oval match of '38? Hutton? Oh yes – he either made a great many

runs or was almost immediately out. I must look it up when I get home.' But on other points the famous memory was crystal clear. 'The girl brought me a cup of tea in the interval. I distinctly told her *without* sugar. In any case, she'd known me for years; had been bringing me my tea without sugar since the summer Tom Hayward scored 3,518, yet when it came my tea had *at least* two lumps of sugar, and was stone cold into the bargain – *if* you can call it a bargain.'

A few weeks ago I got the agreeable news that this book, containing my own memories of Hutton's Match, will fortunately race to press the full length volume on the subject which Hopfinger's publishers have at last persuaded him to give us. In the circumstances I don't think it would be fair to reveal the inside story, the startling revelations that 'Ringside' Hopfinger has in store for his eager public.

To me at least it seemed that a failure to understand the law of averages was the major factor in Bradman's defeat. He had already lost the toss in four Test Matches running. Surely – one can see the innocent Bowral boy pencilling his calculations to show up for the approval of the team's manager – surely that meant that the odds were 4 to 1 on winning it for the fifth game? Only such a miscalculation could account for taking the field with the attack Bradman relied upon. Waite and McCabe, the opening bowlers, surpassed in towering innocuousness even Hendry and Otto Nothling who opened at Brisbane in the twenties, a pair of names as Test Match trundlers sufficiently grotesque to delight simple Australian music-hall audiences above mothers-in-law, kippers and the facts of life. After Waite and McCabe came O'Reilly and Fleetwood-Smith. Then Barnes, Hassett and Bradman. Call it, if you like, a team of two bowlers, and you will be on the generous side: for slow left-hand bowlers have hardly ever achieved success on the three-ply velvet of the Oval. It was hard to resist the conclusion that a team so destitute of bowling could only have been picked in the belief that it was Bradman's turn to get first innings and score so many runs that a position of moral superiority would be achieved which would force the other side to suicide in sheer despair. McCormick was absent with a reputed touch of neuritis. Frank Ward had never been forgiven for failing in his only English Test Match. A wise captain would have insisted on playing him and White, and indeed any other bowler with an Australian accent to be discovered in South London.

It must be admitted that the English side was also weak in attack. Farnes was the best fast bowler in either country. Bowes was still menacing, with a formidable swerve adding danger to his sustained pace. Verity, playing his last Test Match, was still the only slow left-hander really fit for inclusion on a Kennington wicket. After that you came down to Edrich, very far from being the occasionally hostile bowler he has developed into today; Leyland, almost negligible; and Hammond, who had practically given up bowling for his county. It was a Test team certainly short of one stock bowler, such as Douglas Wright, at this time unfit. It could also have spared one of its wealth of batsmen for an all-rounder, or, indeed, for one more top-class bowler of any type.

As it turned out, none of these things mattered. Hammond did something better than march into action at the head of a great attack. He won the toss.

The game began in a lovely mood of irony that suggested that Bradman was going to be forgiven for risking such an Australian side on a pluperfect wicket, in roaring midsummer weather. Edrich, flicking and hooking, looked a batsman of midget stature. The score was still in the twenties when he was comfortably taken by Hassett off O'Reilly. With Leyland playing the unfailingly accurate bowling with a Yorkshire reverence, the score rose slowly but inevitably. It was machine-made cricket, and there was only one thing to admire about it. That was the fielding. Hardly an Australian heel touched the ground before the tea interval.

The morning cricket had only two moments of sharp sensation. Leyland, immediately he came in, was consummately beaten by a huge leg break from Fleetwood-Smith. It missed the stumps by a margin narrow enough to be whistled at. Leyland played several pensive sketches of the stroke he would like to have made while the team changed places at the over's end. He looked bronzed and solid, and I remembered how in Yorkshire's match at Oxford early in the season I had irreverently greeted him, fielding near the boundary, with an exclamation of dismay at the weight he had put on. 'Think nothing of it,' he had replied. 'I shall be down to exactly right weight for fifth Test Match.' Four Tests had gone by without a sign of Maurice. Now here he was, turning up to keep his promise, trimly ready for the fray, and skilful with his duck's waddle as any acknowledged sprinter in stealing the short runs.

The second escape before the lunch interval was more breath-taking than Leyland's little adventure, and might have had further-reaching consequences. Hutton was batting inexorably, patting his singles between mid-on and mid-wicket, or just out of reach of third man. You felt he had no interest in or lustings after such abominations as tend to make the glamour of the game, the swallow-swift cover drive or the soaring hit over long on. And then, of a sudden, just when we were telling ourselves he was destined for a Yorkshire martyr's death from l.b.w. when the light was waning, he lapsed into humanity. There he went, dancing down the pitch, bat flourished behind him, like McLaren of old. The great sneering googly drifting away from Fleetwood-Smith's hand beat him comfortably. He was a yard out of his ground when the ball curved past the wicket and Barnett missed a clear-cut chance to stump him. He score was thirty-nine at the time. He was as unruffled by the incident as he had been in his first Test innings when a ball had hit his stumps without moving a bail, or as his great model, Sutcliffe, had been years before in Sydney, when he survived a similar ordeal.

Then the game began its slow plod towards late afternoon when even Bradman's squat shadow became elongated and Norman. The Australian tactics were now frankly despairing. A field was set to Fleetwood-Smith that suggested that the whole object of attack was to limit the score to singles. To a great extent it succeeded. Leyland hung back in stodgy defence for five balls of an over: the sixth he twitched round his rump for a single, or, suddenly flat-tening himself down the pitch, cover drove in an arc of speed wide of Hassett's right hand.

Hutton batted as if with Herbert Sutcliffe's hand on his shoulder. When Waite and McCabe came jauntily forward to receive the new ball – for all the world like the youngest pupils coyly wriggling up to present bouquets to Royalty – Hutton played respectful dead-bat shots to over after over of stainless long hops. Here and there a ball was gently whisked towards long leg. Now and then an over-pitched ball was despatched – one needs a verb with a smack of the impersonal about it – through the sparrows disputing for crumbs on the edge of the boundary behind extra cover.

The score rose. The runs accrued. There was a heavy shower at tea-time. It bound the wicket nicely. Not a ball could be induced to hop or slither thereafter. And as the afternoon wore on we began to get glimpses of the wristy elegance of Hutton's late cut – the wringing-the-towel motion that put pace on the lifeless ball through the numb outfield.

At last, in the evening, when in three and a half hours apiece each batsman had accumulated his automatic century, there came sudden jerky variations in the internal routine of the play. They were as disturbing as the sight of a caterpillar suddenly falling out of step with itself, halfway down the long, well-drilled procession of its feet. It took the form of a number of fantastic decisions on the part of Leyland to run singles where there were no singles to run. Once he trotted off on a hopeless chase, and Badcock returned the ball with infallible speed and accuracy – to see Waite, the bowler, break the wicket without the ball in his hand. A great cry of indignation went up from the Falstaffian shadow of the gasometer. 'Pull yourself together, Yorkshire! Play a bit careful, please.' Quite right too. We had a bare 350 on the board, and already one wicket was down. What were they aiming at – a collapse?

Hutton and Leyland responded soberly to the well-meant advice. They collected their next half-dozen runs with long-winded discretion. I found myself recalling a little story of an admiring opponent watching young Jack Hearne gently amassing enough neat cuts and deft placements for a century, all in petit-point.

'What a batsman!' breathed the reverent connoisseur. 'I don't see how anyone could ever get him out. Tell me,' he turned to Hendren batting at the other end, 'can this thing be done? Who got him out last?' 'I did,' replied Pat complacently, 'I ran him out.'

The day's play came to an end at last, and we all filed out of church. 'Tomorrow is another eternity,' Hopfinger said to me as we parted in an atmosphere of mutual bereavement. It was all too true.

Monday's play began with a delicious shower. The sun came out on it, and roused none of the baser instincts in that placid pitch. You cannot pervert the Oval wicket: I remembered again how the rain had made it no worse for Australia twelve years earlier when Chapman's team had recovered the Ashes.

The great O'Reilly did all he could to browbeat the pitch into collaboration. He made two hungering fieldsmen advance on tiptoe to silly mid-on, and he persuaded the wicket to give a ball or two an occasional quick left to hip-height. In the circumstances it was as near to assuming an offensive rôle as outraged virtue could go.

Hutton jogged on, mechanical rather than rhythmical. He was without a flaw in his defence, and his driving was firm and effective if never electrifying, while he cut McCabe's shorter ball with something like relish at last. It seemed as if there could be no possible ending to such a partnership. O'Reilly and Fleetwood-Smith, the only possible combat-group in the Australian team, were tactfully mastered rather than dominated. No other bowler looked as if he were giving the sempiternal pair more than decent net practice. And then, when no one could believe that an end could come, Leyland achieved what no bowler could ever do. He flung his right leg down the wicket and rammed home a full-blooded cover drive meant for the boundary. Hassett, wheeling as the stroke was shaped, got his fingertips to the ball, saw it roll away, grabbed again, and sent home a flying return. Bradman saw a chance with his General's eye, and sprang into action to make the most of it. He pounced across the line of the throw-in, palmed the ball, a red blur in mid-field, and in two huge strides had broken the wicket with Maurice waddling imperturbably a few yards off his second run.

The marvellous partnership had raised the score from 29 to 411. It had rarely given the most heartwhole partisan in the crowd a moment's apprehension – save in the matter of doubt as to the running between the wickets. It was true there was not much bowling to master: no better perhaps than you expect to find in a major county side. But that was not the fault of Hutton or Leyland. They were in serene control from first to last. It cannot be proved they would not have mastered any bowling you could have magicked out of the trapdoor to Hell. They were certainly cool enough and confident enough to expect to, as by divine right of their position in the scheme of things.

From the moment of Leyland's departure the game took a turn for the worse – as if to prove that such a thing was perfectly possible.

The incalculable Hammond came in, in a mood of sour seriousness. He sniffed at the pitch. He gardened away at a suspect spot. He made an occasional sombre pass in the direction of mid-off, which counted one run. Suddenly a ray of genius broke through. He scored twelve off an impeccable over from Fleetwood-Smith. It was as if the Headmaster had suddenly relaxed in the realisation that breaking-up day was tomorrow; and had publicly pulled the leg of one of the most trusted of his prefects – not the head boy, for that would be bad for discipline, but the second in the hierarchy. Then magisterial sternness reasserted itself. We were awed with two hours of platitudes at the wicket, which couldn't have been more ponderous if translated into the speech on prize-giving day. There was only one flash of liveliness: a cover drive that took Hammond to his half-century and sprinted away from Bradman in top gear in the race to the boundary. Then, mercifully, there came a miscalculation of a googly. A sober, inept back-stroke; a howl from the inner circle of fieldsmen – and there was the Headmaster walking out, not exactly to go on the scoot through the holidays, but probably to take the chair at some annual conference on the teaching of dead languages at secondary schools.

His departure brought the game to life for half an hour: the longest period of absolutely vital interest it had enjoyed for a couple of days. The English innings might be settled in a Sargasso Sea of inactivity, but at least it had looked as if there were no question of it ever making port in our lifetime. Now, suddenly, the winds and the waves were a-blow. The ship was fighting the elements. She might yet think herself fortunate if she survived wrecking.

Indeed, for one grand, infernal half an hour Australia attacked again. O'Reilly sent back Paynter, who had pecked at a leg-break with a pad in the wrong place. A shower in the tea interval had sent everybody back on the field refreshed for further efforts, and Waite had shown a sparkle of pace that had bowled young Compton, all boyish grin, untidy curls, and big bat held with the jaunty long-handled grip. Before the second wicket fell 400 was on the board. Now three wickets were down, three of the greatest batsmen in England had gone while nine runs were scored. Against the drab timelessness of the background we had seen a flash of the halcyon thing of beauty – a glimpse, no more, but a glimpse of kingfisher's wings, brilliant and vanished away, before we settled down to subfusc eternity once more.

And, as a matter of fact, it wasn't as bad as that. Hutton's mechanical advance had at least been oiled. When O'Reilly came at him, pugnacious as ever, in a new attack, the dour batsman had answered the challenge with a quick human spark of combativeness. The first ball, of flawless length, was glided with improper elation to the long-leg boundary. The next, over-pitched for once, but writhing through the air with its unborn leg break, saw the left foot swing cavalierly down the pitch and felt the hum of the blade projecting it to the fence before extra cover had time to regroup himself for the chase.

After that, to be sure, the great innings dozed a little. There was an uppish shot through the slips when the eclipsing of R. E. Foster's 287 at Sydney was just round the corner. The score was successfully passed. One more record had receded to the unimportance of mathematics. By the time stumps were drawn on Monday night we had 634 on board, and Hutton had batted for rather less than ten hours for 300 not out. It could hardly be said that at any time in this marathon performance he had dominated the bowling. Still less could it be said that at any time the bowling had looked like making the slightest impression on his incarnate impregnability. We went home and to bed rather regretting an unnecessary break in the action of the drama. Surely you could have trusted Hutton to go on scoring a single off one over and two singles off the next all through the night? The routine had become automatic.

It would be interesting to know how many of the 30,000 who filled every nook and cranny of the Oval on the Tuesday had watched some part of the skyscraping innings in its early stages; and how many had turned up, unwearied by this privilege, from the uncomplicated motive of watching an Englishman beat Don Bradman's record Test Match score. These newcomers at any rate got their wish. As he drew near the mighty total there was a moment of shivering nervousness: a moment when a no-ball from O'Reilly put the record at his mercy – and was missed by a foot by a vast, heaving pull that attempted to lift it into the churchyard to the south of the Hobbs Gates. But history was only delayed. The text-book cut off an unrelaxed leg break from Fleetwood-Smith, brought every Australian up for a handshake, and set the crowd cheering with the knowledge that they too had earned a little reflected immortality by their very presence on such an occasion.

Then, a few minutes before he would have concluded thirteen and a half hours at the wicket, Hutton swung a thoughtless cover drive at O'Reilly's fastest ball. It was the merest mashie-shot, and Hassett, taking it knee-high, ended the vastest innings ever played in a Test Match without so much as stinging the palms of his hands. The final stroke was the one those who watched the gigantic innings will remember longest. It was the only surprise they enjoyed in the whole thirteen hours twenty minutes. For the rest, they clapped to the pavilion and all the way up to his dressing-room a batsman who had seized the opportunity of finding himself presented with the feeblest of bowling on a perfect wicket and on the supreme occasion. He had coped with that situation with the coolness and precision of a chess grandmaster winning a game at his leisure, probably by correspondence.

Back in his dressing-room, the world crowded in upon Hutton. With cheque books flourished brave as an army with banners, business men were at the hero's throat, begging him to attribute his success to drinking somebody's cocoa, or using somebody else's night-lights, or wearing yet another's imperishable suspenders. The youth who a few years back had spent his week's pocket money to watch, on tiptoe over the heads of the crowd, the historic innings he had stricken from the record book, dealt with the situation coolly and sardonically. 'I know how long this'll last,' were the words with which he summed up his high hour of triumph. Herbert Sutcliffe and all Pudsey might well be more proud of him for this unshakable realism than for the thirty-five boundaries or even the 143 singles of this three days' work.

With Hutton gone, the English innings continued to inflate to a pointless grandeur. Joe Hardstaff, never less than a text-book illustration of rectangular rectitude in the matter of the staunching forward stroke, advanced with cautious infallibility to a huge score. Wood of Yorkshire, playing in his first Test Match in early middle age, helped him to add more than a hundred runs with glittering attacking strokes in front of the wicket. Then, within the shadow of the ninth hundred, the final exterminating blow fell upon Australia. Fingleton had already left the match as a casualty. Now Bradman, seventh bowler for his side, was to twist his ankle in the deep rut worn by bowlers of long generations past who had toiled in vain through this innings. He fell like a boxer under an anæsthetising knock-out punch, and when they carried him off the field they carried all the heart the Australians had for the fight with him. Now the victory had become too overwhelming. No one, not even the fiercest patriot in whom envy of Bradman had intensified rivalry to the point of hatred, could relish such a consummation.

Hammond declared in a mood perfunctory enough. He would surely have set about embarrassing the Oval score-boards by going for the thousand runs but for the accident to Bradman. His team would have reached the target, too, for 'Joe wasn't going to let 'em off,' Hammond summed up regretfully.

From now on the game lacked savour. Australia's first innings was anæmic submission, except for the stolid excellence of Billy Brown. He set about batting as if the game were all ahead. He dealt steadily and seriously with Verity's spin, Farnes's penetrative ferocity, Bowes's swerve. He was first in, last out, taken by Hammond at slip, with a catch which in the circumstances can only be described as immorally good.

If the first innings was perfunctory, the second was even less in earnest. There was as little spirit in the last stand as in the collapse at Tunis after the long campaign across the desert. Only Barnes and Ben Barnett went to death flourishing defiance. What moments of delight the innings provided all came from the English bowlers and fieldsmen. Bowes unearthed an exciting ball to bowl C. L. Badcock, as usual wielding a bat heavy enough to have been carved out of Tasmanian teak. And there was a wonderful catch by Wood, wide on the leg side. McCabe had feathered a fine leg glide off Farnes at the Vauxhall end. Our wicket-keeper, standing well back, had time to make almost a full left turn and pounce on the ball as it winged past him, finishing the manœuvre with his face to the pavilion.

And so we came to the end, with England victorious by the trifle of an innings and 579 runs. It was too big a revenge to be worth having.

That was Hutton's match – but, of course, its true hero (if that is the word) was not Hutton, but 'Bosser' Martin, the Oval groundsman. In later years this massive, majestic figure bore himself as if less than justice had been done to his performance on this occasion. They had promised him a timeless Test Match, and told him to prepare a wicket accordingly. When England had scored more than 900 he had been hopeful. But, with the wicket as full of runs as ever, the Australian batting had let him down. Whatever had come over it? As far as his pitch was concerned, there was no reason why *any* innings in that match should have realised less than 900. Such was the Bosser's calm philosophy: and we as spectators can only be grateful to the Australian batsmen that they should have been found inferior in stamina to Mother Earth herself.

Indeed, whoever else we blame, we must not blame 'Bosser' Martin that we are not there still. Well, for my part, I have put most of the time spent since those golden days to worse purpose.

Days Without Sunset
1949

Cricket – A Diversion

ROBERT MENZIES

Shakespeare's Falstaff and I have two elements in common; one, over-weight (to which I now plead guilty), the second, the famous passage in *Henry V*, Act II, Scene iii, in which his death is described so graphically; though I am not yet come to that pass.

> A'parted even just between twelve and one, even at the turning o' the tide: for after I saw him fumble with the sheets and play with flowers and smile upon his fingers' ends, I knew there was but one way; for his nose was as sharp as a pen, and a'babbled of green fields.

I will not enter the lists with those Shakespearian scholars who find this passage corrupt; like most unscholarly people, I prefer its errors if it suits my purpose.

For here sit I, thinking about past events and people, fumbling with sheets of paper, a sharp pen (or more accurately pencil) in hand, and about to babble of the green fields of the great game of cricket.

Cricket is a game well understood and frequently well enjoyed by hundreds of thousands of players in a dozen countries, and well understood and sometimes enjoyed by hundreds of writers, to whose numbers I am now a recruit.

Unfortunately, cricket is, save in Philadelphia and a few other civilized places in the United States, not a widely known game in that great country. The late Aubrey Smith, a noted actor and cricketer, gave it some currency in Hollywood, where its essential romanticism had some appeal. But, on the whole, its failure to achieve major status in America is one of those things that have operated to limit that full mutual understanding between the United States and the other English-speaking countries which is so vital in this difficult and dangerous world.

In my time, I must have written a dozen or more 'forewords' for books by celebrated cricketers. I was even honoured by being asked by the famous Wisden to write a piece for its Centenary Year number in 1963.

I am not an expert cricketer. As I said, with, I hope, engaging frankness, in a foreword to Keith Miller and R. S. Whitington's *Bumper* (Latimer House, 1953):

> As a cricket executant, I fell and fall below all standards of decency. The feet, the eyes, the hands, the head, are all no doubt excellent of their kind, but they lack harmony. Yet here is one of the fascinating mysteries of life; so many of my betters have made their centuries and passed on to golf or dog-racing as if cricket had never been. It is occasionally left to people like me to carry with them through life a love and growing understanding of the great game – a feeling in the heart and mind and the eye which neither time nor chance can utterly destroy.

In spite of this serious lack of qualification, the love of cricket has been one of the great loves of my life; and no book of my memoirs would be either complete or credible without some reference to it. Not a whole book (as yet) but at least a chapter.

For cricket has stored my memory with unforgettable images of play and players. It may be of comfort to the philosophic mind to read on the old sundial '*Horas non numero nisi serenas*'. But after all, a sundial is a static thing which is uncommunicative when the sun is not shining. It is one of the glories of cricket that, when one looks back at it, one remembers the hours, not as something static but as something alive, and vivid, and full of action.

Further, I enjoy the company of cricketers; they are, in Dr

Johnson's famous word (though cricket meant nothing to him), the most 'clubbable' of people, full of anecdote and, almost always, of genial goodwill. Without exception, they have always been pleasant to me, admitting me to the dressing-room and the brotherhood, and symbolically promoting me to their own ranks; they have no snobbery.

What is more, I know most of the cricket writers, some of whom are highly literate and literary people, and I read and keep their books, scores and scores of them.

Yet I repeat my confession that I am no expert, except in the sense that I flatter myself that I know a good cricketer when I see one, and find it difficult to forget the great incidents of play.

My American friends cannot understand my strange passion for cricket. 'How slow it is,' they say. 'A game goes on for days, frequently without a final decision. How futile, and how boring!'

I understand this. For in the world of sport, Americans are hustlers. Results count, and results must be got quickly. Take two of their most popular games, American football and basketball, to both of which I was introduced in Virginia last year.

With an interval at half-time, there is an hour's play. In football, there is a minimum of kicking and a maximum of throwing and grappling. The players wear a sort of protective armour around their heads and shoulders and legs; they need it, for there is much assault and battery of a legalized kind; each player will spend a high percentage of his time as one of a piled up heap of players on the ground. Should he become weary of well-doing, the coach takes him off, replaces him, and may later return him at will. But to me the striking feature was that each side has two complete teams, one 'offensive' and one 'defensive', plus, of course, a number of 'spare parts'. When the state of the game seems to require it, the 'defensive' team runs off, and the 'offensive' team runs on, or *vice versa*.

If cricket in England or Australia could command the financial resources of football in America, the adoption of this principle could have fascinating results. Each side could pick two elevens;

one consisting of batsmen only, and the other of ten bowlers and a wicket-keeper!

In basketball, a remarkably fast game, the incessant demand for victory puts a premium on players of inordinate tallness. I saw young men of six feet ten inches as a commonplace; one little fellow of six feet and thirteen stone evoked my sympathy; he looked like a dwarf. One would almost think that players are specially bred for this game. Speed, reach, height are of the essence. Even the onlooker has no time or desire for reflection.

Cricket is entirely different. Except for those playing it, it seems to be a slow and leisurely game. The onlooker has plenty of time for reflection. He can watch the artistry of a batsman without interruption. He is concerned to know what the bowler is doing in pace or spin or turn. He can get an exquisite pleasure from the speed and accuracy and beauty of movement of a great fieldsman. Between the overs (I dislike neighbours who want to talk during an over) he can comment on the present and draw parallels with the past, to his heart's content.

Cricket, in short, is illustrative of the character of player and onlooker alike. It evokes a quiet humour, and expresses both patience and endurance.

Because a player is on view for a relatively long time he becomes a known personality. If he is in the deep field, he exchanges a little badinage with the nearest spectators. And in Australia, if they report that X is 'a good bloke', the word goes round. If he is a batsman, his popular reputation will depend much more on how he makes his runs than on how many runs he makes. He does not need to be even popular, so long as he is 'a character'. For, as every experienced politician knows, it is better to be vigorously hated than to be tepidly admired. For example, I cannot recall any deep public affection for that great Australian all-rounder and captain, Warwick Armstrong; but he was such a 'character' that when he retired from cricket he left a gap like a volcanic crater.

If the cricketer is a bowler, his chances of inspiring hatred or affection are approximately equal. I will illustrate by taking two extremes. I have seen many great fast bowlers, some of them, like

Gregory, MacDonald and Lindwall, Australians; but the greatest fast bowler I ever saw was Harold Larwood, who bowled Australia out in the 'bodyline' series of 1932–3. But, under the somewhat extreme and humourless leadership of Douglas Jardine, he carried out his orders with such devastating speed and accuracy that he quickly became 'Public Enemy No. 1'. Yet, underneath all the passion and furore, Australians took time off from cursing him, to admire him. I know, for I was one of them.

My second extreme is Arthur Mailey, Armstrong's great 'googly' bowler. What a man! He didn't need to be one of the great slow bowlers of cricket history; his talents were manifold – a superbly comic cartoonist, a whimsical writer, a witty conversationalist, a warm friend. Somebody once wrote that his Australian successor, 'Clarrie' Grimmett, the tiny embodiment of accuracy, bowled 'like a miser', while Mailey bowled 'like a millionaire'. These similes are just. That is why, to me, Arthur Mailey was one of the great 'characters' of cricket, a gentle but destructive humorist who could never (I think) have been produced by any other game. I will illustrate this by two first-hand personal observations.

The first concerns the great Master of batsmanship, J. B. Hobbs, playing in a Test Match at Melbourne. When play ended for the day, Hobbs was – as usual – not out, with a century under his belt. Would he ever go out? The next morning, Mailey opened the bowling from the Southern end. Those were the good old days when the Melbourne Cricket Ground had not been converted into a football stadium. At the Southern end, there were elm trees whose leaves, above the sightscreen, twinkled in the sunny breeze. So Mailey, with a bland smile, walked back to his mark, tossing the ball from one hand to the other; turned, ambled in, and sent up a full toss so high that the sightscreen knew it no more. Hobbs bowed respectfully as the ball went overhead. The ball dropped suddenly and steeply, and the bails came off!

My second memory is of a match many years later, when a Test Trial was played at Sydney as a somewhat belated benefit to the veteran Mailey and that great batsman of older years, 'Johnny'

Taylor. Neither had played for many years. On the Saturday, with forty thousand spectators, Ian Johnson, who captained one of the teams, and who was one of the great gentlemen of the game, had an inspiration. After the luncheon adjournment, he brought both teams out on to the ground, and invited Mailey and Taylor, both dressed in their ordinary civilian clothes, to come out to the middle. Both teams lined up at the pitch, and applauded. Ian Johnson then handed the bat to Johnny, and tossed the ball to Arthur. Arthur stood at the stumps, waved both teams back to the boundary, walked back, ambled up with the same old action, and clean bowled Taylor. It was a sensational moment, and we all roared our approval. Five minutes later, Mailey arrived in the New South Wales Cricket Association reserve, stood at the end of the row in which I was seated, and said to me, 'You remember that day at Melbourne when I took four wickets for 364 runs! I now realize the mistake I made. I should have bowled with my coat on!'

It is an amusing fashion among cricket writers, in the off-season, to select 'All-time World XI's', or to name as the 'greatest ever' some batsman, or bowler, or wicketkeeper. I confess that such exercises leave me cold.

Failing any other objective test, the selection has recourse to the averages. Even my friend, E. W. Swanton, in *The Cricketer* of October 1966, while he concedes that 'career records must be treated with reserve, since there is so much in the way of opposition strengths and other factors that they do not disclose', goes on to say that 'they are a prime source of evidence'.

Averages cannot, of course, be overlooked. Brilliant failures cannot be carried indefinitely. And matches are, after all, to be won. And I can claim no authority, for nobody has less. Yet, as I look back over my life, so frequently lit up as it has been by the highlights of cricket, I know that to me the 'greatest' bowler will prove to be that one who achieved his success against the most powerful batsmen (I can still see Maurice Tate bowling to Ponsford and Woodfull!) while the 'greatest' batsman is the one who handled the best bowling under a variety of conditions with success.

If, as in the case of the incomparable Bradman, both averages and success against great bowlers concur, the question falls. (I could write a great deal about Bradman, the master batsman, the superb captain, the very able man of many talents; but I refrain, for I want 'mere mortals' to have a chance. Not that Victor Trumper was in this category, as will appear.) But, though I saw Victor Trumper but once, when I was a boy, I subsequently learned from older and experienced friends of competent judgement enough to realize that the prosaic fact that although his career Test average against England was, on wickets good, bad, and indifferent (by modern standards), the modest figure of thirty-odd, he really 'bestrode the narrow world like a Colossus', and left an imperishable memory behind him.

But, as I have made clear, I am not writing this chapter as an expert, but as an onlooker. For me 'Beauty is in the eye of the beholder'. I have been actively and laboriously engaged in many notable matters, some of which are recorded in this book. But when it comes to cricket, I am that harmless, necessary thing, a born spectator. It follows that I will not profess to offer impertinent judgements as to who were the 'best', or the 'greatest'.

For to me, let me confess it with apologies to my American friends, cricket has been and is a great entertainment. This needs explanation, and perhaps apology. It was once said of the English that 'they take their pleasures sadly'. Well, to the player out in the middle, there may be something dour about a great match. But to me, there is joy in the eye, and in the mind, and in the heart.

It follows that in this brief chapter of reminiscences of cricket as an entertainment, many will be remembered, but few chosen. I will therefore defy chronology and abjure authority, and write something of some of the 'characters' who have entertained me, making my humble apologies to those equally interesting 'characters' whom the demands of space require me to omit.

There have been, I will be told, greater fast bowlers than 'Freddie' Trueman, of Yorkshire and England. Indeed, I can remember some of them; 'Ted' MacDonald, whose run up to the wicket was like the bobbling of silk over a spool; Jack Gregory, whose final kangaroo leap was enough to strike terror into the stoutest English heart; Harold Larwood, whose somewhat ascetic appearance was matched with a degree of accuracy and control which I have never seen equalled (he was the only fast bowler extant who could have carried out Douglas Jardine's orders); and Ray Lindwall, every yard of whose run mattered since he developed speed as he went.

But, of all these, my 'character' is Freddie Trueman, with his curving run, his lank dark locks, his facial ferocity. He must have been a hard man for a captain to control, but he always fascinated me. He will, I hope, allow me to refer to three events.

On the Saturday night of a Test Match at Adelaide, the Australian Board of Cricket Control gave a dinner at the lovely Adelaide Cricket Ground. I was invited on the usual terms; I was to sing for my supper. The weather was hot; Trueman had been bowling from the Lake Torrens end. As he beat his way back to his mark, his head could be seen wagging and his lips moving, perhaps profanely. The genial 'barrackers' of Adelaide – the 'City of Churches' – raucously inquired whether he could 'do with a pint'. His lips moved more eloquently. At the dinner, I hypocritically came to his rescue:

> You know, gentlemen, many people may have thought that
> on his way back into the wind Freddie was using bad language.
> This idea did him a grave injustice! He was, in fact, reciting
> Greek iambics!

Great laughter. But for the next few weeks Freddie's stock question was – 'What did that old b—— mean about Greek iambics? And what the hell are they, anyhow?' But all I know is that he became my friend.

The second event was at my match at Canberra, Prime Minister's XI *v.* M.C.C., a match which I had first established against the West Indies in 1951, and which has become, I think I may claim, a happy feature of each visiting tour. It was my practice, at the end of this one-day 'festival' match, to give a dinner to both teams, a dinner of much hilarity and some superb, if incredible, post-prandial oratory. On this occasion, the Duke of Norfolk was present as M.C.C. Manager, and sat on my right. Ted Dexter, as Captain, was on my left. For the first time in the history of these games, a player's birthday coincided with the date of the match. The player was 'Freddie'.

I had a splendid pewter pot suitably inscribed and, at a suitable time during the dinner, called Freddie up to the top table, said a few words, and presented him with this trophy, on which my signature was duly engraved. Freddie was much affected by this, made a very brief but pleasant acknowledgement, and retreated to his place, muttering quite audibly, 'First time a b—— Prime Minister ever did this to a b—— professional cricketer. It's b—— wonderful.' He was in reality quite moved. But Norfolk, who is the master of the 'dead-pan' face, turned to me and said: 'That was very generous of you, Menzies, but I would like you to know that you have undone the hard disciplinary work of six weeks!' Well, perhaps!

My third anecdote about Freddie concerns the Test Match at Headingley in July 1964. I had dined with the Australian team at their hotel. On arriving at the ground the next morning, I went round to see the M.C.C. team, most of whom I had got to know in Australia. When I had gone round them, and had settled into a talk with Ted Dexter about politics (of all things!), I said, 'Where is Freddie?' A noise behind me identified him, so I turned around. Freddie was just getting into his cricket clothes. I noticed that he had had a haircut; not a close one, of course, but the marks of the scissors were plain. So, in a heavy-footed way, I said: 'Fred, you are a traitor to your country!' He bristled up at once. 'What do you mean?' 'Fred,' I said, 'the answer is simple. You have had your hair cut. And you know what happened to Samson when Delilah cut his hair off!' A broad grin swept across Freddie's face. 'Ah,' he said, with a gleam in the eye, 'I could have done with a piece of that Delilah myself!'

Another great 'character' in my gallery of memories is 'Sam' Loxton, of Victoria and Australia, now a Member of the Victorian

Parliament. 'Sam' is a powerful athlete with, on suitable occasions, a countenance of unexampled fierceness, a heart of gold, and a rare taste for the humour of situations.

I was at Headingley in 1948 when he and Neil Harvey, that quiet artist, were playing their first Test Match against England. On the final day, Australia was set the 'impossible' task of getting over four hundred runs in less than a day's play. For an hour, runs lagged behind the clock; and then Bradman used the spurs. Neil got a lovely century. 'Sam' was in great form, and hit the ball all over the ground. When he was ninety-three he swung wildly at one delivery, and was clean-bowled. Knowing how bitterly disappointed he must be, I repaired to the Australian dressing-room. Sam had just emerged from the shower, and greeted me. 'Sam,' I said, 'if ever I see you try to hit a *seven* before the ball is half-way down the pitch, I will run out and attack you!'

A diabolical grin accompanied his rejoinder. 'Well, you see, Boss, the skipper's instructions were to have a go' (the skipper was Don Bradman) 'and that's just what I did. It's all in the game. After all, Boss' (with a broader grin), 'you've probably made some bloody big errors in your time yourself!'

It has been very rarely that a player, batting in his first Anglo-Australian Test Match, has made a century. Most men who had got so near to that honour and then failed would have been the dejected victims of self-pity. But not 'Sam' Loxton. That is why he is in my collection of 'characters'.

Later in that season, I was able to tell him of a delicious conversation at Lord's. It occurred as Sam went out from the Member's Pavilion to bat. I was sitting between two fairly venerable peers. They were both, as I knew, Bank Directors. 'Sam' was a bank clerk in an Anglo-Australian bank in Australia.

A. 'Who is this fella?
B. 'Our colleague, Loxton, my dear boy.'
A. 'What do you mean, "colleague"?'
B. 'A banker, my dear boy, and in my bank!'
A. 'Oh, splendid! An attractive fella. Good luck to you, Sa!'

And that reminds me. When I get to thinking about cricketers, one thing inevitably leads to another, and not necessarily in chronological order.

In 1938, I had the great good fortune to be in the delightful company of 'Plum' Warner, as a guest of Lord Belper, then the President of Notts, at the Trent Bridge Test Match. And so I saw the great 'Tiger' O'Reilly toiling in vain on the deadest of dead wickets whilst those then youthful masters, Hutton and Compton, made a packet of runs. When England finally declared, with something over six hundred runs on the board, a leg-weary and mentally exhausted O'Reilly came off, only to be greeted by me in a most offensive way – this is a method which the Tiger perfectly understands and practises:

'I always thought you were a spin bowler. How is it that you didn't turn the ball at all?'

O'Reilly: 'D'you know what that wicket is like? You dig a deep trench 122 yards long. You put in a layer of "manure"; you add a layer of soil; you then put down a series of feather mattresses; and you then top it up with more soil; water it and roll it, and then say to us bowlers, "Come on!"'

(He was one of the greatest Australian bowlers; a picturesque talker, and a great 'character'.)

Australia went in to bat, at odds. The pitch had, under the flailing of bat and ball, broken up a little. Puffs of dust began to signal each stroke. A couple of wickets fell. Then McCabe moved into the attack, and played the greatest innings I have ever seen. As usual, he was not overawed by the occasion; he was there to get the runs, and he got them – 232 in 240 minutes! A film of that innings would have afforded a complete course of instruction in the art of batting. If Farnes, who was an accomplished fast bowler, kept the ball up, McCabe drove it along the ground or in the air to unguarded spaces, with deadly ferocity. If he dropped the ball shorter, the rearing delivery found the ropes at fine leg or late through the slips. If he compromised on length, he was pulled or square driven. It was fantastic, and unforgettable. It is credibly reported that Don Bradman called on his players to watch, saying

'You will never see an innings like this again.' I always thought that McCabe's secret was that he loved batting, and was not obsessed by 'averages'. He was a supreme artist, and practised art for its own sake.

I saw one day of the next Test Match, at Lord's. When McCabe went in, he took 'block' at the Nursery end, facing the pavilion, where no sightscreen was allowed to obstruct the spectator's view. The pitch was (and I dare say still is) canted – higher on the 'Father Time' side, so that even a straight ball from the pavilion end would move to the batsman's leg side. Down came a fast delivery, swinging across. McCabe's feet moved a few inches, his wrists turned, and the ball was cracked into the Tavern for six. There was some feeling near me that this was an irreverent action, especially at Lord's. But that was McCabe!

William Maldon Woodfull, Captain of Australia and famous partner of 'Bill' Ponsford in many notable opening partnerships for Victoria and Australia, had the shortest back-lift to be seen before 'Slasher' Mackay. He became known as the 'unbowlable'. His demeanour was modest, but his character was so clear that it was understood by every onlooker. He embodied the spirit of cricket at its best, and was a great leader by example rather than by precept. I will never forget that, just before he was selected to go to England for the first time, the selectors, for some reason best known to themselves, had chosen the bulk of the team before Victoria played New South Wales at Sydney. I was there. For the remaining batting vacancy the choice was (believe it or not) between Woodfull and that great artist, Alan Kippax. Woodfull made a defensive century, to which Kippax's retort was a brilliant double century. In Victoria's second innings, Woodfull made another century, so aggressive in its quality, that he was chosen. They both should have been in the team; but that is (or was) the way of the world.

Woodfull, of course, figured in the great 'body-line' explosion of 1932–3. Woodfull was Captain of Australia. Douglas Jardine, whom I later got to know very well and to like very much, captained England. There had to be some way to defeat the Bradmans and the Ponsfords, and Jardine set about discovering it with almost military method and ruthlessness. The answer was the fast attack, with a fiercely rising ball, on or outside the leg-stump, with a tightly packed leg field. The batsman would be desperately concerned to protect his head and body, and false strokes would be almost a certainty.

Jardine had his instrument to hand. Larwood was a magnificent fast bowler, with a superb control of length, rise and direction. Australia had nobody to compare with him, and therefore could not retaliate. Now, McCabe had shown in Sydney that 'body-line' could be hit to leg with a vengeance; but for that kind of buccaneering business there has been, in my time, only one McCabe.

Up came the Adelaide Test Match. When Jardine marched on to the ground, wearing his inevitable Harlequin Cap, he was roundly hooted. This was an astonishingly bad piece of misbehaviour for Adelaide, which admits to being the most respectable city in Australia. But Jardine had, in the homely phrase, 'bought it'. In every step, in every gesture, in every tilt of the head, on every cricket ground, he showed his contempt for the crowd. He was a cricketing Coriolanus.

I shall never forget the incident which provoked the ultimate crisis, for I saw it all. Up to that time, I confess, I had been on Jardine's side. Why should the fast-rising ball, outside the leg-stump, be any less legitimate than the fast-rising ball outside the off-stump? True, most of the strokes of fine art are on the off; but Jardine had come out to win, not to contribute to art. Something had to be done to counter the all-powerful Bradman.

But what happened? Larwood opened the bowling from the Torrens end, and had early success outside the off-stump. But the indomitable Woodfull was still there, partnered by Victor Richardson. Woodfull moved across rather awkwardly to get over a rising ball on the off, the last ball of the over, was struck over the heart, and fell to the ground. There never was anything bogus about Woodfull; the onlookers knew that he was hurt. Jardine, fielding at point, tactlessly complimented Larwood. 'Gubby' Allen, who was to bowl the next over, ran off the ground for a glass of water.

After a minute or two, Woodfull stood up, but was obviously shaken. Then followed one of the most agreeable exhibitions of the true spirit of cricket which I have ever seen. Gubby bowled a series of almost long-hops, and Victor Richardson played them defensively straight back along the pitch!

Then it was once more Larwood's turn, to Woodfull. An orthodox off-field fell into place, Jardine at point. Suddenly Jardine signalled to Larwood, and swung the field to the body-line setting. It was almost as if he had said – 'This man is a bit groggy; let's dispose of him!' A roar of rage went up from forty thousand spectators. If it had been Sydney or Melbourne, I believe, and said so at the time to 'Plum' Warner, who was next to me in the Committee Box, the crowd would have invaded the ground, and the Test Match might have ended in tumult and disorder.

What happened thereafter is a part of cricket history; angry cables were exchanged; there was much bad feeling; all pleasure went out of the series. Jardine's action was a blunder of the first magnitude. He had in effect announced that 'body-line' was designed as a physical attack; no more and no less. Many years afterwards, he conceded to me that he would like those five minutes over again!

Victor Richardson, of South Australia, was one of those rare athletes who captained his State in both cricket and football, who played cricket for Australia and captained Australia in South Africa! He was a courageous batsman, as the records will attest. But it is as a fieldsman that he lives in my gallery of immortals. Like all very great players of ball-games, he had an eye like a hawk. As a captain, he liked nothing better than to place himself at 'silly mid-off' five or six yards away from the bat. I think that I can confidently say that, in that impossible position, he was never known to miss a catch. I don't say 'drop'; I say 'miss'; for he collected all catches, possible and impossible alike.

In his last year for Australia against England in Australia, some 'expert' commentator in the Melbourne press said that it was 'time for Richardson to go', since, obviously his eye-sight was not as good as it used to be. At the cricket dinner at the Melbourne

Cricket Ground on the Saturday of the Test Match (in 1932–3) I was, as usual, put up to speak. To the astonishment of most of those present, I referred to this press attack, and said that, most reluctantly, I had to agree with it. 'After all,' I said, 'we who have been watching Vic at silly mid-off have not failed to notice that he stands six feet nearer to the bat than he did once. True, he never misses; but clearly his eye-sight is not what it used to be!' Loud cheers from the players; a baleful glare in the eye of the journalist!

Lindsay Hassett was one of the great batsmen of cricket history. To see him play a scoreless and defensive over against Alec Bedser at his top was a memorable experience for any onlooker who had enough wit to know that 'slogging' is not all. But it was even better to see this short, nimble man, reduce the great 'Tiger' O'Reilly to impotence by driving him through the covers and past mid-off time after time. Which recollection reminds me that, some years after they had both retired from first-class cricket, I saw them, during a Test Match at Melbourne, having a friendly drink in the Committee Rooms of the Melbourne Cricket Club. I approached them with all the brutal confidence of a Prime Minister with a majority, and gave tongue. 'I'm just remembering, Lindsay, the day I saw you hit "Tiger" for a century on the Sydney ground.' (Now, don't forget that O'Reilly was the greatest Australian bowler of his time!) 'Oh,' said Lindsay, his face as immovable as that of a dead cod-fish, 'to which of the three occasions are you referring?'

I knew that they were famous antagonists and therefore, in the world of cricket, close friends. I remembered, but refrained from saying so, for even I have had my good moments, that it was a received legend that, on the occasion which I had witnessed, the Tiger, who hated all batsmen on principle, having been roughly treated by Lindsay, walked back past him and said, with all the clarity of a schoolteacher (for that is what he was), 'You little b—— it's not even that you're good looking!'

I remember, many years ago, reading a whimsical description by Neville Cardus (now, happily, Sir Neville), the undisputed

Dean of the faculty of cricket writers, of 'Johnny' Briggs. But I still believe that Lindsay Hassett was the greatest wit in the cricket world.

So you will readily see why he has a double claim upon my affectionate memory.

Then there is that rich character 'Ernie' McCormick, the Australian fast bowler. For a fast bowler, he had, and has, a genial philosophy and a pretty wit. In the opening match against Worcester in 1938, McCormick was no-balled nineteen times in three overs for dragging over.

When the players came off at the luncheon adjournment, the sensation hunters clustered around, hoping for some pithy remarks about the standard of umpiring. They came to the wrong shop for those goods. 'Oh,' said Ernie with a spacious grin, 'it's all very understandable. You see, I come from a country where the States cover enormous areas of land. Here it is different – a great number of small counties. That was where I, as a new-comer, got into trouble. I could never make up my mind *in which county* I was bowling!'

Or again, take the cricketing Indian Prince, the Nawab of Pataudi, who made a century in his first Test Match against Australia. He was fielding in the deep at Melbourne, and receiving good-natured banter from the nearest onlookers. Suddenly a raucous voice rang out from some ill-mannered and beer-laden lout – 'Hey, Gandhi, where's your goat?'

Pataudi turned quietly, gazed speculatively around, and said, 'Ah! there you are. Could somebody lend me a piece of string?' Laughter won the day.

It was on the same tour that Pataudi was warned that 'Eddie' Gilbert, an aboriginal fast bowler who played for Queensland, and whose action was suspect, would possibly 'knock him out' in Brisbane. Pataudi's reply was superb. 'Not at all,' he said, 'when Eddie sees me standing at the wicket, he will say "No, I cannot kill a brother!" and will bowl slow.'

*   *   *

One of the regrettable modern developments in big cricket is that there is too much talk outside the playing arena. For this, the sporting press must accept the major responsibility.

A captain who won't talk to the press is branded as unco-operative, and a 'bad ambassador'. So nowadays he talks; not just at official functions, which is inevitable, but before and after the day's play. He is expected to give his opinion on the appropriate tactics and on his opponents both jointly and severally. He will become an author either in right of his own talent or (very commonly) by trafficking with a 'ghost' who is determined to be neither dull nor prosaic. The teams' dressing rooms are compassed about by a great cloud of witnesses, many of whom have only the remotest interest in the game or the play. The result of all this is to represent cricket as a sort of warfare inspiring bitter enmities, warfare in which the national honour seems to be at stake; victory creditable, and defeat disgraceful.

What nonsense this all is; and how unjust to the greatest of all games, in which the best players, as I have known hundreds of them, are distinguished by character and geniality; warm and sometimes whimsical personalities. It is this fact which has served to make cricket so wonderful an entertainment, so great a source of happy memories for people like me.

When I was a boy, the only way in which a cricket match could be reported was by the printed word in the newspapers. And it wasn't a bad way either; the reporter stuck to the facts, and did not try to write a gossip column!

Then came broadcasting, which worked like a charm when the matches were within broadcasting range, but encountered great problems before the days of short-wave transmission. A Test Match was being played in England. A broadcasting station in Australia undertook to describe it. How? A series of cables was arranged, converted into a sort of direct description at the Australian end. These 'fake' broadcasts were the funniest things in cricket history. Former players were engaged as commentators. Over by over we heard a description, interspersed with a click of bat on ball, arranged in the studio. Then, when twenty runs had been laboriously accounted for, in the better part of an hour, the studio voice would say, 'We have just had a flash score from Leeds; Australia is "no wicket for sixty"!'

After that, it was odd to be taken back forty runs, and pretend not to know what was to come!

Some of the old cricketers found it difficult. The broadcasts on the 'commercial' stations were of course sponsored by advertisers.

At suitable intervals, a laboriously impromptu remark would be made – 'I say, Jack, have an XY cigarette!' But, as I was listening in, Jack, forgetting his cue, replied – 'No thanks, old man; I can't stand them. They give me a sore throat!' So Jack's career ended.

Things are different now, with short-wave and non-stop talk. Some of the broadcasters are very good, though there are some who reduce me to an irritated despair by concealing the score under a cloud of eloquence about irrelevant matters such as the habits of seagulls, the density of the air-traffic overhead, or the antics of the inevitable small dog!

In my County Court days, I had been appearing a good deal before an elderly judge who was not a great lawyer but who had for a brief period been a better than average cricketer. He was somewhat pernickety and abhorred slang expressions, but he was always approachable through his three special hobbies; roses, poultry and cricket. I suppose that purists will say that no advocate should play upon the weaknesses or foibles of a judge. My reply is that any advocate who does not study and know his judge or judges is going to lose many cases, most needlessly.

Anyhow, my story is this. I was for the defendant in a civil action which arose out of events in the neighbourhood of Ballarat, the famous old gold-mining city. My client, as I discovered after a conference with him and his solicitor, was a very decent and honest, but dull, man, quite incapable of stating the facts in any consecutive fashion. Right through the first day of the hearing, the plaintiff and his witnesses were heard. I cross-examined with no particular success. Yet I had a feeling that my bucolic client

was right, if he could only be coherent, and register himself with
the judge. The plaintiff's case closed just on the adjournment. The
judge looked at me, kindly enough (he approved of me because
he thought I spoke good English!) and said: 'Mr Menzies, I think
I should tell you that I find the plaintiff's case and witnesses most
impressive.' With my usual air of confidence, I replied: 'I would
ask Your Honour to suspend judgment until you have heard my
client, who will, I am sure, impress you very much!'

After the adjournment, I led the solicitor and client (we had no
other witness) down to my chambers. All efforts to extract coher-
ence from the client failed. I then produced my cards.

M. 'Mr X, have you ever grown roses?'
X. 'I think my wife has some in the garden.'
M. 'But can you distinguish a La Belle France from a Frau
    Carl Drushki?'
X. 'Not a hope!'
M. 'Do you keep fowls?'
X. 'The wife has a few.'
M. 'Can you distinguish between a White Leghorn and an
    Orpington?'
X. 'Not for the life of me!'
M. 'Have you ever played cricket?'
X. 'Ah! Now you're talking. I played for Ballarat and District
    against Ivo Bligh's Eleven!'
M. 'Good. Conference ended!'

The next morning I opened my case and called the defendant. He
was quite dreadful as a witness. At one stage it became necessary to
ask him about a date. Before he could reply I said, in the most
helpful manner: 'Take your time, witness. I know that dates are
not always easy to remember. Now, if I were to ask you about
the date when you played cricket for Ballarat and District against
Ivo Bligh's Eleven, that would be much easier!'

The judge, beaming with excitement and delight, switched round
in his chair and said, 'Is that so? Tell me about the match. Were

you batsman or a bowler?' And at once they were into it. For half
an hour we had cricket reminiscences galore. By the time my client,
completely relaxed, had returned to and concluded his evidence,
the judge turned to the plaintiff's astonished counsel and said: 'Of
course, Mr Y., you may cross-examine if you like. You have a
perfect right to do so. But I think I should tell you that in all my
years on the bench I have never been more favourably impressed
by any witness.'

It is hardly necessary to add that the defendant won and, I think,
rightly, on the merits. But it was cricket that did it!

While I am in this mood, I crave leave to record another remi-
niscence of cricket and the law.

A case had occurred, well over thirty years ago, in the local
court at Mildura, the famous irrigation settlement in the far north-
west of Victoria, on the River Murray. The Mildura solicitor concerned on the losing side, an old friend of mine, wanted to obtain,
in the Supreme Court, an Order Nisi to review the decision. But
he overlooked the time factor – the Order had to be applied for
within thirty days – and filed his papers and briefed me almost at
the last moment. Alas! It was Christmas time, and the Supreme
Court was not sitting! But there was a Test Match on at the Melbourne Cricket Ground, and Mr Justice Cussen was the President
of the Club.

I hared off to the ground; it was my only hope. The judge was
in the Committee Box. I found my way in, waited until the end
of the over, and then caught the eye of the judge. Happily he was
a patient and generous man. I told him the circumstances. He at
once caught on. 'I quite see the position. Have I your assurance
that the necessary papers are filed?' I assured him that they were.
'Very well,' he said, 'I think the rule is that if you formally apply
within the time, and the papers are in order, I can note the fact
that you have applied, and adjourn the actual argument to a future
date!' I vigorously agreed. He noted the application, turned to the
field, and said with a smile: 'That was a fine bit of bowling wasn't
it?'

*　　*　　*

I could not set down any cricket memoirs without some affectionate references to two of the great men of Lord's, Sir Pelham (Plum)
Warner, and Harry Altham. Both were off the playing list when
I first met them. Each had become a cricket administrator and a
cricket historian; Plum with a clear and vivid memory of events
in which he had played a part, Altham with rare literary charm
and the graces of classical scholarship. Each has now departed to
the Elysian fields.

Over the years, I got to know 'Plum' very well, and learned
without difficulty to love him. He was, in Chaucer's famous
phrase, a 'verray parfit gentil knight'. Cricket was his life. He had
been a great batsman and a celebrated Captain of England. But he
detested rude controversy, was sensitive on all points of honour,
and spoke well of all men, provided they were lovers of what he
used to call 'cricket, the beautiful game with the beautiful name'.

He knew how cricket was going, all round the world. One year
I took to London with me my great friend and colleague, Athol
Townley, now, to my enduring sorrow, dead and gone. Athol
had played for my Prime Minister's XI against the West Indies at
Canberra, and had hit a couple of towering 'sixers'. I had 'Plum'
and a few others to dinner at the Savoy. When Athol walked in
and I mentioned his name, 'Plum' at once came forward with
outstretched hand – 'Ha! Sixer Townley!'

For many years, I have had the respectable habit of putting on a
dinner party in London for my cricketing friends. I always treated
'Plum' as the special guest of honour, and seated him on my right.
I then placed 'Gubby' Allen directly opposite, and had disposed
on the table between them a variety of small movable articles like
salt-cellars and pepper pots. These tactical dispositions made the
party a guaranteed success. All I had to do was to toss in the apple
of discord about fast bowling, or the new l.b.w. rule, and the
contest was on. For you must know that, though 'Plum' was
gentle, he was pertinacious in his views, while my friend 'Gubby'
Allen thrives on controversy, and never has to be talked into offering an opinion.

What a gallery of memories I have of these dinners, with great and good companions like 'Freddy' Brown, Ian Peebles, 'Jim' Swanton, Harry Altham, Rait Kerr and Ronnie Aird, *et hoc genus omne*, and once Lord Birkett, the greatest after-dinner speaker I ever heard.

I rather think that I made a poor start with 'Plum' at Lord's thirty years ago. He had taken me out to see the famous ground. The leather-jackets(?) had been in; the grass was rough, patchy, and worn. I offered the brash view that football should be played on the ground during the winter. Cutting up the ground, I suggested, would let the air in and improve the health of the grass. I delicately mentioned that the Melbourne ground, which sometimes looked like a mudheap after the Football Grand Final, was promptly harrowed, top-dressed, and so attended to that six weeks later cricket was in full swing. 'Plum' was shocked at this blasphemy. His good opinion of me was restored only when, some years later, in the course of a speech, I referred to Lord's as the 'Cathedral of Cricket'.

Indeed, I must tell of my last talk with 'Plum' at the home of his son, John, a close friend of mine, who will, I know, not object to my narrative. The old man was sick, and frail. In fact, I was never to see him again. But John suggested I should come to see him.

'Plum' was seated in an armchair. He gazed vaguely at me; clearly he did not recognize me. But he knew that I was somewhere in his failing memory, and that he must have talked cricket with me. Suddenly he said, loud and clear, 'Who was that splendid statesman from the colonies who described Lord's as the Cathedral of Cricket?'

John promptly identified me, the shadows cleared away, and we launched into cricket talk, which, peace to old Sam Johnson, is just about the best talk in the world.

Afternoon Light
1967

Return from Australia

NEVILLE CARDUS

After an absence from Lord's of seven and a half years, I returned from Australia in June and without loss of time I took a taxi to the only cricket ground in the world on which I can feel at ease and happy. And I saw Yorkshire playing Middlesex. More than that I saw the Yorkshire bowling hit all over the field before lunch, a hundred an hour scored with contumely – and the Yorkshire bowling was not only incapable of taking a wicket: it could not 'close the game up,' to use the canny old term of the North, could not keep the batsmen quiet (the batsmen by the way, being Brown and Robertson). I could not believe my eyesight. What a home-coming!

I had been cautioned in advance before leaving Sydney by flying boat, I had been told by friends in England to resign myself to drastic and solemn changes at home. Monotonous food, queues, austerity everywhere, philosophic doubt, and – as the character in the Chekhov play says – all the rest of it. These hardships frankly did not equal my anticipations, my forebodings. But nobody had warned me about the Yorkshire bowling. Since the days of my childhood I have known it only by certain famous attributes – length, devil, cunning, tenacity, temper and – length, length, and always more length. 'Mek' em fetch 'em' was the doctrine of Wilfred Rhodes. If Rhodes or Emmot Robinson (whom God preserve) had been at Lord's to see their county's attack flogged right and left beyond any powers of prevention, let alone retaliation, they would have suffered agonies which were better not imagined, let alone described, in this article.

There was once a time, and not so long ago as all that, when a Yorkshire bowler would glare down the wicket (and rightly glare) if a batsman struck him or snicked him for a boundary before lunch, or after. A certain amateur, indeed, did one morning snick, without provision, a four from one of the more immortal of the Yorkshire bowlers of the 1920s. It was the last ball of the over, and the Yorkshireman stood transfixed – glaring. The amateur spoke to him with some slight irony: 'What's the matter, George? Do you never expect to see yourself glanced from the leg stump for four?' The answer was rapid and out of the heart. 'No – I don't. At least, not by such a —— batter as thee.'

It is little to wonder at, then, that if Yorkshiremen nowadays cannot bowl a length very few bowlers in other counties observe the first principle of their profession. Frankly I have never before seen so much loose stuff wheeled up and/or propelled along cricket pitches as I have seen in first-class county cricket this summer during the four or five weeks since I returned home. Much of this bowling – some of it to be witnessed in the Test Matches against South Africa – would not have been allowed to go by without being severely chastised and blasphemously counted-out by the crowd if it had occurred in a Grade cricket match in Sydney.

Allowances must be made, of course. We cannot expect at one and the same time great bombers and great bowlers. But surely if we may not for some time to come hope for another Rhodes, another Maurice Tate, another Larwood, another Johnny Douglas, we are at any rate free to demand from paid cricketers some mastery over the elementary points, the A.B.C., which are length and accuracy of direction.

And the question may be asked – *Is* it a consequence of the war that our cricket has markedly declined or is it because of some factor in essential procedure and the conditions and general atmosphere?

Which brings me to the problem I have frequently been asked to elucidate – why from a population of less than London's, can Australia produce year after year cricketers equal to our best? Is it the climate? Is it because young players enjoy the advantage of true practice pitches? These are points not to be settled within easy dialectic of the Brains Trust. First of all some broad idea should be grasped of the Australian cricket scene, or habitat. I don't allude merely to the almost perennial sunshine, but to the organisation and psychology.

To begin with, there is next to no day by day cricket in a normal Australian summer – that is, a summer in which no Test Matches are played. When I became a resident in Sydney I quickly realised that except during three State matches of four days each the magnificent ground at Sydney might as well not have existed at all. It stood vacant under the blue skies, the grass floodlit; a deserted stage. No jumping into a taxi after lunch at one's club with a casual instruction to the driver: 'Lord's.' There is no professional cricket in Australia, and as the sun sinks towards seven o'clock, followed by a swift but magical twilight, there is no chance for evening practice. The more loftily placed heroes of State and Test renown may perhaps be privileged to steal away from office or workshop for a net if an important occasion be brewing. But the average club – i.e. Grade – cricketer seldom gets an opportunity for systematic practice. Coaching as we know it in England does not exist or receive favour. The Australian cricketer learns from experience in the middle. Whenever he does find time for a net he puts into practice there the lessons he has been taught by severe *match* experience. In England we reverse this procedure.

Bradman has frequently expressed the opinion that too much cricket is played week in and week out through an English season. The game begins to change to a routine, a professional job to be done as well as may or can be.

In Australia every Grade engagement on a Saturday afternoon is a fresh challenge. It is a rung on the ladder to Test Match renown. And a State match is a crisis in a player's career; he is almost 'there'. These opportunities come but sparely to the Australian: one day weekly for about seven months with three or four invitations dangling round the corner for the State matches. All the cricket of an Australian season could be put into a month of English summer, given fine weather.

There is no easy-going village or country club cricket in Australia; at any rate, I have never seen any that wasn't seriously conducted. Near my flat is a little bay looking on the harbour; a sort of Fowey by the Pacific. A little cricket ground has been planted not far from a sea of blue. On this heavenly cricket field ordinary casual club teams may occasionally be seen in action: two schools, or a battle royal between police and the General Post Office. But in none of these games have I ever seen crudities. No hoicking by the tail enders. Nose over the line of the ball. Pads well in front.

Even the smallest boys bend down to it. No chins in the air. And of course they all twist their wrists in the effort to spin the leg break and the 'googly.' Cricket seems as much a natural aptitude to an Australian as violin playing to a Hungarian.

I have expounded in another place my main theory about the high Australian standards in cricket. From so few of them the mighty line proceeds – from Bannerman to Bradman. There is not much waste of material.

My theory is that from the moment an Australian youth goes into club cricket he at once finds himself amongst the masters. In England a man might easily take part in good-class Saturday afternoon cricket all his life and never once come into contact with a Test Match player. But a young Australian making his début for North Sydney might immediately be called to go in and receive his baptism of fire against an O'Reilly, a Lindwall. Experience teaches. Example is better than precept.

The Cricketer
1947

Cricket's Last Romantic

A broadcast tribute to Neville Cardus on his 75th
birthday, 2 April, 1964

KENNETH GREGORY

In the whole of recent English literature there was nothing more
remarkable than the cult which grew up during the inter-war years,
the cult of Cardus. Parsons wondered whether they should take
a text from Cardus, the pianist Schnabel enjoyed one of the early
books without having the faintest understanding of cricket.
Birkenhead saw Cardus as 'an enchanter', Barrie sought him out
in front of the Tavern at Lord's. If to many professional cricketers
Cardus was a suspect character who insisted on divining the spirit
within their solid flesh, he was to himself the most fortunate of
men – 'I have met Richard Strauss and Bradman,' as it were the
two master scorers of the century. Today the essays of Neville
Cardus are studied by teenagers for their GCE.

Perhaps before long he will be chosen by some graduate in search
of a PhD thesis – say, 'The Relationship between the Chord of C
major and Hammond's cover-drive in 1938.' So let us for a moment
ponder on the Cardus background and sources of inspiration. He
was educated not at a university but in the Manchester public
library where he immersed himself in the novels of Dickens. He
did not qualify for the Press-box by compiling a tedious innings
for Oxbridge at Lord's, but after serving as assistant professional
at Shrewsbury and occasional drama critic-cum-leader writer on
the *Manchester Guardian* of C. P. Scott. Indeed, had it not been
for illness, he would not have been sent to recuperate at Old

Trafford. Cardus might never have written about cricket. When he did, he was as much at home in the world of the novelists, poets and philosophers as he was in his northern streets. Small wonder he saw cricket not only as a game but as an integral part of the English scene; the English scene, past and present, became irrevocably interwoven with the game's seasonal comedy. In short, Cardus dedicated himself to 'the entrancing art of changing raw experience into the connoisseur's enjoyment of life'. He determined to make his readers see life whole – cricket in terms of music, economics, H. M. Bateman, the Theory of Relativity and much else. That he succeeded was due in part to the passion and persuasiveness of his pen, but also to the nature of his fellow-countrymen. Distrusting the arts, the English found a substitute in cricket – a timeless blend of formal dancing, rhetoric and comic opera. If we allow, as Cardus contended, that cricket is an art form, then it must be permitted its high priest, one who will truly comprehend its mysteries, regard it with an indulgent affection and seek to perpetuate its golden hours. So Cardus was able to do for Spooner and Woolley what Lamb had done for Munden and Agate for the Millamant of the young Edith Evans; he arrested the transitoriness of their medium, fastened upon their manners and movements, and gave them to posterity. In case posterity should require that PhD thesis, I myself have started researching. After all, we should hate misconceptions to undermine the reputation of our author. Posterity might come across a reference to Fabian tactics, find the essay on Sidney Webb and look forward to a critical analysis of the leg-spin bowling of Bernard Shaw. To be honest, the leg-spin potential of Shaw was touched on by Cardus, but the Sidney Webb in question was a Lancastrian who skittled Surrey on 15 June, 1900, the Fabian tactics those of the Roman general who foiled Hannibal. Still, I trust I have shown the need for research, at least where the earlier books are concerned. The one with which Cardus voluntarily declared his innings eight years ago, *Close of Play*, I shall ignore, as its only non-cricketing allusion is to Australian girls who – while pretty – 'are lacking in charm'. This, I hasten to add, is another way of saying that Australian girls do not sound like Elisabeth Schumann, a lady Cardus revered as he did Mrs Wilkins Micawber. The Micawbers bring me to vintage Cardus – *Days in the Sun*, *The Summer Game*, *Good Days* and *Australian Summer* – to the books which, with the classic *Autobiography*, are his abiding legacy. Now, although there are in the Cardus canon only three references apiece to Sterne and Meredith and two to Hardy, the creations of Dickens are mentioned no fewer than eighteen times. The Micawbers, Mr Mantalini, Mr Peeksniff, Mr Chadband and Mrs Gamp were all brought in to emphasise the decline in the art of late-cutting, or whatever. Yet it is strange that although Bach and Edward German, Handel and Mozart, Rossini and Wagner – Strauss's *Till Eulenspiegel* when Bradman was batting – all entered the Press-box with Cardus, there was never a mention of Tchaikovsky. Still, the mind of cricket was adequately propped by Aristotle, Hobbes, Hume, Herbert Spencer and Dan Leno, also a philosopher of sorts. Dr Johnson and Mark Twain came and went, Max Beerbohm was proved never to have entered Lord's, Oscar Wilde was called upon to explain the bowling of Fleetwood-Smith in Adelaide, Lewis Carroll and Albert Einstein . . . But let me end this inventory on a sombre note. At forty-five Cardus introduced Karl Marx on the subject of congealed labour, at sixty he succumbed to Gertrude Stein. Perhaps he had not heard Miss Stein sing.

Probably not, for Cardus believed we must turn to old-fashioned music for mellowness and simple song, as to old-fashioned batsmanship for simple beauty. He was, to adapt Yeats, the last romantic who chose as themes traditional sanctity and loveliness. Looking back to the cricket that bewitched him in his boyhood – the cricket of MacLaren and Trumper, of Ranji, Fry and J. T. Tyldesley – he could readily fathom its secret: 'the age was simple, which was the beauty of it'. He could go further. 'There was an enjoyment of ordinary everyday activities and vistas not known now.' Such a judgement was not, of course, a moral one but a statement of fact. There are technological advances in cricket as in everything else, but they do not necessarily lead to a deeper aesthetic appreciation of the game. The cricket whose hey-

day caught the young Cardus at his most impressionable had
arrived at a state of grace, it had yet to become bogged down in
sophisticated detail. He summed up the essence of cricket, the
satisfaction it affords to both the rudest and most tutored of
onlookers thus: 'When all is said and done, our heroes of cricket
are the creation of the faith which all happy boys live and die in.'
But if, like many other great essayists, Cardus was at heart a
romantic, he was also a journalist and therefore a realist. His
realism was, however, less attuned to the spirit of his age than to
his own discerning vision. Some time after World War II he could
write of 'the amateur influence and the patronage of wealthy
families, now impoverished, [which] enabled cricket to develop
not only as a game but also as an art'. Compare that dispassionate
statement with a recent comment by Mr Alan Ross: 'Cricket, like
the upper classes and standards in general, is in permanent decline.
No one would have it otherwise.' Do we detect whimsical resig-
nation or defiance in that 'no one would have it otherwise'? Cardus,
I fancy, would have responded differently; we know that we cannot
have it otherwise, but we certainly would if we could. That was the
realism of Cardus – northern, hard-headed, devoted to cobbled
streets yet able to cherish aristocracy in all its forms. He could dote
on the past, but moved with the times without relinquishing ideals.
Yes, Cardus moved with the times. Consider perhaps the most
famous of all his phrases – it dates from the mid-1920s – concerning
the Trent Bridge wicket: 'a Lotos-land for batsmen, a place where
it was always afternoon and 360 for two wickets'. Such a felicitous
phrase that Cardus used it again a quarter of a century later. The
Lotos-land, always afternoon, but now cricket reflected the Welfare
State, so Cardus changed the score from 360 to 304 for two wickets.
A great realist, say I, even in his subconscious.

And because he was a realist, he was a master of the relevant
simile or metaphor. I emphasise this because it used to be argued
by those who had not fallen beneath his spell that he over-wrote
and dragged in erudite comparisons for the sake of sight or sound.
Nothing was further from the truth. The apparent embroideries
of the Cardus style were as essential as the figures on a scorecard.

Listen to his tribute to a cavalier Australian batsman: 'Mitchell provided opportunities for hard hitting to McCabe whose tempo suddenly ran away with him as Sir Thomas Beecham's does in the last movement of the Jupiter symphony.' I have an old Beecham recording of this work, and can point out the precise moment Cardus had in mind when he wrote of McCabe's abandonment of strict Test Match counterpoint. If you complain of such writing, you are really in rebellion against C. P. Scott, who once said, 'Our readers must educate themselves up to us.'

Whether or not we educated ourselves up to Cardus, we most certainly agreed with J. L. Garvin that he was 'first in his subject'. But was his subject worth it? That depends on our acceptance of any essayist's subject. We accepted the Cardus vision without question, we had no alternative. In retrospect we may smile at some of his dicta which have become as archaic in their application as Hazlitt's description of Neate's guard in 'The Fight'. How quaint to read that 'the ball which breaks away is more difficult to play than the off-break, no matter how well the latter be bowled'. Yet the truth behind this has not been affected by Laker's skill but by the attitude and skill of the batsmen facing him. We recall what Macartney once did to Macaulay in a Test Match, we know what he would have tried to do to Laker; instinctively we agree with the Cardus dictum, for it has within it the seeds of poetic truth.

It was for his mastery of poetic truth that we reverenced Cardus. For us, he told tales of gods and heroes, of superman like Tom Richardson who bowled 110 overs in the Manchester Test of 1896 and took thirteen Australian wickets. Richardson was the most Herculean of all fast bowlers, on this famous occasion he attacked for three hours, but to no avail.

Australia won by three wickets, and the players ran from the field – all of them save Richardson. He stood at the bowling crease, dazed. Could the match have been lost? His spirit protested. Could it be that the gods had looked on and permitted so much painful striving to go by unrewarded? His body still shook from the violent motion. He stood there like some fine animal baffled at the uselessness of great strength and effort in this world . . . A companion led him to the pavilion, and there he fell wearily to a seat.

How, you may ask, could a companion lead him from the field if Richardson was the only man left there? James Agate professed to know the answer. 'Cardus was seven at the time, but I was there. I recall that Richardson legged it from the field and downed three pints before anyone else could reach the pavilion.' No matter, we still insist that Cardus is a master of poetic truth, which is one reason why he is a classic author. He always wrote humanely, and never far from tears. He could be witty when he chose, but at the expense of his readers, not of the cricketers he loved so well.

At his best he was a supreme lover, for ever fastening his eyes on the beloved, re-acting and analysing, digesting, until for example he had fathomed the secret of Rhodes.

Flight the curving line, now higher, now lower, tempting, inimical; every ball like every other ball, yet somehow unlike; each over in collusion with the rest, part of a plot; every ball a decoy, a spy sent out to get the lie of the land; some balls simple, some complex, some easy, some difficult; and one of them – ah, which? – the master ball.

His green and salad days? Would they might have lasted while cricket continues to be played! Other writers may delight us, yet there is always the suspicion that one has outshone them all.

In paying this tribute, I appreciate I have caused some offence to Cardus. 'I remain to this day subject to occurrent fits of irritation,' he once wrote, 'whenever someone praises my writings on cricket, and then adds as though by an afterthought, a word of recognition of my music criticism.' Ah, the perverseness of the man! Of course he has opened our ears to Mahler's ninth symphony, to Bruckner and the songs of Hugo Wolf. But if he hadn't, we might have discovered their genius for ourselves. A single performance of Mahler by a Walter or Klemperer tells us more than all the books in the world. But without Cardus, the fleeting brilliance – fleeting, because impromptu – of a Trumper or MacLaren would be lost and beyond recall. As it is, I sometimes wonder if Cardus did not create Trumper as some ageless symbol of chivalry. *Wisden* proves, I suppose, that Trumper did exist; Cardus tells us how he existed. Only when writing of Trumper did Cardus fuse the romantic and the realist in his make-up. Trumper, he agreed, is not a name likely to guide anybody towards sweetness and light. But 'Trumper's Christian name was Victor; the poetry in "Victor" neutralised the (let us say) prose in "Trumper"; had Trumper been named Obadiah . . .' Most wondrous fusion of romantic and realist!

It is not fanciful to suggest that writing gloriously about cricket is as worthwhile as playing the game gloriously. What better conclusion to a birthday tribute can I think of than to quote Cardus himself. Substitute the appropriate geographical changes, believe that playing and writing can be synonymous, and here you have Cardus on 'Cricketer' of the *Manchester Guardian*.

I see his long, happy life always with the West Country for a background, a far-off England now, peaceful and simple of heart. Morning after morning the summer's sun rose for him, and he went forth and trod fresh grass. Every springtime came and found him ready for cricket; when he was a boy he learned the game in a Gloucestershire orchard white with bloom. He grew in the sunshine and wind and rain; the elements became flesh within him.

That was Cardus on Grace. And who is Cardus save the Grace of cricket writers?

Knighted in 1967 for services to music and cricket, Sir Neville Cardus died on 28 February 1975, aged 85.

In Celebration of Cricket
1978

Pleasures of the Civilised Mind

NEVILLE CARDUS

It is pretty certain that if 'honours' were awarded according to a national Gallup poll quite a number of titles would be missing from Debrett, 'Who's Who' and whatever. But such a people's referendum would surely support the name of John Arlott for a top place, a safe each-way bet. His name indeed is a household word, his Hampshire, not to say Hambledon accent engaging and persuasive on all topics, sport, politics and on Everyman's way of living. He is Johnsonian in his comprehensive view and authority, with more of urbanity than was the Doctor's strong point.

As a writer on cricket for the *Guardian* he had to face the challenge of succeeding Denys Rowbotham and his predecessor – which was as though a cricketer went in to bat after Hobbs and Sutcliffe. I have always admired Arlott's economy of words, his ability to depict a scene or character as though by flashlight. Myself I needed the oil painter's brush and palette to convey to my readers an event or a personality; Arlott can imprint on imagination by means of swift, accurately seen etching; he has a gift for the word photographic. He is never the literary Mandarin, yet he is one of our most civilised writers.

He is, of course, a full man with a mind well-stocked, acquainted with the finest literature, a mind flavoured with a connoisseur taste for pleasures of the senses, good wine, good food, good talk in good company. In brief, he is a great journalist. If I were an editor I would engage no man whose view was narrowly specialist; I should expect my music critic to interest the musical layman who didn't know what was an enharmonic change. I should expect my financial expert to interest people like me, uncertain what is and what is not a preference share.

And I should insist that my sports writer appealed to readers not fully armed technically but who could respond to soccer, rugger, tennis and cricket and the rest as spectacles, British way of life in British scenes. The ripest compliment I ever received, as a cricket writer, came from the pianist Arthur Schnabel, who did not know the difference between a leg-break and a no-ball.

Arlott can at once, in a phrase, hold the general reader's or listener's attention. Here he is discoursing on Jim Laker . . . 'very English looking, six feet tall, firmly built, fair-haired, fresh-faced, quiet in demeanour, coming up to the bowler's end, with his shoulders hunched, cap at a jaunty angle. He moved to his bowling mark at a constabular stroll and, with the laconic air of one with his tongue in his cheek, pattered along a run of artfully varied short strides. Then, wrist and arm cocked, from a good, sideways-on beginning, he swung through a model, high delivery-arc into the positive follow-through which generated so much spin and life.' Hazlitt on his loved jugglers was not more vividly graphic in words than this.

Apart from his craftsmanship as a writer, and his journalist's sense of an occasion, Arlott has unusually high and even ethical principles. If he is tasting a 1961 claret I feel that not only his physical but his vintage sort of moral selectiveness is at work; that is to say not only taste but high objectively viewed standards are operating in him before he declares the wine a good one. So with sport, topics of all sorts – Arlott's experienced and hard-won values must be satisfied.

His treatment in these columns of the South African rugby team and the principles involved has been an example of his integrity, his cool logic, his passion for fair play considered in a large and humane perspective. Frankly I cannot as emphatically as this reduce any issue to black and white; I am always conscious of greys, neutral tones and enharmonic changes.

Arlott is English and Hampshire par excellence, I can well imagine him quaffing in the company of William Lillywhite on

Broad-Halfpenny Down. The honour now bestowed on him will be warmly greeted and liked everywhere; also it reflects honour on the Prime Minister who recommended that it should be so bestowed.

Guardian
1970

John Arlott was awarded the OBE in the 1970 New Year's Honours.

Not One to Cover

JOHN ARLOTT

'Not one to cover' is a seriously cautionary comment in more circles than one. In cricket it is the batsman's warning to his partner that the fieldsman at cover point is too good for them to expect a single from a stroke in that direction. Cover is potentially the villain or the hero of any fielding story. His specific task is to nullify the most romantic of all strokes, the cover drive: on the other hand, he has the opportunity to be the most spectacularly graceful fieldsman in the game.

Strictly speaking – certainly in the firm opinion of any captain who does not himself field in that position – there should never be one run from a stroke to cover. Yet in practice, there often is. Jack Hobbs – who understood the tactic so well because he fielded there himself – used to 'bait' the opposing cover point. First he would play a series of check strokes to him: hit hard the ball would reach the fieldsman too quickly to allow a single, but 'checked' – played gently – there was time for the batsmen to run one while it was travelling to him. Then, having lured him in too close, Hobbs would unleash the fully powered stroke, placed wide of him and too fast to be stopped, for four runs. It was a joke Jack always appreciated, but cover points never did.

Cover does, of course, make catches – skiers and horribly awkward swirlers from mishits, and stinging skimmers from full blooded drives only fractionally mistimed – but he is predominantly a run-saver. Nyren, speaking from the wisdom of the Hambledon cricket of almost two hundred years ago, wrote that the fieldsman posted 'to cover the middle wicket and point' needed to know 'the exact spot where the two runs may be saved, and that where the one run may be prevented' – the perfect posing of a problem no one has ever managed to solve all the time.

Nevertheless, for the man eager in temperament and fast on his feet, it is the most exciting of all positions: he could probably excel in the deep but, at cover, the challenge is not to save the four or the two, but to save the one: he is as deeply involved with every ball bowled as any close catcher, for even the defensive stroke which trickles the ball out on the off side may give the chance of a quick single in his direction.

Nyren says he must 'play from the pitch of the ball, and the motion of the batsman so as to *get the start of the ball*' and 'learn to judge the direction in which the batter, by his position and motion, will strike the ball, and whether high or low, hard or gently, and before it *is* struck, he should be off to meet it.'

There is never 'one to cover' against a man who meets that demand. The first of them was Vernon Royle, good enough to play for Lancashire in 1873 straight from school, while as an attacking bat, he once finished second in the Lancashire averages: but his great fame was as a cover point. He was ambidextrous, vitally important there since the right-hander's cover drive always tends to curl to the left. The enduring tribute to him was reported from a 'Roses' match. Tom Emmett, that shrewd Yorkshire character, was batting when his partner pushed a ball out to cover and called for a run. 'Nay, nay' said Tom, indicating Royle, 'Woa, now, there's a policeman theer.'

Many of the finest cover points, because of their speed of reaction and certainty of hand, have been translated and posted close to the wicket, like A. O. Jones – who invented the gully position – Percy Chapman, Patsy Hendren and Keith Miller. But Gilbert Jessop, the legendary hitter, who also opened the bowling for England against Australia, fielded there all his life and C. B. Fry, in his analysis of the playing methods of the great, picked him as the pre-eminent fieldsman. Jessop was stockily built and, crouched in anticipation, he was valuably near the ground. As he moved in to pick up, his right arm was in position to swing back and his left foot was lifted so, the instant the ball entered his hand, he was ready to throw in. His throw involved no hint of the 'wind up' which gives batsmen the crucial extra moment of running time. He saved the fractions of a second so often decisive in a run out, by throwing from the elbow down, largely by a flick of the wrist, so that the running batsman, accustomed to the often laborious mechanics of the throw from the deep, was beaten for speed.

From the deep, however, Jessop employed a different, more shoulder-powered, but still low, throw. In 1905, the Australians played Surrey at The Oval on the same three days as were allotted to the Middlesex–Gloucestershire match at Lord's. In the county game Middlesex were soon in trouble on a bad pitch and Gloucester, captained by Jessop, took an advantage by the end of the first day. On the second day the then Prince of Wales – President as well as landlord of the Surrey club – and his two sons arrived to watch play at The Oval in the afternoon, soon after the county began their second innings. It had been arranged that W. G. Grace should sit with His Royal Highness, as well as the Chairman, Lord Alverstoke and, since Surrey were batting, Lord Dalmeny their captain joined the company. Late in the day Hayward struck a ball wide of mid-on to the boundary in the distant – Harleyford Road – corner of the ground, a vastly long hit. Suddenly the ball came back out of the crowd in a fierce, low arc, plumb into the wicket-keeper's gloves. 'Middlesex must have lost' said 'W.G.' 'How do you know that, Doctor?' asked Dalmeny. 'Only Jessopus could have thrown that ball' answered the 'Old Man.' He was right. Jessop, unable to bat because of a knee injury, had left the rest of the Gloucestershire side to make the 14 runs they needed to beat Middlesex and gone to take a sight of the Australians. His cab put him down at the Vauxhall corner gate and he walked in just as Hayward's stroke took the ball into the crowd: and, to W.G. at least, the arc of his throw was unmistakable. We may hope the heir to the Throne was suitably impressed by the 'Old Man's' expertise.

In that match at The Oval, Jack Hobbs opened the innings for

Surrey. The critics of the time, though impressed by his batting, criticised his apparent slackness in the field and, always a model professional, he set out to rectify the fault. Quick-footed, neat and controlled in movement, intelligent in approach, within a couple of years he made himself into one of the finest cover points in the history of the game – so that there was never 'one to cover' when Jack Hobbs was there. For a time, however, he 'kidded' batsmen that there was. He would move in slowly, allow them to take a few runs and then, as they assumed the single, he pounced. In eleven matches of the 1911–1912 tour of Australia, he ran out fifteen batsmen from cover. His accuracy was such that, under pressure and with only one stump to aim at, he would whip all three out of the ground.

As a rule, though, he did not take that risk of overthrows: if the minutest margin of time was left to him, he threw not merely to the wicket-keeper, but slap into his gloves. His friend Herbert Strudwick, who for years kept wicket in the same Surrey and England sides, said 'Jack threw so hard that, if I hadn't taken it, it would have smashed my ribs: at first I used to be a bit alarmed until I realised that it was always going to hit my gloves just over the stumps.'

As the years went by Hobbs ran out fewer opponents: one could observe those he did bring off, his catches and his stops, no one could count the number of runs his reputation saved, runs batsmen *might* have taken but did not dare to attempt because Hobbs was there.

In the days before bowlers set out to close the off side, when the old masters of slow left-arm tempted batsmen to drive into the covers, the post of cover point was even more highly specialised than now. Indeed, Middlesex thought it worthwhile to include S. H. Saville for his cover fielding alone: and Jim Hutchinson, whose career batting average was under 19, and who was a negligible bowler, held his place in the Derbyshire eleven for a decade for his value.

Some great men fielded there occasionally. Sir Learie Constantine, surely the greatest of all fieldsmen, was often needed for his close catching but he was pre-eminent at cover point as anywhere else.

The classic Australian cover was Syd Gregory whose successors were Tommy Andrews and, briefly, before he moved to short leg, Victor Richardson. But their cricket produced a whole succession of players whom memory recalls as all of the same physical mould, of no more than average height, wide shouldered and tapering down to neat, quick feet: all of them would run and pick up into the long, low accurate throw which marks the great Australian outfields – men like Vernon Ransford, Johnnie Taylor, 'Nip' Pellow, Sir Don Bradman, Neil Harvey, Jack Fingleton – all of whom fielded at cover often enough to demonstrate outstanding ability.

Other leading Englishmen in the position between the two wars were Percy Chapman – with the dual advantage of being left-handed and having the strength and timing to throw accurately and fast when off balance, but who soon became a specialist at silly point – Eddie Paynter, Jack Davies and the bubbling Jack Stephenson, an entertainment in himself. At one point in the middle 'thirties Middlesex, for the slow left-arm and leg-spin bowling which they always favoured, could set an arc of superb cover fieldsmen – George Hart, Joe Hulme, Walter Robins and 'Tuppy' Owen-Smith – from short third man round to extra-cover, and still have John Human in reserve and the elder master, Patsy Hendren, standing at slip.

In the post-war years the standard has been maintained by Cyril Washbrook, unmistakable as he prowled the covers, cap tilted, shoulders hunched and wary; Reggie Simpson, slim, poised and graceful; the Indians Gul Mahommed, Adhikari and Gaekwad; Athol Rowan of South Africa, Martin Donnelly and Brunty Smith, New Zealand; Alan Rees of Glamorgan and, when he could be spared from the near positions, 'Tiger' Pataudi.

Now, though cover point is no longer considered so important as twenty years ago, and when cricket standards are said to be deteriorating, the game has produced two men as fine as any who ever filled the position: arguably indeed, the greatest. Colin Bland, the Rhodesian, has so studied and practised the movements of stop, pick up and throw that he seems to blend the three in a single ripple of movement, and his accuracy is amazing. The West Indian, Clive Lloyd, hardly looks an athlete for he stoops and shambles: but he moves like a great cat and throws, on balance with whip, off balance with a kind of push, so that he is as fast in reaching and returning the ball as anyone we have ever known.

Still the wise batsman must say to his partner 'It is not one to cover.'

Cover
(a magazine for insurance-brokers and agents)
50th edition

In His Pomp: Fred Trueman

JOHN ARLOTT

By 1959, Tyson's ankle injury had slowed him and Fred Trueman was without doubt the fastest bowler in England. So far as the world was concerned the Australians Rorke and Meckiff – whose actions were, at mildest, doubtful – Davidson, Wesley Hall of West Indies and, now that Heine had gone, Neil Adcock from South Africa, disputed the title. In England his closest challengers were Brian Statham, Peter Loader – of the dubious bouncer – Harold Rhodes and David White: only Brian Statham for completeness of technique and David White, on his day for sheer pace, cast the slightest doubt on his national title.

So he assumed the mantle of authority with a rare blend of violence, humour, tolerance, experience and brilliance; authority, however, never included conformity; he was not the establishment's man; he could still four-letter-word himself into trouble, still slash the establishment with the sharpest edge of his tongue. Sometimes, too, in his impatience, he had to resort to the beamer, dispatched straight at the point between the batsman's eyes; and once when he was offered even greater violence in return, he not only desisted but doled out a couple of drivable half-volleys by way of compensation. Such generosity was unusual. He normally had bouncers, yorkers and boxers ready for those – generally southerners and fancy caps – who were on his grudge list; and Yorkshire can attribute their run of four Championships in the five years of Fred's 'pomp' largely to the fact that, at the pinch, he would usually summon the knowledge, resource and application – and, above all, the pace – to remove any batsman.

It is true of all bowlers, but more so in the case of Fred Trueman than most, that when he was taking wickets he was never tired; once he mounted the kill he could not be pulled off. When, in 1960, he was – for the only time in his career – the first bowler in England to a hundred wickets, he came to Yorkshire's match with Warwickshire at Bradford nine short and closely pressed by Jackson for the distinction. On the first morning he went, as usual, into the visiting dressing room and chatted up his opponents with his latest stories, opinions and humour, which they accepted with the enjoyment of most teams who did not live with him six days a week. At about eleven o'clock he eased himself off the table to go and change with the words 'Oh, yes, and I only want nine wickets to be first to a hundred – so you buggers can start drawing short straws to see which one I don't bloody well have'.

The Warwickshire batsmen were duly impressed; but Yorkshire won the toss and, after a first day shortened by rain, batted until the middle of Monday before they declared at 304 for nine. Trueman emphasised the validity of his boast by having both Billy Ibadulla and Arnold Townsend taken in the gully from lifters in his first over. The spinners, Jack Birkenshaw and Don Wilson, worked their way through the middle of the innings and he had a couple of catches dropped before he took his next wicket – Jack Bannister, edging to the wicket-keeper – and, when Warwickshire followed on, he still wanted six more wickets and he was tiring. Nevertheless, once Cowan had put out their fellow Yorkshireman, Norman Horner, Trueman swept away Arnold Townsend, Mike Smith, Billy Ibadulla and Ray Hitchcock and Yorkshire claimed the extra half hour. Trueman now was clearly spent and Vic Wilson told him to take his sweater. He protested, was allowed another over, which proved little more than fast-medium – and had another catch dropped – before he came off in high dudgeon and Birkenshaw took his place. 'I'll never bowl for Yorkshire again – and don't send me back to leg slip because if you do I shall drop anything that comes near me – like these bastards have been doing off me all day'. Five minutes later he picked up a glorious swooping catch off Barry Fletcher from Jack Birkenshaw's bowling – at leg slip.

As he threw it up he said 'I'll have another over for that' and promptly bowled John Kennedy. So three wickets were left for the next day and he wanted two of them. When play started late, after rain, Bannister and Geoffrey Hill proceeded with steady competence to bat until lunch and double the score. They even batted on into afternoon before Cowan bowled Hill and Fred, who had refused to be relieved, launched himself at John Fox. He was flagging now and it was a wide, and not very fast ball – the last of an over – that Fox chased and edged to Jimmy Binks to let in Ossie Wheatley, one of the world's natural number elevens. Bannister took a single off Illingworth and so – less wittingly – did Wheatley, before Trueman began his twelfth consecutive over of the day. He was weary but Wilson would not have dared to take him off: he was not to be baulked of this easy victim – though it was by no means certain that he could muster the fast, straight ball that was invariably enough for Ossie Wheatley. He gathered himself, rushed in and bowled: the ball pitched short and at no great speed, wide of the off stump; Wheatley went to 'shoulder arms' and let it pass, but he did not do so quickly enough: the ball hit his bat on the backlift and flew between slips and gully for four. While the field shook with laughter Trueman stood, hands on hips, scowling at the batsman. 'Well,' he said, 'that's the first time I've been left alone for four.' Wheatley was not the most gifted or intrepid of batsmen and, while he observed Trueman's exhaustion, he was not certain that he would not now be given a bouncer of greater pace than his batting ability warranted. So, as Trueman moved up Wheatley began to inch away. The ball proved to be a straight full toss but, in the moment before it would have hit the bails, Wheatley's bat, coming from the opposite direction, demolished the wicket completely and, by a fraction of a second, the dismissal became 'Wheatley hit wicket bowled Trueman 5' instead of 'Wheatley bowled Trueman 5' (his batting average for the season was 4.94). F.S.T. was first to the hundred wickets and the afternoon dissolved in talk and celebration.

England's first choice fast bowler; the main strength of the York-shire attack; trusted and encouraged by his captain; at ease with his fellow players; feeling the power of his bowling and the strength of his position – he became easier than he had ever been since the Yorkshire club left him forgotten in Maltby with his torn thigh ten years before.

He walked into the dressing rooms of Yorkshire's opponents with little of the old doubt, less thought that he was a hated 'Yor-kie'. They were – until they had the bat and he had the ball – fellow cricketers – and an audience: his jokes were fresh to them; he was entertainment; a 'Fred session' became a recognised feature of fixtures with Yorkshire. This was the full flood of confidence and contentment and it was confirmed or perhaps simply reflected – by achievement.

He could not now escape the fact of being a public figure even if he had in the past tried to ignore that aspect of his life. His image now took on some consistency of shape through his personal reaction to public pressures. He regarded himself as an eleven-thirty to six-thirty worker with such variations as playing hours might demand. In that time he was happy to bowl, bat and field to the utmost of his ability; entertain unconsciously – sometimes – by his emotional reactions to play and events; and, more often, deliberately, in clowning, responding to crowd clamour and gener-ally dramatising himself. When play ended he believed that his duty to the public ended also: that his life was his own and that he was entitled to privacy – even in public places – and he never really recovered from his annoyance at the discovery that this was not so.

He was not only a public figure, he was the most effective gate-attraction in English, and probably in world, cricket. Under-standably he was in immense demand, particularly for Sunday matches for charities – usually other cricketers' benefit funds – and so long as those cricketers were not on his hate-list, he would go to trouble to help. With some trepidation I asked him to help with a Sunday match for Peter Sainsbury's benefit. It was to be played fifty miles from Yorkshire's fixture at Bournemouth and an invitation to lunch before, and the local buffet afterwards seemed little inducement to offer. He agreed to come cheerfully and at once. When we mustered for lunch an early arrival from Bournemouth remarked 'Fred might be a bit late; when I came in at half-past-three this morning he was just going out for the second time.' It was a chilling moment: the poster and press announcements that Fred would play would, we knew, have put several hundreds on the gate – and to fail to produce the prize attraction would be to invite trouble for future matches. Ten minutes later – exactly on time – Fred arrived, swept and garnished. He was polite and amusing to the ladies; funny and kind to the children. At the match he bowled fast and – to a youngster – slow; he played some brilliant fielding tricks, hit four huge sixes before he gave away his wicket; sold raffle tickets determinedly; suffered some bores gladly; had a few glasses of beer afterwards and, waving away thanks, left for Bournemouth. As he went one player's wife turned to her husband with 'And after all you've said about Fred Trueman! – no one could possibly have been more helpful or more polite – you men are worse than women'.

County cricketers – by no means all off the top playing level – remember Fred for kindnesses of this sort. In his early days he could be bloody-minded; in his pomp he could afford to be generous and he often was – to his friends.

There is a widely accepted picture of Fred with a heavyweight pipe of tobacco and a pint of beer. He does smoke a pipe, but not heavily – or his wind would not have held out as it did; and he does not drink heavily. It is true that he can be seen for long periods with a glass; that he sometimes lays on a 'cod' drunk act; and at times after a few drinks he has been more belligerent than most. For my part I have known some cricketers who did get drunk – some of them frequently; but I would not put Fred Trueman in that category; he belonged rather in the steady beer-drinker class. He suffered more than most of his kind from drunks and clever chaps who decided that they could use his Christian name and would shout across a bar 'Hello there Fred, boozing again, eh?' – and they thought him rude when he resented it – as he infallibly did. He thought he should be able to sit and drink in a bar or dine in a restaurant, alone or in company, without being interrupted every two or three minutes by a stranger who, cutting into thought, conversation or eating, asks for an autograph 'for my boy Willie' – no one ever met anyone who wanted an autograph for himself. This is a difficult aspect of public life and I have observed it striking the same cord of irritation in two cricketers as different as Sir Donald Bradman and Fred Trueman; I have seen them both put up a defence of their privacy which was not only misunderstood but resented – and reported with embellishments within moments.

He resented, too, the pack of small boy autograph-hunters who pester sportsmen – sometimes almost beyond bearing – for signatures on grimy scraps of paper which clearly are not really wanted; or over and over again for 'swaps'. His annoyance in this instance was frequently that of a physically tired man who had given the day his energies and now wanted rest and to follow his own bent: he did not hesitate to tell them to bugger off or take other spectacular if improbable methods of leaving.

In company Fred Trueman could become excited, lose his judgement of what to say, when and how loud to say it; and most of his gaffes were committed out of embarrassment. As an after-dinner speaker he could be entertaining and usually was; he could misjudge his audience and make both them and himself subsequently miserable.

He did not follow the leisure-pattern usual among cricketers who tend – at the away matches that are half their summer life and from time to time in the winter – to flock together. From the early days of antipathies he tended to go out alone. He was often invited out to the homes of non-cricketers: more often he ended up in a bar or a restaurant where his gregarious nature usually immersed him in conversation.

This was his real relaxation and recharging. He could not face the early bed of some fitness enthusiasts. His body was strong and needed no excessive rest; but his mind buzzed with anxieties, uncertainties, angers, hopes, problems, ideas which would be stilled only by the sleep of the truly tired. He tired his mind by parties, talk, company – of a widely assorted and often unexpected kind – and when he went to his room he was ready to sleep. He lay late abed in the morning, partly because he was that kind of sleeper but also from the sense of the luxury, which comes to all those brought up in working class homes, of not having to be early up and off to work.

The rather shaggy outfits of his youth gave way to restrained suitings, fastidiously neat, trousers sharply creased; shirts gleaming, shoes highly polished. This was his chief extravagance; and he is not an extravagant man: though he has a leaning towards sporty motor cars. Like most who have known the pinch or have grown up in its reflection, he meant to be safe. 'I'm going to have a hundred thousand,' he said one day and, as someone smiled, 'and I'm halfway.'

He did better than most out of cricket; justly enough since he played it better than most; he did well out of the side-products of being a famous cricketer, which are often larger than the direct earnings; and he was there at a time when the rewards for cricketers could be high. Fred enjoyed his 'pomp' – and made it pay.

Fred
1971

Radio Newsreel – POW Style

DESMOND H. JACKSON

I was having an afternoon rest, still suffering from the effects of a severe bout of malaria, when I heard someone speaking to me from the foot of my uncomfortable bunk.

'What did you say?' I muttered as I recognised Reg McWilliams, a fellow Tasmanian, grinning down at me.

'I said, are you going to Radio Newsreel tonight? It's "The Life of Bradman",' answered Reg, who offered no apology for breaking into my siesta.

'Of course I am. Nothing could make me miss that,' I replied. 'Will we go together?'

'Right, I'll pick you up at a quarter to seven.'

I nodded and Reg ambled out of the long hospital hut in which I had been a patient for several weeks.

It was January 1944 and the place was Tarso, a grim prisoner-of-war base camp in the jungle on the Burma–Siam Railway, 130 kilometres from its starting point in Thailand. Comprising a large number of bamboo huts, roofed with matted palm fronds called atap, it was built close to the east bank of the River Kwa Noi and its inmates were mainly seriously ill survivors of railway construction gangs.

As in all Japanese POW camps, food rations were extremely inadequate and discipline was harsh. Immediate physical punishment was inflicted on a prisoner who committed even a slight breach of the strict code of conduct to which everyone was subject and guards, with bayonets fixed, constantly patrolled the camp area.

Death was an ever-present spectre in the dank atmosphere of Tarso and funerals of dead prisoners were daily occurrences, despite the great skill and dedication of the camp's Allied medical officers, who worked tirelessly under primitive conditions, with virtually no drugs or equipment.

Tarso was a sinister hell-hole of suffering and despair: a place where the sick either died or recovered some degree of health, only to be sent away to perform more slave labour for their captors.

But there was one bright aspect – the Japanese permitted the prisoners to have limited entertainment and one of the important weekly events was Tuesday night's 'Radio Newsreel', a show which was usually produced by Major E. W. (Jim) Swanton, known throughout the cricketing world as an outstanding commentator. Like Reg McWilliams and me, Swanton was recovering from a long and terrible ordeal on the railway and soon after his arrival at Tarso he joined the camp entertainment committee.

With the authority of the Japanese, the committee had created an open air theatre, utilising a small concave hill which rose steeply from a flat area at its foot. A stage of bamboo and covered with matting was built on the flat land and the POW audience simply sat on the slopes of the hill.

On Tuesdays, a structure shaped like a huge radio set was placed in the centre of the stage. Also made of bamboo and matting, it was about nine feet tall by seven feet wide. Some two feet from its top, a rectangular section had been cut away and crude lamps burning peanut oil were placed on a ledge behind and below the aperture to give the impression of a lighted dial. Under that, there was a 'speaker' – a large round hole covered with hessian – while wings of high bamboo matting extended from each side of the radio set to the edges of the stage, effectively screening actors and assistants from the audience on the hill.

The weekly 'Radio Newsreel' programmes were entertaining documentaries, read by performers who stood behind the 'speaker' of the radio, and 'The Life of Bradman' promised to be of particular interest, especially to the Australians and the British.

When Reg and I sat down on the hill, it was already crowded

and there was a loud hum of excited conversation. Not so different to a theatre at home I thought. It was a cool night but the sky was cloudless with no wind and most had brought something to sit on as a defence against the early dew. At 7 o'clock, all fell silent and the well modulated voice of an invisible announcer opened the show.

'Good evening. This is the Allied Broadcasting Corporation transmitting from Tarso and tonight Radio Newsreel brings you a cricketing feature about the world's greatest batsman. Our programme is "The Life of Bradman" and will be presented by the well-known sporting personality, E. W. (Jim) Swanton.'

After some warm applause, Major Swanton's pleasing English voice came clearly through the speaker.

'Donald George Bradman was born at Cootamundra in New South Wales on the 27th August, 1908. He was the youngest of five children and in 1911, the family moved to Bowral, about 85 miles south-west of Sydney.'

Already, the audience was warming to the subject. 'In his early childhood, he enjoyed music and showed promise at a number of games – tennis, rugby, athletics and, of course, cricket.'

Swanton then described how Bradman gradually developed his batting talents by throwing a golf ball against a curved, brick tank-stand and hitting the rebounding ball with a cricket stump and by employing a similar method to sharpen his fielding. By this time, each man present was so engrossed in the performance that he had quite forgotten his problems and his unhappy lot.

'While he was still a schoolboy, he was making high scores for the Bowral town club in the Berrima District Association and by the time he was 17, the competition was dominated by Bradman and a young bowler who played for Wingello – none other than W. J. (Bill) O'Reilly.

'In the summer of 1926, Bradman joined St George, the Sydney grade club, and in December 1927 he was selected in the New South Wales team for its Sheffield Shield match against South Australia at Adelaide. He scored a century in his very first innings and so, his illustrious first-class career began on a high note.'

The men on the hill, now completely lost in the enthralling subject, stirred in anticipation. Many, including me, had seen Bradman bat and most knew the basic facts of his story but we all listened as though we were hearing about him for the first time.

'He scored 134 not out against Victoria at the end of his first year and his good form continued into the 1928–29 season when England, led by A. P. F. Chapman, toured Australia. Bradman was an automatic choice for the first Test at Brisbane and the Australian public simmered with anticipation. But, alas, he failed, his scores being only 18 and 1.'

A quiet groan escaped from the audience and I was glad to note that this depressing information was received with dismay by the English as well as the Australians.

'Worse still, Australia, caught on a sticky wicket, was beaten by a record 675 runs and for the second Test, which England won by eight wickets, Bradman was dropped to 12th man.'

From the hill came a spontaneous murmur of disapproval.

'But he really launched his international career in the third Test at Melbourne where he scored 79 and 112. Australia lost that match and also the next – both by narrow margins – but they won the fifth Test by 5 wickets, largely due to Bradman's 123 and 37 not out.'

A cheer went up from the Australians and the Major was quick to put things in proper perspective by referring to the remarkable achievements in that series of W. R. Hammond who amassed 905 runs at an average of 113.

'Just the same,' continued Swanton, 'the outstanding innings of that season came from Bradman who gave notice of his true potential by hitting his first mammoth score – 340 not out against Victoria. And the 1690 first-class runs he made in 1928–29 still remains an Australian record. In the following year, he went from strength to strength and in January 1930, on the Sydney Cricket Ground, he broke Bill Ponsford's world record score of 437 by hitting an incredible 452 not out in 415 minutes. Both these innings were against unfortunate Queensland. That [domestic] season,

Bradman scored 1586 runs in 16 visits to the wicket at an average of 113.'

The listening cricket lovers in the audience lapped up the impressive statistics and secretly yearned for more. Swanton did not let them down. He went on to describe the impact which this cricketing prodigy had on the English public when the Australian team led by Woodfull, arrived in England for the 1930 season. Immediately, Bradman gave a taste of his genius – 236 in the opening match at Worcester and 185 not out in the next at Leicester. Many triumphs followed, including a marvellous 254 in the second Test at Lords and them came the third Test at Headingley, Leeds.

'Australia batted first and when Archie Jackson was out for 1 Bradman came in, virtually as an opener. By late afternoon, he had reached 283, four short of the previous highest Test innings, made by R. E. Foster of England in 1903. The excitement of Bradman passing Foster's score was captured vividly by this historic recording.'

There was a short pause during which a murmur of puzzled curiosity ran through the audience. Then, out of the speaker came the noise of a large excited crowd, over which the raised voice of a commentator could be heard.

'This is an amazing performance,' the voice said, 'no bowler has caused Bradman the slightest trouble and he thoroughly deserves to break Foster's record. Tate has reached his mark and he turns.'

By then the crowd noise had died away and the only sound coming from the speaker was the commentator's voice. On the hill, we were all spellbound.

'Tate is running in and he reaches the crease.'

A split second later we heard the unmistakably sweet noise of a cricket bat meeting a cricket ball, followed by a great burst of applause.

'Good ball,' cried the commentator, 'right on the stumps. But Bradman, using his feet beautifully, has driven it straight to the fence. A wonderful shot for four to bring him to 287, equal to

the record. The ball has been returned to Tate and he is walking
back with a pensive look on his face.'

The crowd noise subsided but it was very evident that the listening prisoners were greatly affected by the vividly realistic and quite
unexpected simulated broadcast. It made us feel that we were at
home, sitting by the radio, listening to a ball by ball description
of a match actually in progress, even though we knew that it had
been played more than 13 years before.

'Tate runs in; he bowls and Bradman pushes the ball to leg.'

For several seconds the commentator's voice was drowned by
a roar from the 'spectators' but it quickly emerged again.

'Only one run but that's enough and Foster's record is broken.
Bradman is smiling broadly and the England players are all round
him, shaking his hand. Now he waves his bat to the crowd.'

The noise of applause increased and as it slowly died away the
prisoners began to clap in spontaneous appreciation of the exciting
commentary and sound effects which Swanton and his small band
of helpers had so cleverly and unexpectedly produced.

The Major went on to describe the remainder of the 1930 tour
and pointed out that Australia regained the Ashes by winning the
series 2–1 mainly because of the predominance of Bradman, who
made 2960 first-class runs during that summer at an average of
98. In Tests, he totalled 974 runs at 139, figures which clearly
demonstrated his formidable influence.

After summarising The Don's great success against West Indies
in 1930–31 and South Africa in 1931–32, Swanton added a romantic touch by mentioning Bradman's courtship of a lovely Sydney
girl, Jessie Menzies, whom he married in April 1932.

Then, with great tact, because the audience was about half English and half Australian, he dealt with the notorious England tour
of Australia in 1932–33.

'That series caused a great deal of controversy and bitterness
and I don't propose to say much about it. England won back the
Ashes by 4 matches to 1 largely because Bradman's average was
reduced to that of a very good batsman. Some said he failed: yet
in 8 innings, he scored 396 runs for an average of 56. It would

have been an excellent result for anyone other than The Don. He was unable to play in the first Test through illness but listen to this recording of his performances in the second at Melbourne, which Australia won by 111 runs.'

Again we heard some excellently simulated ball by ball description, complete with striking sound effects. We listened to Fingleton and O'Brien being run out for 10, making the score 2 for 67. The roar of applause coming from the speaker heralded the arrival of Bradman at the wicket, followed by an expectant hush as Bowes ran in to bowl and then a suppressed groan of agonised disbelief as the delivery smacked into the stumps. Bradman was out first ball and we were as shocked as the Melbourne crowd.

But next came a far more satisfying description because the commentary switched to Australia's second innings with the score at 9 for 222, The Don on 98 and Ironmonger, arguably the least accomplished batsman in international cricket, coming in to bat.

I was tingling with excitement for, on that day, at the age of 12, I was at the Melbourne Cricket Ground with my father, watching my first Test match and more importantly, watching Bradman for the first time.

The vivid word-picture coming through the speaker enabled me to recall very clearly how Ironmonger survived two vicious deliveries from Hammond to complete the over – each time without moving his bat at all. That he was not dismissed was a miracle. And then came the next over with Bradman hitting the fifth ball from Voce for three to reach his hundred.

The approval of the partisan Melbourne crowd thundered through the speaker and was echoed by the men on the hill. The description continued and Ironmonger had just been run out for a duck, leaving The Don on 103 not out, when suddenly there was silence.

Immediately, I saw two guards standing beside the stage. We were back to reality and all knew that if the show was to continue, normal formalities would have to be observed and quickly at that.

The Allied Camp Commander, Colonel Harvey, was sitting

close to the stage and rising to his feet, he gave the order 'kiotske'. The audience stood and came to attention.

'Keray,' called the Colonel. All bowed and the guards acknowledged the salute by inclining their heads slightly.

'Nowray,' called Harvey. It was the order to come back to attention. The guards went behind the screen and we hoped that they would not find something to cause them annoyance. They didn't and shortly afterwards, they reappeared, called 'OK' to the Colonel and stomped away. Protocol had been satisfied and amidst a buzz of conversation, consisting mainly of rude comments about the Japanese, we sat down.

Major Swanton resumed his absorbing story as though nothing had occurred to interrupt it.

'After a phenomenally successful 1933–34 home season, Bradman was back in England with Woodfull's 1934 Australian team. Again, he began with a double century against Worcester but soon afterwards he had an unaccountable lapse of form when he hit only one century in 19 innings. But this unusual situation ended with a vengeance for in his last seven knocks, he scored five hundreds, including 304 in the fourth Test at Headingley and 244 in the fifth at The Oval. At Leeds, Ponsford and Bradman put on 388 for the 4th wicket but England saved the game with the help of some bad weather. At The Oval, Ponsford and Bradman did even better, scoring 451 for the 2nd wicket to enable Australia to win easily and to regain the Ashes by 2 matches to 1. Despite some great bowling by O'Reilly and Grimmett and some fine batting by Ponsford, Woodfull, Brown and McCabe, Bradman was once more the difference between the two sides.'

The Major drew some gasps of dismay from the hill when he described how The Don became seriously ill in England at the end of that tour and nearly died. The audience was visibly moved by this segment because all were involved in a struggle against sickness and disease and we had a strong sense of fellow feeling for Bradman in his ordeal.

Swanton described his slow recovery and how, after missing the 1934–35 home season because of the illness, he resumed playing late in 1935 as captain of South Australia, to where he had moved from New South Wales. We thrilled to a brief description of his dazzling form for his new State – 1173 runs in nine innings, including two triple centuries, one of which hurt me a little because it was made against my island State of Tasmania - 369 in 253 minutes.

'Then came England's 1936–37 Australian visit, by which time Bradman had been appointed a Test selector and captain of Australia. His early form that season was well below his usual high standard and England won the first two Tests. But in the third, the Bradman supremacy asserted itself. In Australia's second innings, Fingleton and Bradman put on 346 for the sixth wicket and Australia won easily. Let us go over to Melbourne and listen to a little of what happened.'

Again, a simulated broadcast enraptured the prisoners, who were treated to descriptions of several highlights of that partnership, in particular an over describing a tense contest between Bradman and Verity, the only English bowler who was able to subdue the great batsman during his long innings of 270.

'Australia also won the next two Tests to retain the Ashes 3–2,' Swanton went on. 'And once more Bradman was the dominating factor with 212 in the fourth match and 169 in the fifth.'

I hoped there would be a ball by ball description of part of the innings of 169 because I watched that match, which was played at Melbourne. But I hoped in vain and the Major quickly moved through the 1937–38 Australian season to Australia's tour of England in 1938.

'And so we come to the last pre-war series. Bradman was again captain and needless to say, he commenced with a third double century, against Worcester – 258. His record against that hapless county was three innings, 700 runs, average 233.'

Gasps of amazement came from the hill.

'Once more he had a great tour and he scored freely against the counties. Hutton and Compton made their debuts in the first Test, each hitting centuries. England had the better of the first two games but both were drawn, largely because of knocks of 144 not out by Bradman in the second innings of the first Test and 102 not out in the second innings of the second. Both were great match-saving performances.

'At Headingley, Australia won by five wickets and The Don's contributions were 103 and 16. His 103 virtually won the match, although O'Reilly and Fleetwood-Smith bowled magnificently. And we come to the fourth and last pre-war Test, played at The Oval. It was a plumb wicket and when he won the toss, Hammond had no hesitation in batting.'

Most of the Australians on the hill stirred uneasily, knowing that for them, an unhappy part of the story was about to unfold.

'Against a weakened Australian attack because McCormick could not play, England batted for almost three days and amassed 903 for 7 declared.'

From the hill, groans of Australian disgust mingled with polite English applause.

'And worse still for Australia, Hutton broke Bradman's record by making 364 in 13 hours of intense concentration. We will replay a recording of him passing Bradman's 334.'

Again, the simulated broadcast captured our imagination and the whole audience joined in applauding the English batsman's achievement. The Australians felt a sense of pride when they heard that the first to congratulate Hutton was Bradman himself.

'Shortly afterwards, when The Don was taking a turn with the ball, he tripped and broke a bone in his ankle. He was carried off the ground and that was the end of his cricket for that tour. Fingleton could not bat through injury and Australia was beaten by an innings and 579 runs. Thus, the series was squared but as holder, Australia retained the Ashes.

'Bradman's record for the tour was 2429 runs with 13 centuries, average 115. His greatness is illustrated by the fact that the next best batsman was Brown with 1854 runs at 58.'

The Major then briefly referred to The Don's subsequent two Australian seasons when in 22 innings he hit 11 centuries, six of which were in succession.

'By now the war had come. In 1940, Bradman enlisted in the RAAF but was seconded to the Army in which he was commissioned. Shortly after, he was again stricken with a serious illness. Despite this, he played in two patriotic matches but scored only 18 runs in four innings. In the last one he was bowled by O'Reilly for 12. We in Thailand are prevented from having news of him and we can only hope that he has recovered. What we do know is that he is by far the greatest batsman the world has known and I doubt that there will ever be a better one. He is also a great captain and a fine man.

'He has already made 92 centuries – about one in every three innings – and about 23,000 runs at an average of 95. Incredible figures. Let us hope that before long, when the war is over, we will all have the profound pleasure of again seeing or hearing Donald George Bradman at the crease in Test matches, displaying once more his extraordinary skills.'

After a short pause, the announcer's voice came through the speaker. 'The Allied Broadcasting Corporation at Tarso thanks you all for tuning in tonight and I hope you have enjoyed the programme. This station is now closing down but first a reminder that the next Radio Newsreel will be presented at the same time next Tuesday night. Make sure that you are listening.'

Well before the end of the announcement, the whole audience was on its feet, applauding with great warmth. Everyone appreciated the excellence of the performance which, by stirring so many exciting and nostalgic memories, had enabled each man to forget for a brief period the awful conditions under which he was being forced to exist.

While Reg and I were walking back to our huts I said, 'Great show, wasn't it?' 'Wonderful,' replied Reg.

We said no more for our minds were strangely at peace and we knew that we had just experienced something that we would always remember.

The NatWest Boundary Book
A Lord's Taverners Australia Miscellany of Cricket
1988

A Good Innings

Written on the 40th anniversary of E. W. Swanton's
first radio cricket commentary from the Oval.

E. W. SWANTON

I am ancient enough to remember the beginnings of sports broadcasting half a century ago – the first talks and eyewitness accounts
and, not least, the first reporting, which soon became known as
running commentaries. As it happened, they coincided with my
entry into Fleet Street proper, at the age of 20. In fact, my introduction to the microphone came in 1934, when I began broadcasting a weekly report of sporting happenings at home, on the old
Empire Service, the forerunner of the BBC World Service of today.

It was not thought at first that the action was lively enough to
make cricket suitable for running commentary – so the BBC
devoted itself, so far as live description went, to football, to boxing, to athletics, to rowing and, of course, to racing. Howard
Marshall – surely the most mellifluous voice ever heard over the
air – was the first cricket commentator. Michael Standing, who
ultimately became director of outside broadcasts, and P. G. H.
Fender, who had been a famous captain of Surrey, came next,
and then I was enrolled – and actually made my first running
commentary on 31 August 1938. I did it quite alone, in a very
small room adjacent to the scorers' box. There was just a microphone, table and chair, and a pair of headphones on which I was
given the cue to go ahead – which I did for half-an-hour, including,
as it turned out, the ten minutes between innings when nothing
was going on except the groundsmen rolling the pitch. Goodness

knows how I whiled away the time, but it seemed to go down all right because I promptly got the contract I was aiming at – to report from South Africa the MCC tour the following winter.

Out I went, then, as a freelance, the first Englishman, incidentally, to go out from home and broadcast the cricket back. For the South Africans, cricket broadcasting was an entirely new thing. Thus, I found myself at Johannesburg on Christmas Eve of 1938, alone again in a tiny box, and gasping for air, because Jo'burg is 6,000 feet above sea level. I talked for half-an-hour back to London, and also throughout South Africa, describing, as it happened, some very dull play. On Boxing Day, the cricket was also very dull and I pictured everyone at home half asleep in front of the fire, when there came a rare bit of luck: suddenly, Tom Goddard of Gloucestershire did the hat trick. Any damn fool of a commentator can make something of that – and, apparently, I did. Tom clean bowled the third victim and so achieved only the second hat trick for England in this century. (Come to that, there has been only one since: by Peter Loader, 20 years ago.) The BBC sent me a wire of appreciation, and that gave me the boost I needed.

The fifth Test against South Africa went on for ten days – and was drawn at the end of it because we had to catch the boat home. The BBC sent me a letter suggesting that, because of the extra five days, they would pay me an extra 25 guineas. Just think of it! Well, it did enable me to show a modest profit on the tour, and I came home more or less fully-fledged, and was engaged next summer to share ball-by-ball commentaries with Howard Marshall and Michael Standing – the first time all six hours of play each day had been broadcast. There was some great cricket in that last series before war brought the West Indian tour to an abrupt end: the youthful Denis Compton and Len Hutton spreading their wings, George Headley at Lord's (neat, wristy, tireless), actually getting 100 in each innings, and Learie Constantine signing off the Oval Test with a tremendous burst; the war now a bare week away.

It was seven years before I was back on the air, broadcasting Test and county cricket. Halfway through that summer of 1946,

I was appointed cricket correspondent of the *Daily Telegraph*, and from that time until I retired, almost 30 years later, I combined the writing and the broadcasting of all Test matches, and much other cricket as well. I still have the letter offering me the first postwar commentary – Gloucestershire *v.* Lancashire, on the Wagon Works ground at Gloucester. My expenses were to be £1 for each night 'necessarily spent away from home'.

Next, in the early Fifties, came the challenge of being in on the first days of televised cricket, and, for many years, I used to alternate between radio and television. The techniques, of course, are very different, and I used to be asked frequently which of the two jobs I preferred. I am afraid I had no clear answer, but I always thought that the sound commentaries were rather the easier. The difference, of course, was that, with sound, one had to fill out the basic details of the play as it was happening, with comment on the players, what they looked like, and their playing background; the tactics and the personalities involved; and, when there was time, a general picture of the ground, the scene, the crowd and the weather. In television, by contrast, the viewer has the picture before him, and the commentator has to add only what the viewer cannot see or may not know. But here there is a difficulty because the casual viewer who is not specially knowledgeable about cricket may need a lot of information which will only irritate the expert.

In at least one respect, we of the old school of commentators were luckier than those today because, when there was no Test cricket, we were put to covering county cricket and the Lord's Week, comprising the University Match (then a major fixture), and the Gentlemen and Players, the classic of the year – which only ceased when it was decided, back in 1962, that all county cricketers should be paid – in other words, no more 'Gents'. These other games enabled the BBC to use quite a panel of broadcasters. It gave us all plenty of practice and enabled the Head of Outside Broadcasters to choose his men from the Test matches from quite a large field.

I must say something of this Head of Outside Broadcasts because, in the early years, he did more than anyone to set the shape and style of sports broadcasting. He was a big man in every way – Seymour de Lotbinière, known as 'Lobby', who stood about six feet seven, and was inclined to add a bit by standing on the fender. Wherever one was, Lobby was likely to be listening and, if so, as like as not, he would have some constructive comment to make on one's performance. Lobby, and Michael Standing, who succeeded him, and after that, Charles Max-Muller and Robert Hudson, were friends to all the games broadcast fraternity.

I suppose some may be wondering how I think sports broadcasting today has changed, compared with the early days. Well, I am sure the pace has accelerated – reflecting the pace of life itself. I am a bit of a reactionary as regards clichés, like 'There's no way . . . that's what it's all about . . . at this moment in time', etc. And I will no doubt be written off as an odd dodderer when I say I dislike the accent in the faster moving sports on superlatives. There are so many 'greats' and 'wonderfuls' flying about that, when something truly astonishing happens, there is no language left in which to describe it. We were taught to make the most of a situation without overplaying it. But I do not think that the cricket commentating team can be accused of laying it on too thick. I listen to them with a lot of enjoyment; and, of course, many of the other commentators as well. Some sports – notably racing – are far better covered now.

All of us, I think, were helped by letters, whether of praise or criticism – provided that the ratio was not too lopsided. I think the times when I brought down the most censure on my head were in 1956, when we retained the Ashes against Australia very comfortably in the end, but were helped by two very bad pitches which gave our superior spinners, Laker and Lock, an overwhelming advantage. I said so emphatically, but some people used to grow – still do, probably – very jingoistic where the Australians are concerned. The other occasion had a much wider significance. It was when the Cricket Council responded to the plea of the government to call off the 1970 South African tour of England. I went on the air that night, in David Dimbleby's *24 Hours* programme, and said I thought it right for the tour to be cancelled because it could only have taken place with the aid of hordes of police, in siege conditions; no one could have enjoyed it, least of all our opponents, and I could not bear the thought of our cricket fields becoming a political battleground.

The most satisfying broadcasts were those when one was able to describe or summarise a really attractive day's cricket – especially when England had had the better of it. After the war, the good times for England were a long time coming, and, for a while, it grew as depressing to continue to relay news of defeat as, no doubt, it was to listen to. On the first day of the first Test between England and Australia at Brisbane in 1950, the prospects for England were pretty gloomy. But, to everyone's surprise, Alec Bedser, Trevor Bailey and Freddy Brown bowled out Australia on a plumb wicket for 228 – a truly splendid performance. In those days, my close-of-play summaries were billed to last ten minutes, and I really put my heart into the happy job of telling everyone back home all about it. 'They'll have enjoyed that,' I thought, as I came out of the commentary box; only to find an apparently disinterested engineer who said: 'Suppose ya know we never got through.' As I recall, I could not trust myself to speak.

The great moment one recalls first, perhaps, was when the Ashes were at last won back, at the Oval in 1953, and one had the chance of describing it all on television, with the screen showing the thousands cheering and waving in front of the pavilion, and Len Hutton, the victorious captain, waving back, and Lindsay Hassett making an appropriate and generous speech over the loudspeakers.

Sometimes, those television summaries – in contrast to those on sound – had to be made under difficulties; from any old spot the camera could switch to, on top of a stand or pavilion roof reached by ladder perhaps, sometimes in the rain. Viewers seemed to enjoy richly the sight of one getting wet. I never minded noise or nearby talk or any other distraction when I was doing commentary, but giving a smooth picture of the day's cricket in two or three minutes, without notes, and with several million looking in, was quite a taxing exercise, and I sometimes thought the last person the producer's aides considered was me. At Old Trafford once, one of these gentry started waving his arms like a dervish, behind the camera, trying, as it turned out afterwards, to stop someone moving behind me. I stood this for a bit, but then pointed my finger (at the screen, of course) and sternly told the fellow to stop it. This obviously seemed pretty strange to viewers, but one lady wrote to say that it had stopped her baby crying!

In those days, one's face used to be fairly familiar, I suppose, and one got used to being stopped by strangers who just wanted to talk about cricket. At the end of one season, rather tired, I went on holiday to the South of France, drove away from the airport, and had to stop to relieve nature. 'No more cricket talk for a bit,' I thought to myself. As I stood there, a chap a few yards down the line called up: 'Hello, Jim, fancy seeing you down there at the pavilion end, you might say, me at the Vauxhall.' As it happens, I am off to France again in a day or two, and don't suppose I will be accosted this time.

Test matches, of course, have a thrill and a tension all their own. But for sheer enjoyment of the job, I preferred sitting and talking, describing the game in a relaxed sort of way, in all the many varieties of ground and environment that help so much to make for the charm of English county cricket: the placid setting of the Saffrons at Eastbourne one day, the grime of Bramall Lane, Sheffield (alas, no more) the next. Most of the urban grounds are agreeable in themselves – Trent Bridge, for instance, and Edgbaston – or are rendered special by great historical associations, like the Oval and Old Trafford. Then there are the beauty-spots: Worcester, with the cathedral looking down; and the Parks at Oxford, in the spring; and, above all, St Lawrence, Canterbury, surely the queen of all purely county grounds. From all these and scores of others, at home and overseas, one has talked cricket over the air since that first, amateur effort at the Oval, 40 years ago. What a privilege it has been; and, apart from certain dramas and frustrations, what happiness one has had!

The Listener
1978

The Dexter Enigma

CLIFFORD MAKINS

I hired him, fired him, and now we are partners in crime – in the fictional sense. After I left the paper we met, by chance, at Lord's and revived an old idea – to write a thriller about a cricket match. This was *Testkill*, a minor feat of invention about a Test match at Lord's between England and Australia. I wanted to call the book 'High Noon at Lord's' but this was shot down by the publisher. A second book, based on golf, will be published in July. We have narrowed the angle; the scene is The President's Putter at Rye where golf blues from Oxford and Cambridge compete in the first week of January. The provisional title is 'Putter' but the publisher doesn't like that one either.

Dexter, as captain of England, entered journalism in 1963 with the blessing of the splendid Billy Griffith, then secretary of M.C.C. I gave him a weekly column in *The Observer* with the encouragement of Michael Davie and the late John Gale. We called it 'Dexter Talking', then 'Dexter Writing' and finally, admitting defeat, 'Dexter'. He was, and still is, a dilemma; cricketer, golfer, aviator, gambler, devoted husband, generous host and aloof companion. I should say at once that, apart from a habit of switching off when he doesn't want to listen, I have never had a moment's bother with him. But others think different. I may be The College of One.

See *Wisden 1961*, 'Five Cricketers of the Year': 'Few batsmen, or writers, announce themselves as Dexter did when batting for Sussex against Surrey at The Oval last summer. His first ball, from the pavilion end, was slightly over-pitched on middle and leg. Feet moved fractionally, head hardly at all, but the bat swung the ball for six over long leg and they fetched it back from the seats under the gasholder.' This observation by Robin Marlar was a hint of things to come. Again from the same source: 'No English cricketer bred since the war has so captured the imagination of those inside, outside and far from the boundary ropes of our big cricket grounds . . . "Lord Edward" indeed. But how apt! A handsome figure, at the wicket he stands stock still. One can sense the latent power. The stance is all-important.'

But there were complications. Take this school report written when Dexter was seven years old. 'He shows promise at cricket, but he must remember he has still much – in fact almost everything – to learn and is not yet in a position to control and give instructions to his fellows, who quite rightly resent it.' Just so. Self-confidence, arrogance, bossiness, indifference, innate athleticism – the blend was there from the start.

I met a dancer and choreographer the other day who was at Radley when Dexter, getting into his stride, was head of school. 'We were terrified of him and, what's more, were rounded up to watch him play cricket.' A dreadful thought, but then Dexter had been playing for the first eleven since the age of 14. Before then he had been a very good wicket-keeper. To add to the damage he was sprinting, playing rackets, rugby and golf and already had an eye on the horses. The fillies came later.

A confusing pattern begins to emerge. But there is also singleness of mind. And not only on the cricket field. 'At Cambridge,' Dexter recalls, 'in spite of sport, which had really taken hold of me by now, the most important decision of this time was choosing my wife. I walked into a room and saw one person, one person only, and moved straight in. It was Susan Longfield, who is now my wife.' She still is, a former model and still radiantly attractive. There's a touch of the Scott Fitzgeralds about the Dexters but only in the sense of 'the beautiful people' – the agony, alcoholism and insanity that plagued the lives of Scott and Zelda is conspicuously absent from the Dexter family.

They live very quietly with their two children, a dog – and a vintage Bentley, a Lancia, a Moto-Guzzi bike and a modest little moped. The latest addition is a greyhound which Dexter bought in Ireland. We went to see it run the other night, in awful weather. It came second. And once upon a time there was a racehorse . . .

In the cricketing context 'the Dexter enigma' (if we may call it that) has, always, been shrewdly observed by Alan Ross. On Dexter's character Ross is very sharp indeed. Take this from *Australia 63* when Dexter was the surprise choice to captain England when, to most people, it seemed a choice between Sheppard and Cowdrey. 'On the surface there was little against him; what remained to be seen was whether he could thaw out sufficiently as a human being and make taking an interest in other people seem less of an obvious effort . . . As a captain, Dexter had proved, mainly at county level, enterprising, wayward, but under pressure or when bored by adversity or lack of success, inclined to dissociate himself from the whole proceedings. He is a temperamental cricketer, and temperamental cricketers depend on the stars being right for them.'

It was to prove a tough, grinding series. Afterwards, Crawford White wrote, 'If Ted Dexter survives the latest broadsides to captain England against West Indies this summer he will be a very lucky man.' Survive he did and the stage was set for the Lord's Test which shook the game, the country and even turned away the public from its devouring interest in Christine Keeler, John Profumo and Stephen Ward.

Ross again: 'What nobody could suspect was . . . that they would be present at one of the greatest innings seen at Lord's since anyone could remember . . . Dexter, all told, batted for only 80 minutes, receiving some 70 balls . . . off these he scored 70 runs.' It was an astonishing spectacle. I was there to see it. England were 20 for two when Dexter came in to face Hall and Griffith. Ross moves in without any fuss: 'Suddenly Dexter was 50, the innings not in ruins, but classically erect, like pillars soaring with eagles'.

Dexter's plunge into politics was mind-boggling. This was one thing no one had considered, not even Dexter I suspect. But suddenly there he was, the Conservative candidate to contest Cardiff

South-East, a seat held by the then Shadow Chancellor, Mr James Callaghan. I remember giving this news to Mr David Astor, then editor of *The Observer*. He looked astounded. So did I, I think. There was some laughter and derision but Dexter was as accustomed to this sort of thing as he was to face bowlers slinging down a cricket ball at 80 miles an hour. He recalls: 'Someone knocked on my door and here it was again, this new experience, this challenge, this opportunity.'

Mr Callaghan, sensibly, kept quiet, but for a short time was known as 'the demon bowler of Cardiff South-East'. Then another eminent man wrote an article in the *Daily Express*, the latest to have a crack at solving the Dexter dilemma. Here is the late Sir Neville Cardus: 'Apparently he is undecided at the age of twenty-eight whether he is (a) a great batsman, (b) an unpredictable bowler, (c) a journalist, (d) a television star (in Australia), (e) a potential golfer or (f) a future leader of the Tory Party . . . It is beyond me that Dexter, a young man with his talents as a great cricketer, should think for a moment of giving up any of his days or nights to Westminster and politics.'

Then on June 24, 1965, Dexter, in true character, was driving home in his Jaguar after a day at the races. He ran out of petrol, pushed and steered the car off the road, lost control and the vehicle ran down a short slope to smash into locked doors. It also smashed his leg. That was the end of his career as a first-class cricketer – at least he chose to make it so. Since then, this eminently fit man has managed to contract housemaid's knee, tennis elbow and a touch of arthritis in the hip. But he goes on jogging along, round the common most mornings with wife and dog as company. He keeps up the golf (and a mighty striker of the ball he is) and still wants to win The President's Putter, a prize that has so often slipped from his grasp with victory in sight.

It's difficult to pin him down, but he certainly has style (though in my view his *prose* style has slipped a bit since he left *The Observer* for the *Sunday Mirror*. But that's journalism; books is a different matter). Dexter's off-handedness – one of his charms – still persists but in the two works of sporting crime/fiction we have written together he has caught on very quickly to the tricks of this highly specialised trade. It's a strange relationship when you come to think of it, and there are some people who believe that it doesn't exist. But it does. If we live long enough (and, who knows, Dexter may be the first to go) we hope to complete the trilogy with a thriller about horse racing. Call it *Fontwell Park*. Dick Francis, beware!

Finally, two brief conversations I had with cricketing knights. 'What do you think of Dexter?' I asked the late Sir Jack Hobbs. He replied: 'Whenever he's batting at The Oval I always find time to go and watch him.' Then he shut up. I asked the same question of Sir Leonard Hutton. There was a classical Hutton response. He bent forward and whispered (I strained my ears to catch the words): 'Well, you see, Clifford, he's a great player but he lacks . . . he lacks . . .' – a dramatic pause seeking for the right word while I stood on fire – 'he lacks what I call . . . concentration.'

The Best of 'The Cricketer' 1921–1981
1979

Sheppard's Master Stroke

ERIC HILL

Successful cricket depends to a great extent on memory – the memory of a batsman's strength or weakness; recalling a particular sort of delivery that only one bowler propels; remembering the last time you saw a pitch like this and how it reacted to the weather. These things can shape the course of a game.

'Chess played with a bat and ball' was how the game was once described, and there is still much truth in this. These are, one might say, the strategic and tactical aspects of the game: the stuff of high policy and practical application. They constitute part of the preparation for the game, and if properly employed can greatly increase the pleasure to be gained from playing. For cricket has shape, sense and a strong flavour of elementary justice about it which immediately appeals to everyone prepared to work hard at the game. There is something to be learned from every cricket match, however minor and lowly.

The groundwork of the game involves careful thought, a good deal of hard labour and a lively appreciation of one's deficiencies. These are the basic essentials, and well worth acquiring; for the cricket connoisseur, given the visionary knack, can get inside the minds of the players he is watching, and see how they might plan to resolve their immediate difficulties. He can put himself in the place of batsman or opposition, and work out several possible solutions to each situation; and always, by watching, he can learn to understand different points of view. This is a fascinating exercise, as perplexing as an acrostic and as absorbing as a chess game. Rightly enough, ability is by no means easily acquired. Neither is the yachtsman's nose for a wind, nor the wine-lover's appreciation of a delicate vintage.

However, on a less serious level, we can at least warm to the stump rocketing halfway back to the wicket-keeper, the walloping leg hit for six or the outrageous snick through the slips. These are the strongest memories. Quick to recall, easy to describe, they are the things that warm the public bar on a chilly November night, or keep the pavilion happy when a squally August north-easter has finished play for the day.

Incidents abound in the mind of any cricketer, of any stature, or any qualification. In a corner of my mind I see W. R. Endean given out at Cape Town in 1957 for handling the ball. A sober, solemn moment this, surrounded by all the paraphernalia of an important Test Match.

At the same time, I see our club's number 11, scared to death, trying to stretch out the last 20 minutes for a somewhat grubby draw. The pace bowler returns, hits him on the fingers – the ball is caught. The shout of victory is drowned by the screams of agony – liberally laced with fearsome oaths of the number 11, as he hops about his crease, pitifully wringing his damaged fingers. All goes quiet before our umpire gives him not out, explaining with quiet aplomb that the bowler ran in front of his line of vision and that consequently he could not give a decision. The match was drawn. The fixture was not continued.

I still flinch when I remember standing trembling at extra cover trying to stop the skimming in-swingers that Charlie Barnett used to hammer at those in the way. I laugh when I remember snicking Tom Pritchard high over the slips at Edgbaston and being instructed firmly by Harold Gimblett, 'Well, look as though you meant it, then!'

A warm glow of satisfaction greets that first time, in an important club match, when I had a slog at the pace bowler and, somehow or another, hit the first straight six of my life. The disbelief, relief, pride and utter astonishment of making the stroke which took me to my first-ever century will last for always. The wonder of undiscovered realms to conquer when the first googly flipped its way between bat and pad to the leg and middle stumps is a memory, too.

The first time the high catch went up, and one set off hopelessly to get under it, is another vivid memory. Keep going, keep going, go for the catch, it could swing the match. The effort of running makes the ball go in and out of focus. Must keep watching it. We're nearly there. Blindly, one dives full length, barking elbows, tearing shirt, greening flannels. The ball is in the hands – a newly discovered moment of triumph.

One's mind naturally turns to the simplest memories, those which concern the cricket strokes. At Frome one year Jim Wood, the Sussex opening bowler, let the first ball of the match slip out of his hand. Gimblett, with the eye of a hawk and able to hit anything at any time, flicked it decorously off his eyebrows. On its way, the vast six narrowly avoided decapitating one of the county's oldest members.

At Taunton, in 1961, P. B. H. May announced his arrival at the wicket with one of the most composed, confident, unruffled boundaries I have ever seen, the ball echoing off the bat as it reached the rope and as someone at last moved off his spot.

I still recall the most audacious stroke to get off the mark. In 1939 Learie Constantine, facing one of the Somerset pace bowlers, cocked his left leg thigh-high down the pitch, and executed a neat leg glance underneath it.

There can be very few batsmen who ever hit the ball harder than Ted Dexter. There is a steely, hating-the-ball, whiplash quality about some of his shots, and the straight six he struck at Melbourne in 1963 against the Victorian leg-spinner hardly seemed to rise 15 feet above the ground. It seemed bent on destroying the Press box, which at the time, was a justified target.

But there is one cricket stroke that I shall remember always. It held the quintessence of this wonderful game. I had arrived at the Melbourne Cricket Ground for the second Test in 1963 just as Coldwell clean bowled Harvey. As I tried to shift my seat a little, I trapped poor old Tiger Smith's elbow between the two wooden arms. Tiger, the Reuter man, was to be my guide and mentor for much of the tour, and I was to be his helper. Just afterwards Ron Roberts fell through the canvas of his seat. It was that sort of day, played out in a gripping, tense aura that I had only known before in the last two hours of a county match.

After my long journey I was so tired, hot, excited and dazed that a strange sort of calm descended on me every now and again. This was the first time I had ever watched Australia *v.* England in a Test match, and to watch in company with such a distinguished bunch of writers, as well as 70,000 other people, was something outside my previous experience. For the first time I heard the classic Australian barracking cliché, 'Ave a gow yer mug'. Gradually my dizzy state of mind passed, as I reflected that it was only a cricket match I was watching. I shall never, however, forget the few hours of that early wonder.

At the start of the last day of the match, England, needing 237 to beat Australia, had made nine for the loss of Pullar. Dexter and Sheppard were in, and McKenzie's first over at the England captain suggested that we should have to wait at least one more match before we could chalk up our first Test win in Australia since Len Hutton's team did it in 1955 – eight years previously.

For an hour, the pair survived, with Sheppard looking much the more settled, and Dexter characteristically attempting to take charge of proceedings.

At 10 minutes past noon, Benaud, who had recently shattered the MCC at Sydney by taking 7 for 18 in 18 overs of 8 balls apiece, brought himself on. He had bowled a couple of sighting overs earlier, but now, one felt, the main psychological battle of the whole contest had started.

Especially, it seemed, did this apply to Sheppard. During the game he had dropped two important catches, allowing Benaud in the first innings, and Lawry in the second, to escape at vital moments. He had made a duck in the first innings, victim of an opening over from Davidson which, with a shade of luck, might have included two more English wickets. The curious circumstances of his selection for the trip in any case was a brooding backdrop to his present performance. Several people, myself included, suggested that he had to make 100 here to stay in the side as well as to win the match.

The taut importance of every part of the play communicated itself vividly to even the least receptive of watchers. I held my breath for each ball of Benaud's first over. He threw one higher in the air than normal, just outside Sheppard's off stump. Sheppard, unleashing his rocklike stance at the wicket, lifted his bat to its full extent. A quick step down the wicket took him to the ball. The position of foot, hands, shoulder and head would have made a wonderful cover picture for the MCC Coaching Book. His full strength went into that shot, and the follow-through was a moment of cricket beauty. The ball, met fair and square in the middle of the bat, skimmed over the grassy, holding turf, and even those two arch-enemies of the opposing cover drive, Harvey and O'Neill, were taken completely by surprise. They had scarcely moved when the ball struck the fence and, remarkably, bounced back a yard or two, a long way from the pitch of this enormous ground.

Everything went into that stroke, in a calculated gamble to put an end to past fears and hateful memories; the strength of wrist and arm matched the perfect coordination of eye and judgement to produce a stroke which called up every ounce of character.

My note-book carried the simple, nervous scrawl, 'Sheppard cover drives Benaud 4, 52 for 1, glorious stroke'. England won that Test, and what was the most thrilling shot I have ever seen was also, in my view, the point on which the result hinged.

The Cricketers' Bedside Book
1966

A Sunday in the Country

J. J. WARR

There has always been a close link between cricket and the stage.
Many actors yearn to play in Test matches and inside every
cricketer is an actor bursting to be set free. The Lord's Taverners
Cricket Club is a nice blend of those two frustrations. Many an
actor can don his white flannels and set out to bat in the company
of a great cricketer. Similarly many cricketers can bend down in
the slips and chat up some household name in the world of entertainment. Most of the matches are played on a Sunday and some
of them have an amusing side.

We were told to pick up the charabanc in Park Lane. A nice
concession to both the Tories and the Socialists in the team. The
match was in August against a village in West Sussex. It seemed a
good idea to get a clean-living, sober and industrious citizen to do
the driving for all of us. Once aboard the coach I was introduced
to the fellow members of the team. There was a member of the
Black and White Minstrels, a Disc Jockey, a Television
Announcer, someone out of 'The Power Game', a very old Eminence Grise of an Ex-Surrey Cricketer who was captain for the
day, a very Famous Actor, a TV Personality, a rather stout man
who said he had played a bit for Berkshire, a former South African
Test cricketer and myself. I could only count ten. Upon enquiry
it transpired that a Famous Comedian was making his own way
down and he would join us for lunch. Also sprinkled around the
coach were various assorted well-wishers and wives.

We set off and before we had reached the Dorchester, Eminence
Grise handed me a bottle of light ale. At 10.30 a.m. on a cloudy

August morning in Park Lane I was reluctantly compelled to decline. Famous Actor accepted with alacrity as did Berkshire and Black and White Minstrel. Meanwhile I noticed that the coach driver suffered from a pronounced squint. It seemed that the only way he could stay on the road was by looking at the pavement.

As we made our slow way through Streatham, Power Game, and Television Announcer joined in the light ale orgy. Just short of Slinfold in Sussex, the early home of the Reverend David Sheppard, Famous Actor insisted that we stop at a pub marked 'no coaches'. Some inner mechanism must have told him that it was open. The irate publican was about to show us the door when he recognised the Famous Actor. The double takes did credit to both parties.

We reached our destination in good spirits. We were having lunch with a local dignatory who poured drinks of such high potency that it even surprised Famous Actor. Meanwhile the Famous Comedian appeared in his Bentley and got out of the car swinging a golf club. The witty fellow, we thought. However it turned out that his manager had told him that he was playing in a charity golf match. 'The show must go on,' he said, reaching for his fifth brandy.

Once at the ground, Eminence Grise negotiated with the opposition captain so that we fielded first. He pointed out that our batting was thin to the point of emaciation and that a good lunch had not helped our reactions. 'What is more,' I heard him say, 'some of my team could do with a loosener.'

The bold band of mercenaries did finally take the field. South Africa opened the bowling very fast down wind and two of the village were back in the pavilion in the first over. South Africa was taken off for bowling too well. I thought it would have been subtle to replace him with Black and White Minstrel. However Eminence Grise had a different sense of humour and he put on Power Game instead. His first ball was very remarkable. Disc Jockey was fielding in the gully and, in the orthodox and prescribed manner, was looking at the batsman at the moment of delivery.

The ball struck Disc Jockey full toss on the knee. He uttered a

stereophonic oath. 'Sorry,' said Power Game, 'I hooked it.' Famous
Comedian nodded approvingly. The next one narrowly missed the
square-leg umpire. 'Sorry,' said Power Game, 'I sliced it.'

With two wides out of two there was a distinct possibility that
he would still be trying to complete the over at nightfall. Thankfully as he came in to unleash the third his hamstring muscle pulled
with a twang that was heard in Hampshire. He limped off to seek
solace in the bar.

Our attack, such as it was, was pressed home. Famous Comedian yorked the village postman on the third bounce and did a
hand-stand to celebrate. Famous Actor persuaded the umpire to
award him a very dicey lbw decision. Eminence Grise presided
over the whole operation from a very fine first slip position.

The village reached 250 and it was decided that a rampant South
Africa, still smarting from being taken off, should be put back in
the firing line. He polished them off in three more overs.

It was our turn to bat. Famous Comedian asked to go in early
as he had to nip off home. One of the side-shows round the village
green was pony rides for children. It was decided that Famous
Comedian should open the innings and ride to the wicket on one
of the ponies. Accompanied by Berkshire, they went to the crease
for all the world like Don Quixote and Sancho Panza. Having
taken guard, Famous Comedian commanded, 'Tether my horse at
cover point and tell him to wait.' He played three golf shots and
retired to a standing ovation.

Disc Jockey entered the fray and snicked the first ball hard to
the wicket-keeper. The village umpire, who was a television addict
himself, gave a memorable answer to the concerted appeal, 'I shall
have to vote that one a miss.'

Meanwhile Famous Actor had disappeared along with the coach
driver. They were discovered in deep conversation in the 'Cricketers Arms' which had been granted a special licence to stay open
the whole day. In an effort to match the Famous Actor whisky
for whisky, the clean-living, sober and industrious citizen was in
the last throes of alcoholic paralysis. He was meant to be driving
us home.

Famous Actor showed no remorse at what he had done. He strode to the crease, erect as a guardsman, and scored a quick forty. We won in the last over of the day with Power Game and Eminence Grise at the crease and Black and White Minstrel acting as a runner for Power Game. South Africa had blasted a lightning seventy and was elected 'Man of the Match'.

Meanwhile a desperate battle was going on to sober up the coach driver. We had intended to leave for London soon after the match. The driver's squint was not fully restored until 11 p.m. and we left for home at 11.15 p.m.

We had been forced to have a tremendous session at the 'Cricketers Arms'. Famous Actor had run through most of the great Shakespearean speeches. Black and White Minstrel had led us in many rousing choruses and Eminence Grise had revealed a quite undiscovered talent for tap dancing.

As we went along through the Sussex countryside, the coach driver was looking at the hedges and steering an impeccable course straight up the road. We knew all was well.

The light ale had not run out and Berkshire spent most of his time pouring it down his old school blazer. Television Announcer tottered to his feet to read the midnight news. Disc Jockey's head was going round and round. South Africa kept complaining that he could not see the Southern Cross amongst the stars.

The coach sped through the night and the driver was so aware of his earlier lapse that he insisted on driving all of us home to our individual doors. When we passed Slinfold, Famous Actor insisted that we should stop at the same pub as on the way down. The inner mechanism was not working so well.

I was the first to be dropped home in St. John's Wood at 1.30 a.m. As the back of the coach disappeared into the still, moonlit night I could just hear Famous Actor, 'Friends, Romans and Countrymen . . .'

Heard in the Slips
1967

Make a Game of It

HUGH DE SÉLINCOURT

In these swift afternoon encounters each game you play may be a
little work of art, complete in itself, and like no other game noteworthy; and also there may be games which, apart from the
weather, a wash-out by rain, are simply not games at all. There's
nothing to catch on to, nothing to be drawn into: you wonder
how a sane man could be seduced into taking any part in a performance so lamentably forlorn and futile. So the phrase *make a game
of it* is fraught with much meaning. 'Ah! I hope we make a game
of it.' 'Yes: that's the thing: sure. Win or lose, who minds? So
long as we make a game of it.' Seldom a Saturday passes without
those words being used in those taut moments before a match
when the team so casually assembles, loafing up, their careful non-
chalance the measure of their suppressed excitement.

It was a hot afternoon in June, a real hot summer afternoon in
June, with a shimmer of heat haze on the not too distant hills,
when Tillingfold played The Vagrants, a touring side from
London. A perfect day for cricket. And when Gauvinier reached
the ground soon after two, he found most of the visiting team,
who had been taking lunch at the 'Black Rabbit' in the village,
about on the ground, having a gentle knock, very gentle; bowlers
soon sat down laughing, to be joined by the man with the bat,
who, prodding them with gibes and his bat in vain, himself subsided soon on the good green turf to chew grass and to wait – a
pleasant summery sight.

Old Sam Bird in his shirt-sleeves made his careful way through
the gate from the road, in good time for the solemn rite of knocking

in the wickets on the pitch chosen and marked out on the previous evening. He was all one large inner beam of immense satisfaction at the prospect of the game.

'It'll be middlin' hot out there, I take it.'

'Scorching. Can't be too hot for me.'

'They look a very likely lot. But I've heard nothing whatsoever about whom they're playing and how they've done. Nothing. It's early for a side to be touring. Things have all changed though since I played. Why, there ain't no such thing as distance now, as you might say.' And his voice sank to a conspiratorial depth to enquire: 'And who is this new man Carswell as we've got playin' for us? Not the V. T. Carswell as played in the 'Varsity Match a year or so ago: Took fifty odd against Oxford, if I'm not mistaken.'

Sam Bird follows cricket with avid interest. He knows the county teams for the past forty years and more: his memory remains young and retentive for fresh names. He turns the pages of Wisden with a damped thumb and reads with the reverent care with which Thoreau's old lady used to read the Bible, page by page, a chapter every morning, and when the last page is reached begins once more with the first.

'Yes. That's him. He is staying with the Flints. Dead keen to turn out for us. Stiffen up the batting a bit. We're a real good side. It ought to be a marvellous game.'

Which offered, of course, too good a chance for old Sam to miss.

'I have often observed, Captain, that the best sides on paper often put up the poorest show. What I believe they call in the papers, the glorious uncertainty of cricket. There was a side called The Vagrants as I remember in the 'nineties, but that was some years ago . . .'

'Half a minute, Sam.' Gauvinier hurried off to join a group of the visitors moving towards the pavilion: a genial crew revelling in their luck with the weather. Two days' country-house cricket at a place some forty miles away he'd barely heard of, that filled Monday and Tuesday; you could always get games on a Wednesday and Thursday, according to early closing; Friday blank for bathing, and finish up on Saturday, having made a week of it. Hoped they were infringing no copyright with the name. Yes: they drew on various clubs in London and round about. Four or five could manage the whole week. 'Thanks to old Jack Martin here, we've never been a man short. Oh, to-day, yes. Quite a decent little side.'

'Ah, forgive me: just a moment. There's a man – yes, *the* Carswell – staying here. No, he doesn't turn out regularly . . .'

Gauvinier strode off towards the oncoming General Durslake, who was escorting with understandable pride (though his usual manner, you might have thought, precluded the possibility of *more*) the redoubtable Carswell on to the field, whom Gauvinier took to at once – small, mild, retiring and very neat – his head indeed became almost hang-dog in horror at the General's full-throated pronouncements as to the good fortune of the village in having a player of such calibre in their midst, 'which you, I am sure, Mr. Gauvinier, will be the first to bear me out in—' Gauvinier smiled and hummed and coughed and ha-ed at what he hoped to be suitable moments, and as soon as possible:

'Care to come into the pavilion?'

'Thanks. See you later then, sir.'

And a little later a low murmur reached Gauvinier's ear. 'A dear old boy, but oh my God, he does give tongue.'

A remark which was lapped appreciatively up but left unanswered, as Carswell was introduced to various members of the team, much awed at the proximity of so distinguished a performer, until the irrepressible Freddie Winthrop was heard to mutter: 'Sorry to let you down, skipper, but I've just had wires from Hobbs and Larwood and Jardine to say they can't get out of the games they're booked for.' And the general laugh broke the ice.

'Jolly decent to find me a place. Always wanted to turn out for Tillingfold. Beaten Raveley this year?' He looked up from lacing his cricket boots to enquire, and Gauvinier left him, obviously liked. Left him to find the opposing skipper and toss.

He found the skipper and won the toss and elected, with a laugh, to bat.

Old John McLeod, the best secretary that any club could have
(alas! he no longer played: that sudden stoop was too much for
his jovial rotundity; his wife, too, may have . . . but we won't go
behind his old back with horrid surmise) – old John McLeod came
bustling up with beaming, rosy face, panting and laughing: 'Well,
fancy you winning the toss now. But it doesn't do to be too pleased
about that: the toss isn't the game. Oh no. Not a bit of it. Still,
you've a fairish sort of a middlin' decent side – on paper – though
no beautiful nice steady opening batsman to break the bowlers'
hearts for them and leave dreadful wild sloggers like you to make
hay and enjoy themselves swiping and slashing. But what an afternoon. What a beautiful, lovely afternoon, to be sure. Summer.
Summer. Summer.'

He trotted off, and Gauvinier wished like hell that he were still
able to turn out. He knew well enough how the old fellow hated
the bodily disability which kept him from playing, and how his
indomitable old spirit triumphed, so that his presence on the field,
watching, added to the game's enjoyment.

'Ah well! I've had my innings, boy; and it's an allfired miserable
sad thing not to be playing any more: but devil take it, don't pull
such a long face, boy. I'll enjoy watching more than most of you'll
enjoy playing . . . such an earnest lot of grousin' rascals as never
was. Who'd blame 'em with such a skipper? Not me.'

Dash it! Well, anyhow, he was still lively and about, the Lord
be praised.

'I've won the toss all right,' Gauvinier called in to the pavilion.
'Will you get your pads on, Carswell, and take first knock. Ballard,
there, will be with you. Number three, Alec?'

'Eleven? Skipper?' asked Freddie.

'Ass! No, seven. And I'm six, and we'll just have a nice little
stand together.'

'Not if you get taking a dip at the first ball.'

'I'll bring the list back. Yes, four as usual, Walter: five, Jim.
And Bill, you don't mind going in last, do you? Just time for a
few sixes into the road, you know. A bit low down, William.' He
took a boy aside to speak to, the son of a builder; very nervous,

but a good bat, who had not done himself any justice yet on the side. 'You'll be ten, I'm afraid, to-day; but we've rather a strong side out. Change your luck, very likely. We shall want all we can get, you know.'

'Dad says he reckons it the best side that's ever turned out for the village.'

'I don't know about that; but he's not far wrong. Tea five and draw seven. Is that all right? Yes. Rather, we've got one. Sam! Umpire's coat wanted. If you've not burst 'em both. All right, Francis. I'm coming. Tea five then, draw seven. Number ten, then, laddie, this time . . . Sorry, didn't I tell you, Mr. Morley? Eight.'

He strode off to the score-box, waving the list at a frowning Francis, passing Sam, who was explaining the boundaries to the umpire while he assisted him into the borrowed white coat, which had been taken from a locker and tossed out of the pavilion. 'Fower to the hedge. Six over. Them flags over there – 'Sam pointed sadly to the pernicious outfield. ' 'Tain't right or proper, strictly speaking, but we has to judge 'em best we can. And now perhaps, if it's all the same to you, we might be makin' our way . . .'

The two umpires in their white coats, fingering beans in pockets, walked slowly out on to the field: the great moment of beginning which made small boys on the instant and for the instant, still and staring, in a sort of awe as at something dimly sensed as inevitable like fate. 2.35. And not only small boys felt a tough clutch on their inside, winding their nerves tight with anxiety as to what the next minutes had in store.

The visiting captain was setting his field. The red new ball was being thrown about. The stumper came on last, pushing on his gloves. Yes, a likely lot, as Sam Bird had wisely said. They certainly looked it.

A sad voice was heard in the pavilion. 'Well, anyway, I hope we make a game of it.' And a sharp expostulation: 'Good Lord! Some fellers. Gloomy. Well, talk about a funeral.'

A tense stillness followed the round of clapping that sent off Tillingfold's first batsmen to the wicket. Ballard, tall, dark, beautifully made; a real class bat, he'd been making a lot of runs. Ballard

was taking first ball, facing the road, to a tall left arm bowler with
a lovely loose action. Two slips. Third man – deep extra cover –
square leg very close, mid-on nearish, well in front of the bowler's
wicket: a silly point a bit behind . . . likely to bump them apparently. Play.

One watches the first ball with a queer intensity. He had been
'putting a few down' very much the same as he now bowled: very
little faster. Ballard played it full in the centre of his bat, a nice
shot towards cover, jumped forward crying 'Wait!' Carswell, mis-
hearing, started to run. 'No, wait,' came the shout. Carswell half
hesitated – and Ballard calling, 'Oh, come on then,' ran, as Carswell stopped and turned. Ballard slipped trying to get back and
was easily run out. Just a foul misunderstanding. Promptly taken,
there would have been a comfortable run. Neither would have
been run out, as is often the painful case, if either had done almost
anything but what he did do. And Carswell was clearly most
forlornly upset, not liking a little bit on his first appearance for a
side to have run out the side's most useful bat. Yet the justest
judge would have found it difficult to apportion the blame for the
horrid accident fairly. A nerve-shattering piece of bad luck for the
village, not soothed very much by old John McLeod, who
declared: 'What a miserable, wretched, disgusting thing to happen
with the first ball. Still, mistakes will happen.' And he remembered
with excruciating vividness the awful moment when he, such a
good judge of a run too, had run out the great Waite – in that
never-to-be-forgotten match against Raveley when he had carried
his bat through the innings. 'They'll be shook up,' he moaned to
Gauvinier. 'Make bad worse, they'll be that shook up.'

But Alec John put his first ball confidently to leg, gave a confident call, took a confident run – and old John was comforted and
murmured contentedly, 'Ah, that's better, that's better!'

And Carswell took centre and faced the bowling.

Then happened what is probably a small record in the sad annals
of cricket misfortune: for Carswell drove a half-volley so hard
back that the bowler jumped to one side to avoid it, and did not
jump clear, for the ball struck the sole of his boot, was diverted

yards on to the wicket, and Alec John, backing up, was run out. 1–2–1.

The game had been in progress for five minutes, five doleful minutes for Tillingfold. There was just nothing whatever to be said about it. Carswell must have wished he'd seen a black cat or something before his innings. Had he walked under a ladder? Anyhow, it's no good being superstitious, of course; he had to continue his innings, and the first over was not finished yet. No doubt he tried to pull himself together, but *it* was too much for him. Who could blame him? He played forward, correctly enough, at the next ball, but no one was really surprised that he played an inch or so inside it and flicked up an easy catch to short slip. There is that against which the strongest spirit cannot stand. 1–3–1, on a perfect wicket, on a perfect day. The stars in their courses were fighting against Tillingfold, and that, too, not in the black hours of the night, but in brilliant full daytime sunshine. Such catastrophe has an odd effect on some: they are forced, as it were, to side with misfortune and pretend to find their team's discomfiture funny: and to greet with ironical cheering any ball that did not take a wicket.

It turned our lusty stumper, Jim Forman, savage. Always inclined to be reckless at the start, he now let out in fury at the remaining balls of that first fatal over, missed them completely, and survived: a sight so lamentable as to dim with sorrow the more judicious eyes. Walter, at the other end, was dogged and tight and feeble, poor chap; making nice harmless bowling look quite deadly in its guile. He got a lucky one to leg, and Jim could hardly wait to take centre before continuing his display of rage. It is rarely wise to ask for it: he asked for it loud and clearly: and of course on this dreadful day he got it. For he let full fly and connected, driving the ball hard at mid-off who, standing rather deep, stretched out a large right hand and brought off a beautiful catch, which the enraged James by his manner seemed to suggest (oh! so wrongly) was another slice of foul bad luck. 2–4–0.

Gauvinier went in, hoping humbly, but without much confidence, that he might be kept from being merely silly; for there

was *that* at work determined to make the side look ridiculous. The
score struggled painfully into double figures without further loss,
when Walter, at length feeling less dogged and tight, took his first
hit at the left-arm bowler, quite a good shot, but a shade too soon,
and, getting under it, gave deep extra cover a nice catch to hold,
and he held it. 13–5–6.

Freddie Winthrop came in, hurrying. He and Gauvinier had on
several occasions made a pleasant stand together when a stand had
been needed. Would they again? The worst of it was that these
horrible opening minutes – eight minutes, still, to three, old John
McLeod looked at his watch with anguish to observe – had trans-
formed the doings of the afternoon from a game to a calculated
torture. 'Ah, got to take your medicine!' as one spectator remarked
to a rueful player.

And the score dragged slowly along – still in its futile teens, for
all the grim persistence of Freddie and Gauvinier at the wickets.
Came a half-volley outside his legs at which Gauvinier smote, and
which he missed; the stumper jumped to stop it with his pads and
the ball shot off his knee on to the wicket: 'How's that?' The
umpire's finger was instantly and rightly raised. As Harry
informed Harriet in the song, if she died unwed 'you've only got
yerself to blame'; there was no need to have missed the ball, no
need to have dragged his right foot so far over the crease in missing
it – still it was unfortunate. 16–6–5.

Altogether too much, the whole dreadful business, for the next
man: he took a wild dip at his first ball, which was straight and
set his middle stump leaning. 16–7–0.

And father was exhorting his son William: 'The wicket's perfect,
boy; the bowling is nothing to mind. Just you stay quietly there,
as though nothing had happened and you were batting number
one as you used to bat at school and should by rights bat here . . .'

Gauvinier passed out of earshot, unable to bear the excellence
of the precepts given; somehow it seemed the wrong moment to
indulge in them. And when it came, as it quickly did, to William's
turn to bat, father kept on with his counsel, yards out with son
towards the crease, who uttered an unfilial but explicable: 'Oh,

that's all right, Dad!' which being interpreted with gesture and omissions must be construed far more strongly than the mere words can suggest.

Well, there they were, Freddie Winthrop and William, batting: the last frail gossamer hope – for Bill, ah, Bill! he hit sixes or got out; always, pretty well, got out. And nobody rebuked Jimmy, the stumper, for starting to put on his pads. 'No sense in hanging about.'

The team were all hardened in advance by this time against the ignominy of being skittled out, and felt that the sooner they went into the field to give the visiting side their care-free batting practice, the better. There was nothing to bowl against: no hope of getting them out cheap, hitting mightily, declaring, and pulling the game out of the fire on the second knock. Spirits sunk to their uttermost ebb. The batsmen were gloomily, almost angrily, watched; their puny little efforts to prolong the agony were not really liked! A run here, a run there, a couple of byes – what was the use of that? And they were running very nicely; Freddie was quick; no doubt about that, very quick. Not much good now, though how excellent it would have been with a hundred or so on the board: a good little stand of twenty or so for the ninth wicket. But their pluck now served to sink others deeper into sorriness and gloom. Yes: William put them to leg with a neat shot, quite well, but not quite well enough to justify father's ecstatic perpetual cry of 'Oh, beautiful stroke, boy! Beautiful stroke!' You couldn't help unkindly feeling that so long as his boy showed up well, nothing else much mattered. In fact horrid thoughts were everywhere present, like a swarm of gnats, eager to bite.

And meanwhile thirty was hoisted by eager little boys, which drew a cheer, disgustingly tainted by derision. Even the bravest watched fascinated, of course, but utterly refusing to think it was any good, utterly refusing to hope.

And forty went up. A new bowler was put on, who presented William with a full toss to leg and a long hop, which were both quietly despatched to the boundary for four. Then a swiftly run, snatched two past cover and fifty went up. There was no derision at all in the cheer which greeted it. Jimmie the stumper began to unbuckle his pads; then stopped, thinking very seriously, 'If I takes them off they'll be certain to get out,' and buckled the straps up again. That was not superstition, of course, but plain common sense.

But, oh Lord! what's this? Look at Freddie! Such a shot. William's fours must have excited him too much; what was meant for a dashing drive struck inches too high up on the bat and soared up softly to a pleasant height to drop sweetly down into the hands of mid-on, a sitter if ever there was a sitter: down indeed it sweetly dropped straight into mid-on's hands and sweetly through them to the ground: to a roar of joy, as Freddie turned back laughing to the wicket, which he was beginning most woefully to leave.

Spirits rose with an almost painful jerk at this large slice of luck thus suddenly and unexpectedly presented. The miasma passed off in one great gasp of delighted astonishment, and in one great shout of joy as Freddie, not to be put off, leaped right out at the next ball and slashed it wide of mid-off licking along the grass to the boundary. All eyes were bright, all faces eager and happy, as the score mounted, easily and smoothly, to sixty. Every run was cheered, and every run increased the tensity of excitement, as gradually it became evident that some sort of a game was after all to be made of it. Sixteen when William went in. Good boy, it's sixty now. And little old Freddie. 'What price the Doddler!' as Sid Smith (alas! a mere spectator now) shouted from the pavilion at the top of his loud, clear voice. Old John McLeod was beside himself: 'You never know at cricket! You never do know at cricket! Was there ever such a beautiful nice game? Don't dream of declaring till tea, boy; don't dream of declaring till tea! Ah now, there, bless my soul, if those boys aren't putting seventy up. And that dear good foolish woman of mine wanted me to go to the pictures. Did you ever hear of such tomfoolery in all your life to miss a game like this? Oh, well hit, boy, well hit!'

William had made a lovely shot to leg, a quick tap, beautifully timed. Missed, as it had been, that shot was his undoing: his left leg came well in front, and l.b.w. he'd been with sickening frequency. Now it was his making; the bowler kept on plugging 'em at his legs, swearing to himself (you could pretty well hear him!) he'd get him leg before this time. But it was William's day, not his.

And eighty went up, which, as old John hurried round assuring everybody, was every bit as good as 120 on almost any ground but ours (where the dreadful outfield turned many a safe four into a two or even a sorry one). A quarter to four. Those two good boys had been batting for as near the hour as made no matter. A new bowler was put on: an oldish chap. He seemed to know what he was about, for he instantly brought two men on to the leg side, knowing apparently to the exact inch where he wanted them to stand (Sid Smith called out cheerily, to a general laugh, 'Ah, body-line bowling's barred, sir!'), closish square, and dropped mid-on back ten yards – with a very deep mid-wicket. The leg-side trap took a few minutes carefully to set. He then proceeded, with a stiffish action, to bowl a full toss well outside the off-stump, which must have disconcerted William, for he took a lash at it and missed. The bowler swung his arm round to loosen it, and laughed. He gave the impression of being anxious to have his bit of fun, and almost everybody watching was in the happy mood to think him merely funny. Along came a highish full toss on William's body, who swung out to sweep it on its way; but the ball hit far nearer the splice than the centre of the bat and dropped into the hands of the carefully placed short leg. Who laughs last . . . 'I knew it! I knew it!' wailed father. 'Oh, boy, what a pity! Nearin' your fifty, too, and the hundred not quite up.' 83–9–47. And many were hoarse and sore-handed with appreciation of young William's performance.

Bill hurried out, half running, half walking. The horrid trap had been set apparently all specially for William, for the field was rearranged – more usually, by which Sid Smith, knowing Bill's methods, was immensely tickled. For Bill's repertory of strokes is confined to one terrific wipe; he has a marvellous eye when it functions – must have; quickness of foot, too, when they do move

– must have. Yet no one knows, himself least of all, why or when or how he does anything with the bat. He's just a miracle.

Whack! at the first ball; nowhere near it; wicket still stands. The bowler thinks another like that will just do. Along it comes. Whack! This time, though, hit clean and sweet, soaring into the road, off the off stump. The old bowler, surprised but unshaken, puts down a perfect-length ball on the middle peg: harder and higher and well over the road, that one – to frenzied yells of delight from every little boy on the ground. From eighty-three to ninety-five in two hits, when every single run was of priceless value! Ah, yes, here it comes, slower, tossed farther up for Bill to hit across, and he hits across it all right and misses it, and the ball misses the wicket by barely half an inch, but misses it.

Follows a maiden, for Freddie is aware how near we are to the hundred and simply can't do more than stop 'em, knowing one beat from Bill will do the trick, and send the hundred up; superstitious, too, about Bill's inability to hit any ball without the lure of the road to help him.

It is difficult to believe that a good-length ball on the middle stump should be jam, pure and simple: one step out with a swinging crash, and the ball soared over both hedges far into the orchard on the other side of the road. 101. The bowler could not believe it: must be a fluke, not to be repeated. He sent down an even better ball, slightly faster. Whang! The same shot, considerably higher, but dropped safely in the road. 107.

'Oh, go it, Bill!' 'Just one more, please.' 'Let 'em have it!' 'Here comes the old 'bus!' Yells came and shouts from the crowd, in a state near mania now with excitement and the sheer mad fun of it all. Young Bill, of all people, helping himself to sixes, off a toff team, too. ''Struth! Look at that! Would you believe it? The best of the lot, that one.' They stood up and leaned forward and yelled through cupped hands at him, 'Well hit!' 113.

The old bowler pulled himself together and managed at last to send down a slowish half-volley on the leg stump, a gift of six to a batsman, but a fatal ball to Bill, who hit, of course, yards across it and was bowled. 113–10–30. Not enough, but not bad considering that at one time it was about two to one against Tillingfold making twenty.

Carswell had got caught up into the wild excitement; keen as a prep.-school kid, Gauvinier noticed with glee. He'd been sitting with the team in the pavilion, the General having gone off for bowls; he rolled a cunning wood.

'We must do 'em in. After that ghastly start! Too priceless!'

'There'll be three-quarters of an hour before tea.'

Tillingfold rather prided themselves on being good in the field, and it was clear so soon as ever the innings started that no runs were going to be given away from slackness, or catches dropped through inattention. Every man was alert, on his toes, in his place; all keen and glad that the side had done so well, although only three of them had had much fun at batting. You could feel the vibrant keenness if you were sensitive, as Gauvinier was, to the feel of a side. Carswell's good fielding had been remarked upon at Lord's. He never fielded better than he did against The Vagrants on the village green, and his neat, good work was appreciated, though not on this occasion written about in the newspapers. The batsmen took no risks; there was no hurry; they played themselves carefully in against bowling (Ballard one end, Gauvinier the other) that needed watching. Runs came very slowly during the first half-hour, and then Ballard, with a beauty that came in from the off and took the leg bail, clean bowled. No. 1. 11–1–5. Twenty was up by tea-time.

But almost directly after tea, they began to attack the bowling. Nothing reckless or unsound about their play; just determined aggression, which set every man on the field more tightly on his toes, more alert for a possible chance. It was good cricket. By forty Gauvinier had a double change, taking off first himself, then, an over or so afterwards, Ballard. In the fifties he went on again, and off his second ball young Carswell brought off a catch he will never forget and few will forget who saw it held, running full tilt back from cover, just reaching it with a stretched right hand. 58–2–23.

That magnificent catch started a change that was dramatic in its suddenness. It looked a certain four as it left the bat. 60 for 1, with two men going strong looked wellnigh hopeless. 58 for 2, looked better, and when Gauvinier yorked down the leg stump of No. 4, 58 for 3 began to look promising. He put Ballard on again, and Ballard, terrifically on his mettle, shaved the wicket with his first ball and scattered it with his second, which came in a good foot from the off, a real beauty. 58 for 4. Tillingfold were certainly going to make a game of it. The excitement grew in tensity. The new man started off, as though he'd been batting for an hour, with perfect confidence: a two past mid-on, a neat four to leg, then lashed a short one on the off well past a slower cover, but Carswell, moving with neat swiftness, brought off another superb catch, a less spectacular, but to a trained cricket eye, an even better catch: sheer alert knowledge took him to the right place and made the thing look almost simple, which would have appeared no catch at all to almost any other man on the ground; for he started to move practically the moment the bat struck the ball – an exquisite bit of work. His prowess in the field had atoned for his mishaps at the wicket. 64 for 5. There was now a sporting chance of an actual win, if this excellence of attack could be maintained.

The Vagrants felt the pressure, knowing full well the importance of not losing another wicket yet. An advantage gained that once begins to slip away is apt to go with a rush. The game was held in tensity, as in a tug of war the pullers lean back stretched and straining and no inch of ground is given by either side. One batsman faced the pressure dourly to wear the attack down slowly, and played a maiden over. The other batsman was resolved to burst through the pressure, to meet attack with attack. He jumped out to hit Gauvinier; two balls he missed, two balls he drove hard to fieldsmen, the fifth ball sent for four, and the last – a huge hit – was skied, a terrific height, and Gauvinier held it ten yards behind the umpire: he had to look down to avoid the stumps, then up again and take his place for the ball, which did eventually drop (it took a long time) and fall into his hands; a catch he was pleased, as the service says, to have and to hold. 68 for 6.

And off Ballard's third ball the dour man was caught at the

wicket. 68 for 7. Whereupon The Vagrants definitely began to feel
the hardness of the wall at their backs. But the incoming batsman
showed no sign whatever of this. He stepped briskly to the wicket
and said, with cheerful casualness: 'A real good little game
this!' And the answer was not a growled, ferocious: 'A damn sight
better little game when you've had your blasted stumps knocked
down for you!' The answer was an equally casual: 'It is and no
mistake!'

The strained pull with no inch given on either side began again
after The Vagrants' totter towards the fatal line. Seventy went up
and slowly, run by run, each run fought for, the score moved
nearer and nearer to eighty. What had at first seemed certain to
be no game at all had turned out to be a superb game – a very
game of games. And then suddenly, with two fours and a six, the
lost ground was regained and ninety went up, and at ninety-one
the eighth wicket fell, mid-on leaping out to and holding a fast
one.

The excitement was so great that everybody, playing or watching, could not help hoping that the next man in would have a go
to knock the runs off or get out (preferably, get out) and not
keep up the almost unbearable suspense. The next man in thought
otherwise. There followed two maiden overs with no semblance
of a chance; after which the two batsmen walked to the centre of
the pitch and had a little conference together. It at once became
clear what they had conferred about. For the second ball of the
next over was pushed slowly towards mid-off and an immediate,
very quick, very short and perfectly safe run was taken: a tip-and-
run shot taken with tip-and-run immediacy. The effect was to
intensify the already tense atmosphere. The next ball was pushed
towards square leg and an instant run taken before the bewildered
fellow had decided which end to hurl the ball. Carswell at cover
moved a yard or two nearer praying for his chance. It came – he
leaped in, flung his return at the bowler's wicket, with the man
feet out, missed the wicket by inches and gave two overthrows,
as Freddie could not nip back in time to be in place for backing
up.

The thing became excruciating. Every man was wound up tight, on his toes and more, tumbling almost over them.

And the score was nearing the hundred. The pace slowed down again. They refused to take further risks: it was a sudden burst to surprise the field and rattle it. Two painful maidens slowly passed. Two runs in the next: three in the next: and the hundred went up. They looked set, and Gauvinier changed the bowling. Half an hour more to go: and then suddenly, surprisingly, the end came. The batsman who had suggested the short runs, for the first time in his innings, stepped out and cracked two successive sixes into the road.

The Vagrants made 133 for 9 and Tillingford were beaten, but in a game which no one who had played in it would forget for its excellence (quite lurid in its incident), after a start which made it look as though it must be burnt for ever into the mind for its feebleness.

Cornhill Magazine
1936

The Norfolk Worthies

HENRY BLOFELD

There is nothing quite so good as the past. All cricket lovers talk with reverence of the incomparable hundred on an impossible wicket which their hero made long ago. Of course, comparisons are never possible and how dull it would be if the unanswerable became the answerable.

Bradman = Grace? Trumper = Compton? Larwood = Hall? These are equations which can never come out. Yet most ardent cricket lovers have heroes of another kind. Lesser heroes maybe, but the first heroes and these are even more permanently etched on the mind.

My cricketing life started seriously when I was eight. This was the first summer I was allowed to go with my parents to watch the annual Lakenham cricket week. Lakenham is Norfolk's charming ground in Norwich. It was and still is one of those permanent institutions which so many people are slaves to, willing slaves of course.

The glamour of marquees and vast crowds – all of 4,000 – and white-flannelled cricketers chasing about followed by exciting backwashes of applause, made a big impression on me. Very soon I considered myself as important a part of Lakenham as the players themselves. If we were late any morning in starting for the ground I was tearful at the thought of what I might be missing. I knew the averages to four decimal places. When a newcomer made his first appearance I was swift to evaluate or maybe devaluate him. Even in those days I am afraid I preferred the old names and the old faces.

For me the Norfolk cricketers were deities and Lakenham was their temple. My friends at my preparatory school were not as impressed as I would have liked, but there was a certain W. J. Edrich whom they all knew about. When I told them he had started with Norfolk one or two eyebrows were raised and I cashed in where I could.

Lakenham is a surprisingly rural ground to find in a city or even on the edge of it. There are enough trees on the South and West sides to keep the red brick houses at bay. The East is entirely wooded. In the North-West corner stands the large and impressive white pavilion. Occasionally I was allowed in with my father. Proudly boasting my 10/6 junior member's badge, but feeling a little weak at the knees none the less I climbed the half dozen or so steps onto the large raised forecourt.

At each end of the pavilion were the two dressing-rooms which bulged out giving it a bracket effect, and in the middle was the long room, it seemed huge, where the players had their meals. The bottom two panes of the dressing-room windows were frosted, but sometimes I saw some of the players standing up and looking through the top panes. The Norfolk dressing-room was on the right and I always looked there first, even when they were fielding. If it was Clements or Thompson or Rought-Rought or Boswell or any of the others I just stared enraptured. The left-hand dressing-room belonged to the enemy. At best they were lucky cricketers; they got wickets with bad balls; they appealed too loud and they always had the umpires on their side. I looked at them out of the corner of my eye.

The East side of Lakenham was home. Here there were and still are eight or ten small round white tents which are hired by individual members. They were old, they had always been old. When it blew the guide ropes came down, when it rained the water poured in and when the sun shone they were like an oven. Inside each was a pile of deck chairs and one of those collapsible tables which never stood on more than three legs whichever way round one tried it. Take the teapot off one side and the chocolate cakes slid off the other.

The week began on the old August Monday and the first excitement was to see which tent was ours. My father's name in bold black capital letters was fastened to the back of the tent. Who were we going to be next to? The car was parked behind the tent and we carried in the picnic lunch and the binoculars. The tent was opened and the deck chairs brought out. I liked to get there a bit early. I always had a bat and ball with me and I often persuaded some unsuspecting person to 'give me a few' at the back. A friendly face might say, 'It won't be long before you're out there', and my day would be made.

I was back in my chair at least by twenty-past eleven. I sat with my binoculars nervously between my fingers and the scorecard on my knees waiting for a glimpse of the umpires. Every second minute someone would look round the edge of the tent to say hullo to the family. My mother would give me a dirty look and I would jump up and shake hands. More often than not she would say, 'You sit in Henry's chair, he'll get another.' And I would miss the magic moment when the umpires came out of the pavilion, stopped to synchronise their watches with the clock and walked slowly down the steps. My family never understood the importance of these moments.

So the scene was set. Norfolk cricket just after the war was in a bit of a state. In the 1930s we had had a side which everyone said would have held its own in the County Championship. Now the war and anno domini had torn it apart. After captaining the side in 1946 M. Falcon, who first played for Norfolk in 1907 and captained it five years later, had retired. D. F. Walker and T. G. L. Ballance had been killed; Bill Edrich's two brothers, Geoffrey and Eric, had gone to Lancashire; G. R. Langdale now wore Derbyshire colours and R. C. Rought-Rought the eldest of the three brothers had called it a day. The heroes of yesterday in fact, but I was too young, my heroes were out there in the middle.

Thompson may once have been about the quickest in England, but now he contented himself by hitting vast sixes onto the bowling green behind the sight screen at the North end. Whenever his colossal figure came striding out everyone leant forward in their chairs, or at least I did. He was captain too and there was a certain amount of mystique attached to that.

I never watched him through the glasses as that way I could not watch the ball when he had hit it. To me the joy of six-hitting was to follow the flight of the ball. When Thompson bowled in post-war years the unkind 'medium' crept into any accurate description of his bowling. But so what, it was the sixes that mattered. Occasionally my mother would say, 'that was a nice one', but I always thought it a great deal better than that.

Clements was another who quickened my pulse rate. He scored the only Norfolk century in my first year and so I expected a lot. In those days it did not pay to expect too much. But Clements was an all-rounder and when he was brought on to bowl his left arm spinners I felt that salvation was near. I am sure I dreamed of following in his footsteps. Clements was a particular hero.

Then there were the other two Rought-Roughts, D. C. although he retired in '47, and B. W. So many of my parents' friends had come as much as anything to see each other. I could not understand this. 'Oh, that must be one of the Rought-Roughts' they would say looking over their shoulders. 'B.W.' I would chip in quickly. I never knew how people could talk through an over when Clements was fielding on the boundary no more than five yards away.

Every now and then a batsman would hook or cut, the tents were square on, and the ball would come to the boundary near us. The elderly, at least they seemed old, usually made a poor show of fielding and throwing back. Occasionally it came near enough for me to leap out of my deck chair, get behind the line and wait with my feet splayed out in a wide V as I had been taught. My throwing was not so good. If there was a boundary fieldsman I returned it to him underarm. If not I tried overarm; it would have been infra dig not to, but it did not always work.

Boswell was the professional and he had come from Essex before the war. He was another giant, but he was not so far away as the others. To start with he was always smiling and then he took the Easter coaching classes. Each April hundreds of small boys including myself collected in a large drill hall where there were two indoor nets. 'Bozzie' as he was known – it was Mr. Boswell when we spoke to him – told us when to put our pads on, when to get our left legs to the pitch of the ball and when to make less noise. But most important of all he said, 'well played' when my turn was over. Once he smiled at me when he was fielding on the boundary.

These were the major heroes. For a year or two they were uncontested although there were moments when maybe Thistleton-Smith, Cunliffe or Beresford came into the reckoning. There was one snag to all this. It was incredible, unbelievable really, that such fine cricketers could not lift Norfolk away from almost the bottom of the Minor County Championship.

When we drove in through the gate behind the pavilion our membership tickets were inspected. There was an agonising pause while the gateman counted heads and then tickets and checked again. His arithmetic was often poor. Even when we were waved on there were about thirty yards to cover before craning my neck out of the side window I could see the scoreboard.

On the first morning of a match when we arrived a little late it so often read 4 for 1 or 15 for 2 or something like that. Now when the scoreboard came into view the sight-screen blotted out the pitch. At this point the road turned right and then left and so it was another ten seconds before I knew who was batting. Inevitably it was Norfolk. When the score was 70 for 0 my hopes were again dashed by the figure of Thompson walking enormously back to his bowling mark. Yet I was never more than momentarily disillusioned. A third wicket partnership of 39 or two wickets in the nineties restored hope.

I was very excited when Eric Edrich came back from Lancashire. As soon as I heard the news my list of heroes grew. Behind the stumps he was like a rubber ball. He picked up the most impossible catches, but he would appeal too loud. I rather enjoyed it, but some people thought that to throw the ball miles in the air and to scream wildly was rather too professional. He made a lot of runs as well and he and Clements often got them together. Then it was like a dream.

There was one match at Lakenham, against Kent II, where they were both in great form. It was a remarkable game of cricket. Kent made over 300, but Norfolk and Clements and Edrich in particular fought back splendidly. Clements missed the magical hundred. (How I longed to stand in the middle holding my bat aloft as the crowd cheered.) Anyway runs still came.

Only a handful were needed for the lead when suddenly a large cow came down the pavilion steps and ran onto the field. The players fled as she cantered round the square. The crowd also took evasive action as the animal turned its attention to them. By now its pursuers from the market had arrived and soon the cow was trapped in a corner. But not for long. She shook herself free and dived into the allotments by the wood on the east of the ground.

A quarter of an hour was lost and of course everyone thought it was hysterically funny. I am afraid I found it very irreverent. The game was held up at a thrilling stage, the wicket might have been harmed and worst of all the batsmen's concentration upset. Fortunately there was a happy ending. Norfolk just reached 400, an exclusively pre-war luxury, and Edrich was left not out with 170. It helped me to forget the cow.

Nineteen forty-nine was the last year with all the old familiar faces. With the 1950s came new and younger players, and Norfolk cricket grew just a little more fallible. By now I had seen a Test Match at Lord's and well . . . I was getting older. I began to see that Clements = Compton was not any sort of equation after all.

Best Cricket Stories
1967

Test Century

GEOFFREY MOORHOUSE

The Centenary Test which starts at Lord's next Thursday will, it is safe to say, be an occasion that every cricket watcher in the country would like to attend. A seat by a television set will be small compensation for anybody who will be unable to tell their grandchildren that they were actually present when England played Australia in the great anniversary match at the headquarters of the game. Cricket has cherished its traditions more than most sports, and nothing in the long history of the game has ever roused as much feeling as Test matches between Englishmen and Australians. This is the strongest as well as the oldest major international rivalry, its origins lying in historical events that have nothing to do with cricket, but which the game has perpetuated; this is where the love–hate relationship between the old colonials and the old imperials has been maintained most steadily, fiercely, warmly and dramatically. Neither the Poms nor the Aussies take kindly to being beaten at cricket by any team, but when one defeats the other the sense of triumph and dismay can assume the proportions of an independence celebration or a national calamity.

It is, in fact, something over a hundred years since the two sides first met. Combat began in Melbourne in 1877, a game that was celebrated three years ago by another centenary match on the same ground, memorably and brilliantly fought to precisely the same result as in that very first Test which the Australians won by 45 runs. They led by two matches to one when their cricketers came here in 1880 and played the first Test on English soil. This was hastily arranged at the Oval on 6, 7 and 8 September at the end of a tour that had been improvised from start to finish, with the Australians at one stage advertising for fixtures because the English counties already had their summer programmes booked up. England, led by Lord Harris, had the three Grace brothers in the side and W.G. hit 152 in the first innings. That was topped by the Australian captain W. L. Murdoch with 153 not out, but in the absence of their great fast bowler, Fred Spofforth (hurt in a game at Scarborough) the tourists were beaten by five wickets before crowds which, according to Wisden, were the largest ever seen at a cricket match – close on 45,000 over the three days.

When the Australians next came to England in 1882 to play a single Test, again at the Oval, 'The Demon' Spofforth was in full working order and finished the game with figures of 14 wickets for 90 runs, bowling with such ferocity that every English batsman might have echoed what The Hon Edward Lyttelton once said after facing him: 'I give you my word that for several overs I stood on the brink of the tomb'. One of the most famous cricket matches ever played, its fortunes fluctuated tightly (Australia 63 and 122, England 101 and 77), and its climax was so nerve-racking that one spectator died of heart failure and another chewed right through his umbrella handle. Spofforth was carried from the field shoulder high when the last Englishman was bowled eight runs short of victory. Within a week the *Sporting Times* had published its famous mock obituary of English cricket: 'Deeply lamented by a large circle of sorrowing friends and acquaintances. RIP. NB – The body will be cremated and the ashes taken to Australia.' Thus a great myth was begun, to be given reality after the third Test at Sydney in 1883, when England took a 2–1 lead in the series. A bail from the match wickets was burnt and its ashes were sealed in a tiny urn which was presented to England's captain, The Hon Ivo Bligh, who later became Lord Darnley. This is the mystical trophy for which English and Australian cricketers have played ever since, though the urn never changes hands whoever wins a Test series; having been left to MCC in Darnley's will, the Ashes have been on display in the cricket museum at Lord's for many years, and there they are likely to stay.

The two countries have now fought 239 Tests, the Australians winning 92 to England's 79, with 68 games drawn, and some finishes as desperately close as that at the Oval in 1882. In the fourth Test at Old Trafford in 1902, Australia won by just three runs, after Victor Trumper had scored a brilliant century before lunch on the first day at almost a run a minute, and after poor Fred Tate of Sussex had not only dropped a vital catch on the boundary but, last man in for England, had got himself bowled out as well.

Particular players on both sides will be forever associated with certain matches, for great feats or significant failures, or simply for displays of enormous character. Warwick Armstrong, a huge man from Victoria, is remembered not only for leading Australia to the only clean sweep of a full series that has ever occurred (5–0 Down Under in 1920–21) but for his protest at the Oval a few months later against the English authorities' decision to limit the 1921 matches to only three days each, instead of playing to a finish, however long that took, which was the habit in Australia. When the fifth Test was heading for an inevitable draw, Armstrong left his fielding position close to the wicket, strolled over to the boundary and began to read a newspaper. Eddie Paynter, of Lancashire, will never be forgotten for his performance at Brisbane in 1933, when he got out of a hospital bed with England up against it, and began an innings of 83, with the aid of egg and brandy taken between overs at the crease, that laid the foundations of victory. Sydney in 1946 was where Godfrey Evans, keeping wicket for England for the first time, didn't let a single bye get past him in Australia's match-winning score of 659 for eight declared. Brisbane in 1958 was where Trevor Bailey batted remorselessly for seven-and-a-half hours to make only 68.

Those names, and the events attached to them, are among the regular currency of Anglo–Australian Tests; there are many others, and volumes have been written to do them all justice. But in a game which thrives on statistics (down to the calculation someone has made that after the fourth Test at Sydney in 1975, no fewer than 864,000 empty beer cans had to be cleared from the ground), the absolute dominance of some players is reflected in the record books.

The most lustrous name of all remains – possibly for ever – that of Don Bradman, whose batting genius originated in childhood when he would spend hours at his home in New South Wales hitting a golf ball against a wall with a cricket stump. Throughout his first-class career he was to average a century every third innings he played and, although he made only 19 runs in his first Test match against England at Brisbane in 1928, he rarely failed to produce big scores after that. By the time he retired 20 years later – bowled by Hollies, second ball, in his last English Test – his overall Test average stood at 99.94, and against England alone it was 89.78.

It was to counter Bradman's devastating efficiency with the bat that the Englishmen resorted to the strategy of bowling dangerously short and fast down the leg side in the notorious 'bodyline' series in Australia in 1932–33, which all but ruptured diplomatic relations between the two countries. The chief instrument of 'leg theory' was the Nottinghamshire bowler Harold Larwood, but the strategy was wholly that of his captain, the austere Surrey Scotsman, Douglas Jardine, who became the most detested man in the southern hemisphere as a result. Fielding on the boundary at Sydney one day (an act of moral courage in the circumstances), he brushed away an insect which flew round his face, when a voice from the crowd yelled: 'Leave our bloody flies alone, Jardine. They're the only friends you've got round here.' Humour, one of cricket's great graces, has generally broken in even at the most belligerent moments.

Bradman had hit the world's record Test score of 334 just before his 22nd birthday at Leeds in 1930. Len Hutton, curiously, was almost the same age when he made 364 at the Oval in 1938 – still the highest individual score between the two sides – and England crushed Australia by an innings and 579 runs. This is one of two matches that Englishmen prefer to dwell on most, the other being the setting for the most astonishing piece of bowling in the history of cricket.

It was Jim Laker of Surrey who turned the fourth Test of 1956 at Old Trafford into a legend that almost certainly will never be surpassed. England had the very best of a wearing pitch to score 459, and in the event they could have won the match by an innings with little more than half those runs. Laker was virtually unplayable from start to finish of Australia's batting, as wind and sun aided his baffling flight and finger spin. His Surrey colleague Tony Lock took one wicket in the first innings, but Laker collected every other Australian scalp in the match – 19 wickets out of 20 for only 90 runs.

Three great moments stand out in the Test matches played at Lord's. In 1934, Hedley Verity, with left-arm spin, took 14 Australian wickets – including Bradman's – between noon and late afternoon on the same day. In 1953, the obdurate Bailey and Willie Watson came together on the last day when England were 73 for four and heading for defeat. For over four hours they hung on against an attack which included Lindwall, Miller, Davidson and Benaud, and saved the match. In 1972 it was a novice's name that rang out from this ground – the 25-year-old Bob Massie, playing in his first Test for Australia, swinging the ball in extraordinary fashion to dismiss 16 Englishmen for 137 and take his side to an eight wickets win. Lord's, indeed, has usually been a good place for the Australians, who have lost only one Test there (Verity's match) since 1896.

They will therefore go into the Centenary Test this week with a distinct psychological advantage. England might well wish to be playing at the Oval, which has been kinder to them and which historically would be a more justifiable venue; but Lord's can accommodate several thousand more spectators and that, more than anything, has given it what promises to be a splendid occasion. A number of cricketers will be playing who deserve to be listed with the all-time greats of Anglo-Australian Tests. The Australian captain, Greg Chappell is one, and so is their fast bowler Dennis Lillee, who may well be making his last appearance in harness with Jeff Thomson to form one of the most effective of all speed combinations. ('Ashes to ashes, dust to dust,' wrote a

Sydney cartoonist after the pair had wrecked England during the 1974–75 series. 'If Thomson don't get ya, Lillee must . . .'). Of England's likely players, Boycott, Underwood and (already) Ian Botham belong with the legendary cricketers. Many more of those will be watching with the rest of us, including old-timers like Bill Ponsford, who will be in a party of nearly 100 ex-players and officials flying across the world for this match. Another legend will, sadly, be performing in his last Test – John Arlott in the commentary box, who retires after 34 years of illuminating and embellishing the game. What everybody will hope for above all is that this occasion comes as near to perfection as the Centenary Test at Melbourne did three years ago. And all Englishmen should pray that the result, like the one at Melbourne, is the same as in that Test a hundred years ago.

Radio Times
1980

The Global Pavilion

SIMON KUPER

Like many Dutchmen, Spike was 6ft 8in tall, had buck teeth and lived off state benefits. He believed that the rat race was evil and so, as a matter of principle, had not worked a day in his life. As a child, Spike joined a cricket club in Leiden, the small town in Holland where he and I lived. By the time I knew him he was in his mid-30s and had been around so long that he could remember watching our first team being bowled out in 1967 for the lowest total ever recorded in Holland. The two runs were byes.

Spike was a good off-spinner. He spent the winter watching Test cricket on the BBC and twirling a cricket ball against his index finger to create a callous before the season began. He played every week in summer.

On Sundays we took part in vicious league matches against posh Anglophiles from The Hague, or against working-class Pakistanis from Amsterdam. Mid-week, we met a succession of English touring teams full of middle-aged men who spent the whole week drunk on Dutch beer but still beat us comfortably.

Spike at least had an English mother. Most of the Dutchmen in our club had ended up cricketers by accident. Some simply felt like doing something different while others had parents who wanted them to play an upper-class game. Our first team opening batsman was a general's son named Meindert Jan van Erp Taalman Kip. We called him Kip.

The other players came from the football branch of our club. Older Dutch football clubs – and ours, founded in 1892, was one of the first – tended to have cricketing wings.

A regular, stalwart batsman was Piet Kantebeen who was in his seventies. His batting technique was exquisite: acquired in the 1930s, it was straight out of a Jack Hobbs textbook. Piet's brother Ton had scored more centuries than anyone else in Holland but he and Piet had had a row years before and no longer spoke. As a result, Ton, who was nearly 80, moved to a rival team down the road.

Ex-pats made up the numbers. My father taught at Leiden University, and Vernie February, a South African refugee who was in his department, became a valued team member. Another regular was a Bangladeshi engineer called Zulfikar who sprinted into our ground one Sunday afternoon after he had spotted us playing from the road. He didn't know that Dutch cricket existed, or how rough it could get.

As all games are played on matting or artificial grass, even a 13-year-old can bowl a pretty frightening bouncer. No one walks unless caught high in the gully after scoring a century, and wisely so: an umpire does not give a teammate out unless he's had a row with him.

Rows are common. Spike retired in the end, driven out by a player he regarded as an idiot. Spike's main problem was that the idiot was friends with the civil servants who were setting about depriving him of state benefits.

The Netherlands, with its 5,000 registered players, is, in my view, by far the best cricketing country on the Continent. Roland Lefebvre plays for Glamorgan and Andre van Troost for Somerset and the Dutch national team meets England in next year's World Cup. Most of the team's players are Dutch, one of whom, Tim de Leede, is a year older than me and grew up in a small town near Leiden. In 10 years, we once got him out before he reached the fixed retirement score: he was 11 years old, I was 10, the retirement score was 40, and he ran himself out for 39. In one match when he was 16 he grew so bored that he began batting left handed. He retired on 50 with seven sixes.

In Europe, only Holland, Denmark and Corfu have a reasonable number of native players. Corfu has four teams named Byron,

Gymnasticos, Phaex and Ergaticos. And the names get better still: the writer Michael Green claims to have been bowled out on the island by an off-spinner named Prometheus.

Under Queen Victoria, British businessmen and sailors took cricket and football around the world. But in most places only football caught on. AC Milan began life as a cricket and football club, but cricket in Italy is now fairly dead. There are 20 or so Italian clubs. They favour big hitting, fast bowling and loud appealing, but they are not very good. Nor are they like us: they call silly mid-on *mezzo-accesso stupido*.

The French are more familiar with cricket than are most Europeans, but they have traditionally been wary of the game. In 1979, French customs officials at Calais decided that a cricket bat was a 'sporting engine without mechanical movement'. Its owner had to pay 1.25FF in duty.

When the MCC came to Paris in 1867, a Frenchman is supposed to have told one of the players: 'It is a magnificent game, but I cannot understand why you do not engage a servant to field for you instead of having so much running about to do yourself.'

The Emperor Louis Napoleon had a greater understanding of the game. A few days after he had visited the Paris Cricket Club to have the rules explained to him, a batsman at the club tripped while running and broke his arm. The police were about to suppress the game as dangerous when an appeal to the emperor saved French cricket.

Today, the English middle classes play in the Dordogne, Pakistani and Sri Lankan students in Paris, and some actual Frenchmen in the north.

Although there is not much cricket in Russia, one of the more surprising revelations of the Cold War was that in 1983 Victor Popov, then Soviet ambassador to Britain, had played cricket for St Anthony's College as an exchange student. The Soviet Embassy refused to comment. Apparently Mr Popov had slipped a disc while diving for a ball.

German cricket is played almost entirely by ex-pats. The British Army on the Rhine is still the best team in the country, however depleted and, at a recent European Cup, a nephew of the Nawab of Pataudi opened the German batting.

The Munich Cricket Club plays in the town's Englischer Garten. The park's other customs have apparently given rise to a rule whereby a batsman cannot be given out if, in the umpire's opinion, he has been distracted by a sexy woman jogging in the outfield.

Charles Darwin could have explained why cricket failed to survive in most environments. Football not only requires less kit, but is also easier to learn to play well. Without coaching, you may become a Pele, but you would probably never be able to bowl a googly.

The Anglo-Argentines play cricket in a leafy suburb of Buenos Aires called Hurlingham. It has several English-language schools and polo fields, and the only lawn tennis courts in Latin America – in fact, it is rather like Dulwich.

Tony Lewis, the former England captain, recalls the MCC tour to South America of 1964. One night well inland in Argentina, Lewis and Alan Smith, the Warwickshire and England keeper, were teasing an exiled Scotsman named McKay. McKay lived on a huge farm and had not been to Britain in 25 years. The Second World War was over, Lewis and Smith told him, and had he heard of Peter May? Suddenly McKay turned to the keeper: 'It's nay good, Smith. I've got to come out with it. You, keeping wicket for Warwickshire. Why the hell do you stand back to a trifling medium pacer like Cartwright?'

In nations such as Israel, the United Arab Emirates, Canada and the USA, cricket is pretty good but played almost entirely by expats. Drive through New York boroughs on a Sunday and you will see some fine fast bowlers – most of them Jamaican.

In 1967, on a matting wicket, the MCC played the West Indian League of New York in Red Hook Stadium, Brooklyn. The League included several recent Shell Shield cricketers. On the same tour, in a game at Staten Island, the MCC came up against Wes Hall's brother. C. P. Snow thought inswing bowling might have been invented by the great Pennsylvanian fast bowler J. B. King at the turn of the century.

King had learned from life as a baseball pitcher, and on his last English tour, in 1908, he topped the national bowling averages with 87 wickets at 11.01. Arthur Lilley, the Warwickshire wicket keeper, claimed that King could throw a cricket ball in a way that made it rise again after it had begun to dip.

Pennsylvania used to be a rare site for American cricket, but today few native-born Americans play. One exception is Richard Adelstein, an Ivy League academic who picked up cricket while at Oxford. Back in the States, he joined a West Indian club playing in a Connecticut-Canada league. After a year or so it was found that to be insured he had to become a club member.

The obstacle was Byelaw Four, which stated that every member had to have at least one parent of West Indian origin. The byelaw now reads: '. . . at least one parent of West Indian or Polish origin'.

'Cricket Abroad'
Cricket – West Indies Tour
1995

Cricket on Corrugated Iron

MARSHALL LEE

Names such as Garda, Barnes, Chotia, Stamper, Rubidge and Omar if not yet household were at least on cricket people's lips, so to speak, during the historic 1976/77 season in the Transvaal and when the *Rand Daily Mail*'s Sy Lerman, reporting on the confident early performances of Sacboc players in the integrated new non-racial leagues, said it looked as if they'd been doing this sort of thing all their lives, well of course, they had been.

Theirs is a promise that has been around for a long time, if only we had cared to look and do something about it. Why, I saw Morris Garda make a provincial century back in 1969 or thereabouts. Curiosity took me to Johannesburg's Natalspruit ground 'down there by the flyover at the bottom of End Street' to watch the Transvaal Sacboc side against Natal.

My first impressions were mixed. I was appalled by the ground itself – a grassless, matting wicket, corrugated iron sort of place that a 6th Division white cricketer would have hesitated to play on. But I was also surprised by the quality of the cricket I saw.

Apart from Garda's hundred, I remember the bowling of Hoosain Ayob, some fine catching, and a youngster called Chicken Bhamjee who, if my memory doesn't fail me, was keeping wicket for a Transvaal Colts side on the adjoining pitch.

Ayob, even in those days an experienced provincial bowler, impressed with his pace, direction and easy action. But whites only noticed this College cricketer for the first time when he turned out for Kohinoors and bowled them to a Premier League victory against Pirates.

Chicken Bhamjee, brother of the controversial Abdul, grew up to become rated by some as the best wicket keeper in the country. But for political and/or personal reasons we probably won't see him in action, which is a pity for he is undoubtedly a quality prospect.

From the first outing I recall other things. I think I even met a Mr Varachia who has also come in from the backyard to make a name for himself among administrators.

In any event, on the strength of one afternoon's watching I became an instant authority, at least among the ignorant, on black cricket. I was told that I was the first white cricketer and journalist to have made an appearance at one of their games since that famous match some years ago in which Johnny Waite's XI was beaten.

As a one and only test of strength, this game frequently popped into conversations. Just as the one match I watched became the basis for much of my cricket talk. Oh yes, I dined out on my experience, convinced that among the 'untouchables' there was a lot of wasted talent.

Whites who favoured the status quo – and in those days the white cricketers were largely united in their reactionary feelings – used to hide behind the belief that the 'Indians' were just not good enough.

Even D'Oliviera was scathingly reduced to a second rater. You'd be surprised how many top cricketers said Dolly wouldn't make the Transvaal B side, who believed his choice for England was political. Certainly some of them found it hard to believe Wisden, which revealed Dolly's Test average to be in the first three or four of all contemporary South Africans.

These sort of arguments on merit meant the moral questions could be kept out, not because of the colour of their skins but because they weren't up to standard.

Here again, as far as D'Oliviera himself was concerned I was prepared to believe my eyes. And I enjoyed an argumentative advantage in the middle sixties over many cricketers who had not been to England. Although I actually only played with him once (in an SA XI against the Nawab of Pataudi's Oxford University XI) I saw enough of his ability that season to convince me.

It was around about then that I decided to become a sports writer, to give up my three-piece suite, lawyer's office existence, return to South Africa and radicalise sports writing. Plainly my stance (in between what I hoped would be passages of Cardusian lyricism) would be non-racial. I would become the muse for mixed cricket, rugby, everything!

Well it didn't quite happen like that. I was seduced in other directions and came eventually to the *Rand Daily Mail*, where I, as Features Editor, encourage people to enter the Tuesday Jackpot.

On the way I had a few swipes! – suggested that people would one day say Peter Hain did more for South African cricket than Wilf Isaacs. Almost sacreligious then, people admit it now, including some of those to whom mixed cricket was anathema and impossible only a few years ago.

One article I wrote, in *The Star*, was a profile on Abdul Bhamjee. He was, in 1970, in a challenging mood – calling on all-comers with his champion College Club. They were winning everything within their reach, but though they applied (and nagged) they could not win a place in the Premier League. Bhamjee was way ahead of the time. And the TCU had to squirm to say no. The Government wouldn't allow it, they said. That sort of thing.

The Bhamjee article drew an ironic comparison with Ali Bacher. Both men were A.B., both were opening batsmen. Both were captains of Transvaal. Their complexions were (and still are) similar. More important, their principles were coming together.

'Better late than never,' said Bhamjee, who was understandably sceptical of active white support for his views.

'There is no legislation that says we can't play together,' said Bhamjee, who had a simple solution to the whole problem: 'If you really mean what you say then let's play. It won't be the end of white civilisation.'

But nobody was prepared to risk our civilisation at that point. On the contrary, this simple straightforward approach was interpreted as the reaction you'd expect from a 'troublemaker' – a reputation incidentally that has been entrenched.

The Press have contributed to Abdul's stormy petrel image. After all, he was the only black cricketer in Johannesburg they'd heard of in 1970.

'Now I need a full-time office just to answer questions,' he said then. 'And when the newspapermen phone me I say: "Where have you been all this time?"'

Yes, where?

Anyway, behind the journalist's trick that gives the impression one is a know-all, I was hopelessly ignorant of the quality, structure, depth and nature of Sacboc cricket. The names didn't help either. They came in a foreign language and my knowledge didn't extend much further than Bhamjee, Howa or College Cricket Club – until 1976 the only club of which whites had heard.

Bhamjee is important in this piece because it was he who persuaded me to become a player again. There was more to principles than simply expounding them at dinner parties or under the Country Club oaks.

In the comfort of my white privilege I was merely an armchair cricketer batting for non-racialism and proving nothing.

'Come and play,' said Abdul.

It was easy to say no. After all, my serious cricketing days were long over, my wrist (an operation y'know) was weak, I was getting on, I couldn't get to practice, I had better family things to do than make nought on Sundays. What would I prove anyway?

So I got up and put my pads on. And what did I prove? Besides the fact that my doubts were valid? Well, I didn't set the cricketing world alight, neither as a batsman nor as a political sensation. Nor can I claim (and my egotistical me would like to) that I in any way hurried the advent of 'normal' cricket.

But by welcoming me and Colvin Henderson in their club, College cricketers proved simply that we were breaking no laws, we could play together and it didn't matter a damn except, I suppose, who won. Above all, it just felt better this way, and if we had any hopes it was that others (more spry perhaps) would follow the example.

We at least knew we were playing normal cricket, though we prefer to say just 'cricket'. Where else but in this daft country would one have to say 'come on chaps, let's go and play some normal cricket?'

The qualification should be redundant. As it is, it can be read as a euphemism for cricket that is not quite normal at all.

Having said that I can hardly say that the cricket I began playing three years ago was what I, or other whites, could call normal. Normal for us whites is what Jackie McGlew would call 'the green sward'.

This was cricket on baked clay, broken glass and stones. A matting wicket. Bloody elbows. No change rooms. Two matches going on at the same time on the same ground. A right of way practically across the pitch.

Anyone who has played or spectated at Queen's Park, Vrededorp, will know exactly what I mean. Here College and Crescents players have played out their greatest dramas, sometimes hitting sixes over the trees, always putting on their boxes in the street and frequently bumping into square leg from the other game whose territory overlaps as far as the other pitch.

My debut, in keeping with a number of other of my debuts, was disastrous. I made two. I floated down the wicket after one of the slowest balls I've ever seen and was stumped.

A columnist in *The Star* a few days later said something like 'What about merit selection?' I must say I felt like a token! However, we stuck it out and though I dropped the odd catch I got round to holding my own.

I even managed to eat lunchtime helpings of curry and rice with my fingers, and with growing proficiency. It took only a game or two and it seemed we'd been playing together all our lives. But I still wasn't at home on the baked grounds.

In retrospect the experience was invaluable and my sentimental streak will always enable me to look back on my College days with fondness. How else when I gained so much?

Apart from the facilities (at least Queen's Park had character unlike the deserts called Gravel 1, Gravel 2 etc in Lenasia) the thing that was most striking was the enthusiasm and competitive spirit of the matches.

As bitter as many of the players might have been politically, this did not interfere with their wholehearted approach to the game. They were prepared to dive into catches and much of the batting was no less positive.

It was difficult to assess properly how good the teams would be outside their backyard.

But it was obvious that there was enough talent around to bolster the Sacboc stand for mixed merit cricket. What was lacking, and is still absent, was the sort of depth enjoyed by white league teams with their school nurseries, coaching facilities and reserve strength. Even the top teams did not field second teams except I believe, Crescents.

College for years had been the leading team propelled by the aggressive Abdul Bhamjee, a forceful opening bat whose flaws were hidden behind his capacity for runs. And it is sad that he appears to have missed out on the Premier League cricket for which he fought to enter for so long.

In the confusion over the introduction of mixed cricket and the extremely questionable grading of Sacboc teams for the TCU league, Bhamjee and his College side are out in the cold. Some of us, however, joined other clubs and are trying to enjoy the benefits of the changed situation.

More than that I guess we hope to put some non-racial reality into the game and expose any 'multi-racial' label as a waste of time.

It is heartening that the Transvaal Cricket Union felt the same and kept their bargain to play ordinary cricket and not be part of 'multi-racial' sport.

I personally needed these reassurances before I would participate in the new set-up. And one of the assurances was that Transvaal sides would be picked without fear or favour on merit alone. Even if it meant picking only whites.

Fortunately to make it nicely kosher, Garda, Solly Chothia and Tiffie Barnes came quickly and were good enough for representative selection. And had Chicken Bhamjee been available, Ali Bacher and the selectors would have had little difficulty putting in a fourth Sacboc man.

By the end of the season others had joined the queue in the selectors' waiting room and will get their chances.

The lead has been given at Provincial level and it is now up to the white clubs, also, to accept players on ability. Not until there is easy integration at club level will cricket be truly normal. And as long as clubs are referred to as 'Indian' or players as 'Coloured' the longer it will take to remove 'Multi-racial' from the game.

Meanwhile the face of Transvaal league cricket has changed and cricketers have discovered each other. And though I have reservations about the depth of the 'Sacboc' sides, they have already shown that they are capable of playing good cricket. Some of it has even been inspired. In particular, I think of the first Premier League game in which I played: Crescents against Old Johannians. Apart from the highly respectable scoring – Old Johnnies made 302 and Crescents 273, the game proved the all round quality of Tiffie Barnes. He bowled 42 overs and his four for 90 would have been even more impressive had there not been dropped catches. Then he followed up this performance with a score of 140 when Crescents batted. Some cricketer our Tiffie.

If there were problems and unresolved political hassles on the debit side in the first season, they were heavily outweighed by the credits. On the field it's true some of the heart was knocked out of the weaker teams, early on.

But they picked up the pieces. And took guard again. Crescents, in particular pulled themselves from disaster to a position where they were confident enough to challenge any side in the league. They were playing very good cricket indeed and the results prove it. Certainly if they had been able to start the first season as they left off, no side, not even the Old Edwardians and Old Parktonians could have taken them lightly.

In their first 13 matches Crescents lost 12 and beat only Rangers.

In their last 8 matches they won 5, drew one (against top team Old Eds) and lost only two. They won 4 of their last 5 games – the loss ironically to Rangers.

The Crescents transformation was remarkable, lifting the side from weak to formidable. Against teams such as Jeppe, University and Balfour Park, they turned colossal first round defeats into comprehensive second round wins. There was no luck here. They outgunned their opponents in all departments and had they not been victim of a sieve-like cover that turned the Lens Stadium wicket into a quagmire they would have easily beaten Rangers. As it is they lost that game by 6 runs after removing the Rangers batsmen on a plumb track for 132.

Among all the ifs and buts and remaining obstacles and prejudices, there is one thing I believe; that the Crescents example is the signal for the future. Which explains I guess why I'm humble and kinda proud about my association with this team.

When it was struggle all the way down to the bottom, it was consolation to say: 'Don't worry, we're the leading team in the country. We are the only fully non-racial team in South Africa.'

Non-racial the team certainly is with Indian, African, Coloured and White, and the blending of the individuals into such a viable, spirited team has set the pace for other cricketers. The recipe has worked. And now to my friend Abdul I'd like to say: 'Come on let's play'.

Cricket in Isolation
1977

The Gully, the Maidan and the Mali

MIHIR BOSE

When I started writing this, the kindly man who edited it suggested to me that I explain how a 7 or 8 year old in India takes to cricket. We know how he does so in this country but surely the Indian process is very different? Indeed it is. If English cricket is essentially rural and village cricket, in George Orwell's picturesque phrase of the light falling towards evening and a ball hit for four killing a rabbit on the boundary, Indian cricket is urban. Its roots lie in the lanes of India's teaming cities and on the broad patches of green, called the maidans, that occasionally break up the monotony of concrete. Talk to almost any Indian Test cricketer, particularly of the last thirty years, and he will trace his cricketing roots back to the maidan and the gully. The wonder of the maidan is well captured by Gudhi Kunderan, in this recollection of how he started playing cricket:

> Since my parents moved to Bombay, when I was eight years old, I hadn't seen cricket in my native place. None of my family members (have) ever seen or played cricket in their lives. The first time that I saw a cricket match on a maidan in Bombay I fell in love with the game . . . this is the only game we could play on the maidan, apart from running, to play any other game in Bombay (in) those days you had to be a member of big clubs, where you could play tennis or other indoor games. But I had no opportunity as such.

An evocative picture of Kunderan, the villager moving to the big city and being claimed by cricket, sufficiently early for India to have a remarkable wicket keeper and batsman. Similarly, gully cricket, often with a tennis ball, was part and parcel of the make-up of almost every Indian cricketer – as much part of Viswanath's batting, as Chandrasekhar's bowling, or even Azharuddin's rise to fame. It was gully cricket at the old MLA ground of Hyderabad that started Azharuddin off and he and his mates getting together and forming a gully team provided him with his first taste of cricket.

All this can be simply stated. But how does one convey gully cricket? It does not have the natural cadences or the rhapsodic melody that comes naturally to English cricket. It can be hard, brutish, often messy, though with a beauty of its own. It would be tempting to draw shrewd analogies between cricket in England and gully cricket in India, as has been attempted with beach cricket in the West Indies. But I can best convey it by reminiscing about the gully cricket that I played at Bombay's Flora Fountain – the very heart of this great city.

The centres of the world's major cities are well etched in the mind: New York's Times Square, Paris's Champs Elysées, London's Piccadilly Circus. But even now I feel a curious magic about Bombay's Flora Fountain. We called it the heart of the city and so it was. The Flora the fountain commemorated was lost to history, even the various ladies who made up the fountain could barely be discerned and only occasionally did their mouths and nostrils and breasts spout water. As a child I could remember Flora Fountain trams but as the city removed trams, the fountain took on its more recognisable Indian shape of a haven for urchins, layabouts and stray dogs amidst a large parking lot. Round about it swirled Bombay's commercial traffic.

We used to say with pride, and occasionally from my mother, a little disgust, that all roads led to Flora Fountain. My mother's disgust was due to the fact that our house acted as a magnet for all sorts of visitors, most of them uninvited. To me, from my bedroom window, it seemed to provide a panoramic view on the world: here the cinema, there the bank, here the school, there the playing field, here the sea, there the restaurants. Much has changed in Bombay in recent years as Manhattan-style tower blocks have gone up and the city has fallen prey to property developers. The rhythm of Flora Fountain hasn't changed.

Flora Fountain at seven in the morning is expectant: the sound of a passing bus distinctive. By nine it is a cacophony of noise as cars, buses, taxis, handcarts, lorries and horse-carriages make their way towards the various business houses round the area. By twelve the hubub is pierced by the rhythmical chants of the 'box-wallahs' balancing tin boxes on their heads and carrying hot lunches for the hungry clerks. This must be the most remarkable food service in the world, with almost each individual office worker in Bombay receiving and eating the lunch faithfully prepared by his wife at home. By three the constant afternoon noise is again pierced – this time by a different cry, that of the news vendors selling the evening papers; 'Evening, Evening, Bhumi'. By six the noise has hardly abated but now the centre is a maze of queues as commuters patiently wait for their buses. By nine the streets are virtually deserted, or as deserted as they ever get in India, and such is the contrast in noise that a fast-moving taxi braking hard can produce a jolt. It is twelve before silence really falls and then the streets surrounding Flora Fountain are a sea of human bodies: the homeless of Bombay making their beds on the pavements. It was a rhythm I had grown up with, yet it so fascinated me that even on holidays I would often sit at one of my bedroom windows and observe the pattern, so regular and yet so capable of wonder.

Our flat was on the second floor of an office block almost exactly opposite the Flora Fountain. The block itself was one of a chain of linked houses which stretched across what the American would call a 'block', and for reasons that I never fathomed out, all the houses in the block had names associated with the sea. Our house was called Sailor Building but I had never seen any sailors in it, the house next to it and linked with it was called Darya Building, which literally means 'the house of the sea'. Down below was Bombay, with its swirl of traffic, its hawkers and its almost end-lessly fascinating variety of shops. Just past the American dry food shop and the picture gallery, which appeared a bit too highbrow and snooty for us, ran a lane where my father's company had its main Godown, and just to the right of this lane, past the cold drinks shop, the betel nut place and the area's most elegant tailor, was my friend Hubert's magical cricket gully. From my flat to his gully was no more than two hundred, perhaps three hundred, yards – a walk of less than a minute, yet our worlds could not have been more different. It was our amazing St Xavier's School which brought us together but it was cricket, and gully cricket, that cemented our friendship.

There was nothing sweet about Hubert's gully. The entrance to his gully was narrow, as if it were a pencilled afterthought of the architect designing the area. On one side there was a high wall that enclosed the Parsi *Agiari* – the Parsee religious place, a formidable barrier. The other wall opened with the area's sewer and ended with Hubert's house. The sewer part of it was open, while underneath Hubert's house was situated a press which reeked of gum and paste and sticky molten substances, a shop of sorts and then a gymnasium where in the evenings the local boys – poor but enterprising – could be seen developing their puny bodies.

The structure of Hubert's gully was of some importance. Its narrow entrance meant that cars – or in fact any form of transport – was never particularly welcome – the high wall of the Agiari and the definable boundary of the open sewer on the other gave the area the appearance of an enclosed space. It provided a sort of mini-cricket field all to ourselves, where Hubert and I, mimicking cricketers we had admired, could play out our fantasies. Even here our relationship was defined: I, the Bengali Hindu, assuming the names of Indian Test cricketers, while Hubert, the western Indian Catholic, invariably assuming the names of English or Australian cricketers. Years later he was to tell me that he had gone to watch his first cricket match – the 1956 Australian Test match at Bombay – in expectation that one of the Australians would go down with stomach trouble and Hubert, from the cheap-priced East Stand, would be drafted in to fill the breach. To me the fantasy in the story was Hubert being asked to play Test cricket at all. It did not seem strange to me that Hubert, whose skin colour and appearance were not all that dissimilar to mine and millions of other Indians, should expect to play for Australia – with a name like Hubert Miranda that seemed very natural.

Neither Hubert nor I had ever been properly coached in cricket. At weekends or holidays we watched proper cricket on Bombay's maidans. I had read a few instructional books, seen a bit of Test cricket and generally discussed the game with my friends. Now Hubert's gully fashioned all this into a very strange game. I emphasise, it appears strange now but then it seemed most natural, even the stench of the sewer which was always strong in our nostrils. Our pitch was the road – stone chips and coal tar: three lines drawn on the wall that divided the gully from the rest of the world were our wickets. The road was sufficiently long to simulate a full-length cricket pitch and, conveniently at the point where the bowler's crease would be located, there was a manhole with a cover. It seemed ideal to mark the spot of the bowler's wicket. Beyond that there was another few yards where the bowler could indulge in a run-up and, if necessary, this could be increased by running parallel to the wickets, alongside the gymnasium, a run that was not only quite long, but rather elegant since it provided a curve as you approached the wicket.

The hazards of the gully seemed to increase our appetite for play. Though we had drawn the wickets on the wall as straight as we could, the wall markings as wickets meant that there was always an element of doubt as to whether the wicket had actually been hit or not, doubts that were not always easy to resolve since the bowler's interest invariably clashed with the batsman's. To this was added the hazard of the sewer. The very nature of the gully, a wall at one end, shops at the other, meant that we could only bat at one end. This meant that the sewer was our permanent square-leg and a firmly hit ball, or even a rustic swing, down the leg-side, often landed right in the middle of the sewer. not that we were squeamish about going in to collect our ball. We, generally Hubert, would balance on the wall and precariously fish out our rubber ball. However, this did cramp our leg-side shots and our general tendency was to play on the off-side.

Both Hubert and I had played our early cricket with a hard ball and were petrified of being hit on the legs. So our normal tendency was to retreat from the ball down the leg-side and poke it away on the off-side. In Hubert's gully this was also a very paying stroke. A mere five yards from the wicket was the wall of the Parsee Agiari and to stab it in front of us and towards cover, our most favoured stroke, ensured it would hit the wall. The convention Hubert and I had devised meant that any hit on the wall of the Agiari was worth two runs. We occasionally managed to drive straight ahead, hit the doors of the gymnasium or the printing press and this counted as four, a mighty hit landing on the first floor verandahs outside Hubert's house counted as six. Very occasionally our swings cleared Hubert's house, which was roughly mid-on, and disappeared somewhere into south Bombay.

Every now and again it cleared the high wall of the Agiari. The Agiari was cover, to sewer's square leg, but here the problem, if anything, was much worse. From the sewer you could retrieve the ball, the Parsee Agiari was a total loss. To approach the Agiari with its closed wall and forbidding atmosphere demanded a courage which neither Hubert nor I possessed. We had occasionally tried it and had been mortified by being confronted with Parsee gentlemen, skull cap on their heads, and wearing the all-white Parsee garb of vest and loose trousers, standing sternly at the entrance, almost defying us to try and retake our ball. In histories of Indian cricket, much is made, and rightly, about the role played by Parsees in fostering it. We knew little about this history, our knowledge of English cricket history was substantially more than that of the Indian one and for us, Parsees, at least the Parsees of the Agiari, were not initiating our cricket but destroying it.

There was one other source of interruption. I have said the seclusion of Hubert's gully made it ideal. But it could not be entirely protected from what went on in the wide streets surrounding it, and every now and again the interaction of the Bombay police with the Bombay hawker stopped our games. Hubert's gully, as I have said, was a mere two hundred yards from my home, and the main road through south Bombay which ran right up to Victoria Terminus, the gothic Victorian building which was Bombay's main railway station. All along the pavement, from our block of buildings right up to Victoria Terminus, a whole group of hawkers sold their goods to the public. Their place of business was the pavement, their method of selling highly fascinating and their whole operation quite illegal.

The problem was that the hawker was not left unmolested. He had to contend with the police, not so much the man on the beat, who probably received a regular sum of money from the hawker called *hafta* which allowed the hawker to carry on his pavement business. It was the sudden police raid, in a very black police van, which caused the hawker and our cricket, problems. Sometimes the local policemen would tip the hawkers off and they would take precautions but occasionally the raids came as a surprise. No sooner did they see the police van approach, than the hawkers quickly gathered up their things. Hubert's gully, a quick run away from the police, but secluded enough from the rest of the world, was a very convenient hiding place. Suddenly in the midst of the most tense India-England Test match, with me as Umrigar trying to avenge myself on Hubert Trueman, we could find that we had suddenly acquired an extra wicket keeper, or a couple of slips, or even a hawker-fielder at silly mid-on. It would become impossible to continue playing. Occasionally the panting hawkers, running for shelter into the gully, would be chased by the police fanning out from the van. Armed with *lathis*, they would rain blows on these unfortunate hawkers and frog-march them, whimpering and complaining, to the police van. I must confess that such was our dedication to Test cricket, that we shed few tears about this. We were definitely on the side of the police dealing with 'hawker nuisance', a favourite Bombay phrase, as this meant we could carry on with our cricket.

Of course when all else failed, when it rained, or it grew dark, or Hubert's gully was somehow occupied, there was always the landing outside my flat. It was no ordinary landing, reflecting the fact that the house was never meant to be lived in but just used for offices. Our flat had really been carved out of a large office floor, the main and best part of it – facing the road – was our flat and the one at the back, my father's office and store room. The result was that when you arrived on the landing outside the flat, any number of doors faced you. The first one as you came up the flight of stairs was a door that led to a row of toilets. Next to it was a much larger door which was always shut, a third led to our kitchen and then finally there was the main door. This started off by being a rickety, rotten door, smeared with heavy chalk marks which denoted wickets. It slowly developed into a better-looking, more permanent door, against which we placed a specially constructed set of wooden stumps fixed to a base.

Its advantages were obvious. It was enclosed and gave the feel of an indoor wicket, we could easily play at night as the landing was fairly well lit. It was, however, much narrower than Hubert's gully and did not give us the same feel of a cricket pitch. The landing itself formed the wicket at the point where the staircase from the floor below curved on to our floor, marking an imaginary bowler's wicket. But this severely restricted our run-up which had to be of a curving, slanting type to have any meaning whatsoever. The only way we could increase our run-up was to open the door that led to the row of 'loos' immediately behind the bowler's wicket. Running along the length of this and emerging from darkness, one could gather some speed and simulate the feel of what we imagined was a quick bowler.

As in Hubert's gully, cover was again a problem. In Hubert's gully it was the forbidding wall of the Agiari. Here, cover point was a window. At some stage early in our India-England-Australia Test matches, a window had been broken and never replaced and a sizzling cover drive, or what passed for it, meant the rubber ball whizzing through the open window and dropping two floors below right down the common sewer of the three buildings. To collect this ball was an extremely difficult feat and invariably I had to seek the assistance of some of my father's servants, or, more usually, have it replaced.

But perhaps the gravest problem with my landing was that it was, after all, a landing of a flat and, therefore narrow. A leg-side stroke was almost impossible since the wall on the leg-side was a few inches away from where we took guard at the wicket. And then there were the problems of the two staircases – the one that came up from the floor below and the one that went to the floor above. Very often a straight drive that beat the bowler would ricochet off the wall and go bouncing down the wooden stairs – right down to the flat of an old lady, who would complain piteously.

It is possible Hubert and I fashioned a unique form of cricket but I doubt if our experiences were all that different from many of the midnight children growing up in India in the 1950s and 1960s. If anything our experiences of cricket were typical of India then, and now.

From gully to maidan was a natural transition. In fact we journeyed back and forwards between the two forms of cricket very often, as do almost all those who play cricket in India. The maidan is, probably, the most evocative place in Indian urban life. It has been called the equivalent of an English park but this is grossly misleading. The only similarity it has with a park is that it is a vast, open area, very often at the centre of cities. But beyond that there are no similarities. It is not merely that the grass in an English park is much greener and finer than that of the maidan, but that whereas an English park is an oasis of calm, a shelter from the hustle and bustle of city life, the maidan reproduces Indian city life with all its noise and clamour. The grass is matted, raggy, struggling to stay alive amidst the dirt and rubble. Flowing through the maidan are little canals, the surface is pock-marked with ditches, even what looks like small ravines and the whole area is filled with people from every walk of life. It is amidst such confusion and noise that Indians learn to play their cricket.

Photographs taken at the Fort William maidan in Calcutta, on the rest day of the Calcutta test, illustrate what maidans and maidan cricket are like. There is the maidan cricketer who fancies himself as Dr W. G. Grace, a pavilion under the tree,

tea with cakes from a tin box, the bewildering variety of cricketing styles and dress and above all the sheer wonder of playing
cricket on a ground so inhospitable you might think it would
deter walking, let alone the pursuit of such a delicate game. But
just as the lotus, that great Hindu flower, springs from the dirtiest
and most inhospitable of surroundings, so does Indian cricket
arise, grow and blossom on these maidans dotted all over the urban
landscape.

Nowhere can maidan cricket be better appreciated than Bombay,
particularly south Bombay, where I grew up. That area is dominated by three great maidans: Azad, Cross and the Oval. Azad,
meaning free, had the distinction of being the home of the club to
which Vijay Merchant, one of India's great batsmen, belonged.
Opposite is the Cross, so called because at one end of it there is
a huge cross bearing the inscribed legend INRI. Azad is a regular
venue for many of the matches played in the inter-schools tourna-
ments of the city. Cross often attracts large crowds to watch
famous Tests, or ex-Test players playing in the inter-office *Times*
shield tournament. This competition, organised by the leading
local daily, *The Times of India*, is very well reported and, at times,
an even better draw than the Ranji trophy. It costs nothing to
watch and it is not unusual for a few thousand people to gather
along the boundary edges, sometimes spilling over onto the adjoining roads, to watch the stars of today and yesteryear do fierce
competitive battle. This is what may be called *mali*-dominated
cricket.

Malis generally live in the shacks that dot the edge of a maidan
and efficiently police the pitches on the maidans. These pitches
are distinguished from the rest of the field not merely in the normal
cricket sense, but by special arrangements. No sooner is a cricket
match over than the mali comes trundling in with wooden staves
and ropes and encloses the whole area of the pitch. It would not
take much to remove the wooden staves and dismantle the rope
but such is the aura possessed by these illiterate, but shrewd guar-
dians of the pitches of the maidan, that nobody dares. Also playing
on these is part of a package that you have to earn. Along with

pitch comes a tent, specially erected for the match, and acting as a pavilion and changing rooms. A tent that comes with a little cubicle attached to it and serving as a lavatory. It is when the malis start erecting the tents that the people on the maidan know that a proper cricket match, on a proper pitch is about to be played.

The maiden pitches are also used for net practice – mostly on weekday afternoons. The Azad maidan lay between school and home, and on my way back from school I would occasionally pause to watch these cricket nets and find nothing surprising in the fact that the batsmen, with their boxes happily attached outside their trousers, practised at the nets. Today when I revisit Bombay, and occasionally visit Azad maidan, the sight of hundreds of batsmen in full cricket regalia proudly displaying their boxes as they practise the forward defensive stroke seems odd, even faintly obscene. Then it was part of normal mali-maidan-cricket.

Most of my maidan cricket and, for that matter, most people's, was played on dirt tracks with some grass on it which formed the space between the pitches. This wasn't the only impromptu part of our cricket. There was the problem of equipment. I had been generously provided with full cricket gear, some of it from my father, and some of it gifts from friends and relations. But most of the members of my team were not quite so happily placed, and in most of our matches we had at best two pairs of pads, and very often just three pads. I mean not three *pairs* of pads, but one pair of pads and another solitary pad! So for much of the time, since most of us were right handed, we wore a pad on the left leg, leaving the right unprotected. Gloves were a scarcity and, though I had a set of stumps, only very rarely did we play in matches where we had two sets of stumps. Generally we had four stumps which imposed its own constraint. Three stumps would constitute the wicket at one end, the solitary stump the bowler's wicket at the other end. This meant that at the end of overs the batsman would cross over, not the wicket keeper or the fielders. Again the bat which had been a gift of a friend of my father was our prize bat, and very often the non-striker would have to do with a broken bat, or a wooden plank. At the end of an over, or when it was his turn to bat, he would exchange his bat, or plank, for a proper one. These are, of course, personal recollections but they mirror cricket as it was played then and now.

Not surprisingly maidan cricket gave rise to a new vocabulary. Thus maidan cricket uses the expression 'runner' in a totally different way from the common cricketing meaning of the term. In cricket a runner is one who runs for a batsman who has been injured during the game and cannot run for himself. In maidan cricket the number one batsman is called the 'opener', his partner is called the 'runner'. Very often in this class of cricket there are only three stumps and the stumps at the bowler's end are indicated by a pile of *chappals* – Indian slippers – heaped at the spot where the proper stumps would be. The runner is the one who immediately takes up his position at the chappal end.

There is also 'twoodie'. In maidan cricket boundaries have to be laboriously fixed. There is often very serious arguments about where the boundaries of the ground are. This is not surprising since the ground is not marked out, there are very many matches taking place all at the same time and the square-leg of one match is the cover point of another match. Often there are objects on a maidan which conveniently indicate a boundary: a roller, a tree, perhaps the spot where a pitch has been protected by the mali's wooden staves and ropes. But very often there are insurmountable objects on the ground too near the wicket to classify as a four and a hit to the object is denoted as twoodie, meaning two runs.

But perhaps the most major innovation of maidan cricket is the reinterpretation of the two-fingered salute. Now, normally in cricket the index finger of the right hand raised upward into the heavens is seen as the traditional mark of the umpire's decision in favour of the fielding side. This is all very well when the umpire is giving a decision in favour of the fielding side. But what if he is signifying not out? How does he do it? He could say 'Not out', but in maidan cricket this is considered not enough. So an innovation has been introduced whereby one finger raised to the heavens is out and two fingers raised to the heavens is not out. In maidan cricket, the umpire wishing to turn down an appeal doesn't say 'not out' or shake his head – a gesture which in India has a very different meaning – but raises two fingers of his right hand.

But what sort of cricket is this maidan game? Let me reminisce again and talk of the maidan cricket I played as I grew up in the 1950s. For some reason, and may be because I provided much of the essential gear – stumps, bats, gloves, pad – I was the Captain of my maidan team. In the early years I also provided two very important players: Shankar and Arjun. Shankar was my father's driver and Arjun one of the many servants whom my father employed. Both of them were young men in their prime and though they hadn't really played cricket properly, their ability to clout the ball hard and bowl it faster than we could added considerably to the strength of our team. This enabled us to boldly challenge older boys and hold quite an advantage over most teams. Later, as work commitments made Shankar and Arjun unavailable, I formed a team that perhaps reflected that area of Bombay rather well.

Apart from Hubert, whose cricket skill was perhaps slightly inferior to mine, there was Bala. He was some years senior to us and of his origins we knew nothing. One day while we were practising at the Oval he had turned up and become part of our team. He would often come in bare feet, or at best wearing thin, fragile chappals. I think his father was some sort of labourer and his family lived in a *chawl*, a tenement not far from Flora Fountain though, prudently, we made no enquiries.

Then there was Eddy. He was the same age as Bala but came from the same Catholic milieu as Hubert, though from Goa and, of course, was much more sophisticated and cleverer than Bala. Both Eddy and Bala, I believe, appeared for the matriculation at the same time, with Eddy doing somewhat better than Bala. This gave Eddy and Bala a certain awe in our eyes. In school, matriculation was always being held up as the great exam that would crown our school career, passing it was considered essential if our lives were to have any meaning, and we hoped to follow the example set by Eddy and Bala.

I was personally intrigued and enchanted by Eddy's infatuation with *The Guns of Navarone*. This was around 1958 and *The Guns of Navarone* had just been released in Bombay. It was proving immensely popular and easily notched up a Silver Jubilee, twenty-five weeks of continuous showing. Eddy, if I remember rightly, saw it half a dozen times and appeared to have memorised every scene. His particular favourite was the moment when David Niven and Gregory Peck discover that Peck's girl friend is really a German spy. Eddy, in a typical Goan accent, that would now be described as a take-off of Peter Sellers's Indian one, would love declaiming David Niven's speech to Gregory Peck urging him to kill his girl friend. 'Do it for England', Niven urged Peck in the movie and this became Eddie's war cry during our matches. Eddy, who was quite a decent bat, would often share stands with me and in the middle of a stand, as we crossed over, or consulted in the middle of the pitch, Eddy would seek to encourage me by quoting Niven's speech and saying, 'Do it for England.' I don't know how often we 'did it for England' in those matches but we found nothing incongruous in Eddy's exhortation.

But perhaps our most colourful cricketer was Ching, the Chinaman. It was an indication of our cricket, or at least of my team, that we never really discovered his proper name, nor even made any effort to do so. He lived not far from the dock areas of Bombay and had been introduced to the team by Bala. The most distinctive thing about him was not his origin, which we accepted without question, but his style of play. His most effective, in fact his only, stroke would be to cross his legs in front of the wicket and then hold his bat in the gap formed by the crossing of the legs. If he kept the bat straight then he would drop the ball dead centre. Occasionally he would twist the bat either on the leg-side, squirting the ball through fine leg, or on the off-side, sending it through slips. I think the shock of the style proved so great for most bowlers that they often found no way of dislodging Ching.

Bala, Hubert, Eddy, Ching and I would form the hard core of the team. We would be supplemented by other players, cousins of Eddy's or friends of Bala's but at times we struggled to complete the team. Then total strangers would be incorporated into the side. Some of them just people lounging at the Oval while we were about to start the match. This gave our already exotic team an even more exotic flavour and probably accounted for our success.

Some of our most colourful matches were played against a team made up from the residents of Rehmat Manzil, a large block of flats on Veer Nariman Road, the road which runs past the Oval and houses most of Bombay's restaurants. Many of the boys in the team were from my own school, some of them from my own class, and they were the archetypal 'building' team (all being from one building). There was Gupta, who happily allowed everybody to mispronounce him as 'Gupte' thus appropriating some of the glory that was attached to the name of Subhas Gupte, India's legendary leg-spinner and a hero of our youth. The cricketing similarity between Gupta and Gupte was remote, since Gupta's leg-breaks very often turned out to be gentle up and down stuff. Worse still, not all members of Gupta's team accepted his captaincy, though the gravest problems for him were caused not by his middle-class school contemporaries, but by Sammath, the son of the 'building' durwan, an Indian-style porter. Durwans in India generally hail from Afghanistan or the North West Frontier provinces and are called Pathans. Most of them are called not by their names but by a general term, Lala, and this Lala was a tall, fierce man who fitted every Indian stereotype of the Pathan and looked capable of fulfilling his job of protecting the building. Sammath, his son, in our cricket terms was just as fierce – a tearaway fast bowler who took a long run up and appeared to deliver the ball with exceptional speed. Unfortunately for Gupta's team, Sammath also had the fast bowler's temperament and did not like being taken off at any time. This caused some merry rows between Sammath and his Captain Gupta, much to our joy.

No doubt individual memories of maidan cricket will differ. But in essence I doubt if it has changed all that much. It is still the world of twoodies, runner, the V-sign signifying not out, the mali as a shambolic man but with real power protecting his pitch from the assaults of the multitudes and the maidan team made up of many elements reflecting urban Indian life.

The Maidan View
1986

Abdul Qadir: Cooling Down

SCYLD BERRY

Abdul Qadir lives in the Dharampura district of Lahore. I went to visit him there before England began their cooling-off period in Sahiwal. In the First Test he had recorded the fifth best figures for an innings in Test history; and though he faded thereafter because of an internal ailment, he finished with thirty wickets in the series, three times as many as the next man, Iqbal Qasim (three of whose first four wickets should not have been given out). Qadir was now that rarest of cricket phenomena, a shock and stock bowler in one, in effect a Malcolm Marshall capable of thirty-over spells at less than two runs an over. Most of us will never see a finer wrist-spinner.

The name of Dharampura is significant for not being a Muslim one. The quarter, on one side of the railway track from Lahore to Karachi (socially, the wrong side), used to be inhabited by Hindus and was vacated on Partition: it therefore had something of the stigma of an abandoned ghetto when poor newcomers took it over. Qadir's father came from the village of Marghas, near Peshawar, in order to find work in Lahore, before his eldest son was born. He was the Islamic equivalent of a cleric, and rose in time to become the imam of the Dharampura mosque.

The family used to live in a back lane off one of the side-streets of Dharampura, in a tall and rambling brick house. Kim used to explore by night the rooftops of similar houses in the old city. When Qadir became established as the best performer of his kind, he thought it the duty of the Pakistan Board to advance him a loan for a new house. A dispute ensued, of the long-running kind which only the BCCP seems to be able to sustain with its players, during which Qadir was sent home from a tour of New Zealand. Whatever the Byzantine intricacies, Qadir eventually got his new house, in the main street of Dharampura, and a shop attached to it, 'Imran Qadir Sports'.

Qadir had risen from his afternoon sleep even as the sun had set. At six o'clock he appeared in his sitting-room, wearing the pyjamas which are widely worn in the sub-continent. After a little talk, he spread himself out on some cushions in front of an electric fire, so that a track-suited one-eyed man of about sixty could give him physiotherapy. At this stage Qadir thought the pain in the right side of his back was muscular; not until later was he diagnosed to have kidney stones.

He is a man of moods. He kept saying, 'I am a mood bowler' and, more than once, 'It's all up to the mood'. This moodiness he ascribed to his being by ancestry a Pathan (and his mother tongue was Pushto). But he was not best pleased when a feature I wrote about him for *The Observer* was quoted back in a Pakistani newspaper in such a way that it made him seem keen to emphasise his distinctiveness from Baluchis, Punjabis, Sindhis and the rest. Like many Pakistanis, he feared Balkanisation and wanted to play down regional differences. Qadir did not claim he was Pathan to gain any kudos, simply to explain his temperament. It was Pathan to bowl in a brooding mood in the Faisalabad Test when his body and mind were troubled. It was Pathan to flare up in the Karachi Test and to run to the boundary fence in mid-over to shout at an abusive spectator. He said his full name should have been Abdul Qadir Khan.

A younger brother of Qadir's plays as a batsman for WAPDA, and he himself has three sons: Abdul Qahir, Imran Qadir – named, of course, after his captain and friend – and Suleiman. He has a daughter too, and it was Pathan of him to keep the distaff side of his household out of the sight of visitors in his sitting-room (male well-wishers were forever dropping in for a while, simply to sit in the presence and watch). Plenty of silver medals and trophies were on display. On one wall of the sitting-room was a framed copy of a poem in Urdu which sang the praises of 'Abdul Qadir the Googly Bowler'. Another photograph showed Viv Richards and Malcolm Marshall visiting his sports shop soon after its opening, and trying to be patient with the hordes. 'Business is not – pause – not that bad', said Qadir, as he lay on his back while the physio kneaded him. He did not sound perturbed.

False modesty is not part of Muslim etiquette. 'I bowled superbly,' Qadir admitted of his performance in the first innings of the Lahore Test – never better. Earlier in the year he had been dropped from the Pakistan team on their tour of India, and he had not been in the mood in England either until the final Test. But after that tour he had trained hard, driving to the Qaddafi Stadium in his Honda Civic, running round the outfield, doing 25 press-ups and 25 sit-ups and then repeating the dose. 'It was my ambition to do well in the World Cup,' he said. He likes one-day cricket for the reason that batsmen have to play strokes against him and cannot hide behind their pads. Qadir was annoyed, surprisingly annoyed, that Gatting should have been strokeless in his second innings of the First Test when he batted 130 minutes for 23 runs. He had challenged the England captain by saying to his face: 'Why are you batting like a kid?'

'Off the field I'm very modest, very friendly, like my father – he was the real hero of my life. But on the field I'm a different person. I'm trying to get the batsman out all the time. This is Pathan.' Qadir in fact used to see red when he was hit to the boundary: such was the intensity of his anger the blood would rush into his eyes, as it did with Imran, another of Pathan ancestry. He had not been able to control this phenomenon until three or four years back. 'Now I'm thinking it's part of the game to be hit for four. I am a spinner. I shouldn't react immediately.' England, during the series, seldom gave him cause to see red.

The Googly Bowler sat up after a quarter of an hour of massage. He has long ears and an expressive face which is usually handsomely smiling or darkly clouded. At the time he had a haircut which didn't suit him as it made him resemble Laurel scratching his head when Hardy was about to make him cry. Tea was brought in by a young boy in the household retinue – Muslim families can be very extended – while Qadir mentioned that he had picked up the game of cricket in the streets of Dharampura from the age of twelve. He had been a fast bowler at first, which had suited his temperament; leg-spin he had picked up experientially, as he had gone along.

Samosas were offered around as well. Qadir took one, with some spicy sauce from a bottle, then a second. He loves his vegetables, especially his lentils, and eats them with roti bread. When staying in hotels he does not mind that Tuesdays and Wednesdays are designated 'meatless days' in Pakistan: for reasons of national economy, not of religious stricture, red meat cannot be bought or sold then. Though almost a vegetarian, Qadir is a strong man, especially in his shoulders. Hitting Courtney Walsh for six in the final over of the qualifying match in Lahore had not been so very demanding for him, but the rupees were still flowing in from business firms and individual admirers. These shoulders may also play a part in giving his bowling its distinction, for most of his kind leave it to fingers and wrist. One technical alteration he had made was to cut down his leap at the crease, and this new poise in delivery had led to his extraordinary steadiness of length. He continued to tug his left arm down as he delivered, and to tuck it into his side as if he were about to shake somebody's hand with it: that gave him his bounce. Indeed I have never seen a ball so full of energy as those which Qadir propelled out of his hand after a long arm swing, a heave of his right shoulder and a snap of his wrist. The ball had a battery-charged life of its own.

The samosas were offered round again, for generous hospitality is another Pathan characteristic. I asked him why he had turned down an offer to play county cricket. 'If I join a county I'll bowl against your young players and give them experience. My country has given me respect, money, everything. I'm not going to sell my art for my country. Money is not everything.' A bazaar rumour, on the other hand, printed in a newspaper, had it that Surrey's offer was not high enough. Who knows? Men's motives are mixed, and the more so in the East. Again I asked him why he had not arrived in England that summer along with the rest of the touring team and barely in time for the Second Test. The bazaars, naturally, had their supply of rumours. 'I cannot say,' he said. 'It was a family matter.'

I don't believe Qadir is governed by gold-lust. He had, after all, given away the car which he had won for being the leading bowler in Pool 'B' of the World Cup. At the Lahore semi-final General Zia had presented him with the keys, which he had promptly given back, asking the president to give them to Imran as a farewell gift. 'It was a shock to Imran,' Qadir remembered. Somebody motivated by money and with his own business to run does not get up at ten o'clock, as Qadir confessed he did on non-match days. I concluded that pride drives him, pride in himself and his country – when he is in the mood, that is. Pride blinds too; hence his appeals for some lbw decisions, such as those against Gatting in the Lahore international and Test, which he would otherwise have regarded as absurd.

By the end of the series against England, Qadir had taken 145 Test wickets in Pakistan, at half the cost of his 46 Test wickets ahead. The nature of Pakistani pitches accounts for a lot: if a ball squeezes your finger against the unyielding ground, nothing gives except your nail. Elsewhere, even in India and the West Indies, pitches are no longer hard but slow, grassy, tired old things which assist nobody bar the seamer. The umpiring, however, has not been a negligible factor. Of his thirty wickets against England, eleven were lbw. Of his wickets in Pakistan over all, more than a quarter have come from such decisions, against one-eighth abroad. Yet there can be no doubting the greatness of his bowling. In the words of John Emburey, the one England player who came to read Qadir: 'He is the greatest spinner I've seen.'

This superiority of Qadir's only made the umpiring more vexing. They had said about Bhutto after he had won his last election by means of massive rigging: 'It was so unnecessary – he would have triumphed anyway.' It was the same here.

A Cricket Odyssey
1988

Sri Lanka

SHIVA NAIPAUL

Sri Lanka was suffering from its worst drought in 30 years. In the countryside around Colombo, the waterless paddy-fields baked in the sun. Village wells were drying up. Outbreaks of cholera and typhoid were being reported. In the heart of the capital a permanent haze of red dust overhung Galle Face Green. The talk everywhere was of the rain that would not come. But up in Kandy they were expending 10,000 gallons of water daily on the field where Sri Lanka would soon be playing its first Test match with an Australian touring cricket team.

'You will observe our priorities,' an acquaintance (who happened to be an enemy of the present capitalist-minded government) remarked. 'Who cares if the country goes to rack and ruin? So long as the cricket fields are green, what else matters?' Cricket, enjoyed by perhaps 20 per cent of the population, was part of the oppressive class structure that was slowly but surely going to strangle Sri Lanka. As such, it ought to be abolished.

At that juncture I was sympathetic not so much to the Marxist logic of the argument as to its conclusion.

Next afternoon at the Singhalese Sports Club, the headquarters of the Cricket Board of Control, my Press card was scanned with an odd mixture of suspicion and inertia and returned to me with a shrug.

'Everybody here,' said a non-reactive individual, 'is damned busy. We're all damned busy.' On the walls were fading photographs of vanished teams, vanished heroes. Turning my back on all those damned busy people, I walked out to the airy balcony.

Down on the playing field, a wicket was being watered. A rosy dusk was beginning to illumine the sky.

These private Colombo clubs, of which there are about 25, have traditionally controlled cricket in Sri Lanka. Those who take their cricket seriously tend to be urban and overwhelmingly middle class, though some attempt is now being made to change this, to broaden both its social and geographical appeal.

In a society where 1300 rupees a month (about £40) is considered a good wage, and where half of the population earns 300 rupees or less a month, the financial attractions of modern cricket (and I leave aside the kind of bait dangled by the South Africans) are obvious. If you have the talent, it offers an alluring vista of escape from the debilitating and endless struggle for existence. It is so much better to be a successful cricketer than to be earning a pittance in the Survey Department after 25 years of service; it is so much better to be a cricketer than an unemployed, not-too-literate university graduate. Cricket holds out a possibility of international recognition denied Sri Lankans in most spheres: the island offers little glamour to the vast majority of those condemned to live there.

How wonderful to be a 'teen star' like Arjuna Ranatunga – who scored a half-century against the Australians in a one-day match – and have this sort of prose appear about you in one of the local newspapers: 'Ranatunga, the whizz-kid of local cricket, smashed an exhilarating 55 in 39 deliveries to send Sri Lanka soaring to a magnificent four-wicket victory.' The Australians had met their match in this 'Wizard of Ours . . . the teen star who bopped them.'

If Ranatunga had not been a teen star, his thoughts, like those of so many other Sri Lankans, might have turned towards the Middle East: in Dubai it is possible to earn eight or nine times the average Sri Lankan wage. (The whore-houses of Colombo, I had been assured, had been emptied by the Middle Eastern exodus.) The 30,000 migrants living in the Gulf states are a valuable source of foreign exchange and a buffer against social unrest – always just round the corner in Sri Lanka.

For those who are able to play it, cricket offers a fantasy of possibilities – a fantasy that has begun to acquire a new solidity with the granting of Test status. Cricket is not played in Sri Lanka because of any post-imperial nostalgia. The clubs are only nominally oases of exclusivity. Many are shabby, fly-blown places, battling to make ends meet. The young men who play cricket may, by the standard of the island, constitute an élite. But they are a peculiar and modest élite; an élite on the make.

Again and again I was told with a mournful air of pride that Sri Lankan school cricket was considered among the best in the world; that the best schools gained prestige less from their academic performance than from their performance on the field. So what happened to all that talent after school? It ran off and disappeared because precious jobs had to be found; families had to be maintained. The struggle for existence took precedence. But now, with Test status, with the odd tour by teams of international class, it was hoped that this would gradually change. Young men could now join the Army, the Navy, the Air Force, the police – and continue to play cricket for the teams fielded by their employers. I stared out into the deepening, rose-red dusk, watching precious water soak into the turf.

The Australians dominated the sports pages of the newspapers. They had sent a good team. Nearly all the big names had been included – Greg Chappell, Dennis Lillee, David Hookes, Rodney Hogg, Kepler Wessels. Chappell was saying all the right things: he had heard so much about Sri Lanka and had always wanted to visit the island; he and his team had no intention of underrating the opposition. It was all terribly pleasing. In turn, the Sri Lankans could point to Sir Garfield Sobers. He had come to advise them, to exhort, to boost morale. 'Togetherness' was one of his major themes. He spoke of the damaging effect inter-island rivalry had had on West Indian cricket. He appealed to his charges to consider Test cricket a 'national duty'.

The local commentators, falling into the spirit of the occasion, described his remarks as opportune. What Sir Gary had said about the West Indies was, apparently, all too sadly the case in Sri Lanka. Players and selectors had suffered from 'unfair and vulgar criticism'. An unnamed Sri Lankan cricketer commented, 'I, for one, just feel like chucking in the game . . . if hoots and bad remarks are all we get from our own people for playing for the country.' The atmosphere was charged with a pre-connubial tension. I was reminded of the irritability, the excitability, that precedes an Indian wedding.

And yet, in the end, it all turned out to be slightly deceptive.

On the day of the first one-day international, the police issued extensive traffic regulations. I feared the worst. My imagination conjured up images of chaos. I saw multitudes thronging the approaches to the Sara Stadium, I saw bad-tempered policemen on bad-tempered horses. I saw stampede and mayhem. It was not at all like that.

The Sara Stadium turned out to be located in the midst of one of Colombo's most squalid squatter colonies. In the doorways of dark-interiored hovels lurked young men and women with painfully meagre bodies. Children splashed in fetid pools, squatted in the roadside dust. The morning air was tainted with the smells of ordure.

'Bad people, sir,' my driver murmured obsequiously.

'Why are they bad people?'

'They should not be here, sir. It is not their place.'

'Where is their place?'

He did not know and he did not care. We were watched with lethargic hostility from the doorways. Nearby rose blocks of mossy apartments bordered by broad, stagnant gutters, ornamented with mounds of refuse. A few days previously there had been stampede and mayhem in this locality. The blocks of flats ringing the stadium are occupied by Air Force personnel and their families. Assorted disagreements – I was not able to discover the exact points of contention – had arisen between the Air Force families and the squatters. The former, losing patience, had opened fire on the latter and gone on a rampage. Some of the hovels were burnt down, squatters were killed. The Army and the police had moved in, establishing a kind of martial law in the vicinity. Reflections on Test cricket and national duty receded as we crawled past groups of soldiers armed with rifles. I stared at a colourful portrait displayed on the roadside. It commemorated a squatter child murdered during the disturbance.

Within the stadium, the crowd was disappointingly small and subdued. There were reasons for this. Tickets were expensive, some costing 200 rupees; the match was being broadcast on the radio and televised. Also, it happened to be the Singhalese and Tamil New Year and so large numbers of people were 'out of station', enjoying, in this season of drought, the high-altitude delights of the hill country. A line of low stands fringed part of the ground, conveniently overlooked by the Air Force tenements – they probably had the best view of the game. I hoped they would not suddenly take into their heads to open fire. A licensed jester, with a Sri Lankan flag, paraded the perimeter of the field, shouting encouragement. Occasionally, a fire cracker exploded.

At lunch, the Sri Lankans were pleased. The Australian total was modest and half the side was out. The afternoon drawled on ('Good shot, sir, damned good shot'), pursuing its luminous path to dusk.

It seemed that Sri Lanka could win. When the possible became probable, the crowd livened up, detonating their fire crackers with selfless prodigality. When the probability became a certainty, the police converged on the boundary.

I quite forget who won the Man-of-the-Match award.

Observer Colour Supplement
1983

Kanhai: A Study in Confidence

C. L. R. JAMES

Writing critically about West Indies cricket and cricketers, or any cricket for that matter, is a difficult discipline. The investigation, the analysis, even the casual historical or sociological gossip about any great cricketer should deal with his actual cricket, the way he bats or bowls or fields, does all or any of these. You may wander far from where you started, but unless you have your eyes constantly on the ball, in fact never take your eyes off it, you are soon writing not about cricket, but yourself (or other people) and psychological or literary responses to the game. This can be and has been done quite brilliantly, adding a little something to literature but practically nothing to cricket, as little as the story of Jack and the Beanstalk (a great tale) adds to our knowledge of agriculture. This is particularly relevant to the West Indies.

A great West Indies cricketer in his play should embody some essence of that crowded vagueness which passes for the history of the West Indies. If, like Kanhai, he is one of the most remarkable and individual of contemporary batsmen, then that should not make him less but more West Indian. You see what you are looking for, and in Kanhai's batting what I have found is a unique pointer of the West Indian quest for identity, for ways of expressing our potential bursting at every seam.

So now I hope we understand each other. Eyes on the ball.

The first historical innings (I prefer to call them historical now) by Kanhai was less than 50, for British Guiana against the Australians of 1956. Kanhai had not as yet made the West Indies team. He played well but what was remarkable about the innings was not only its promise but that he was the junior in a partnership with Clyde Walcott as senior.

It is a commonplace what Clyde Walcott has done for the cricket of British Guiana. In reality, in truth and in essence, the thing should be stated this way. The tremendous tradition of Barbados batting, the fount and origin of West Indies cricket, through Walcott had begun to fertilize another area in the Caribbean. Kanhai was the first-fruit. Some like to lay emphasis on the fact that he comes originally from the Courantyne, the home not of depressed sugar-workers but of independent rice farmers. There may be something to this. I do not know British Guiana well enough to have on this matter an opinion that is worthwhile. I prefer to remember and to remind of the fact that Christiani coached on the Courantyne. Now Christiani was one of the most brilliant of the brilliant school of West Indies batsmen. Of an innings of 107 not out that he played for the West Indies against the state of Victoria in 1951–2, A.G. Moyes said that it was the most dazzling innings of the Australian season. So that the burgeoning Kanhai inherited not only the universality of Barbados batting but was able to absorb also the individualism of one of the most brilliant of West Indies individualists.

Kanhai played effective innings which resulted in his being selected for the 1957 West Indies tour in England. I am not making a chronicle. I remember, however, the batting that he showed in all the Tests in England. West Indies was scrambling for openers and much of this responsibility was thrown to Kanhai. He bore it without disgrace, with spasms of alternate toughness and brilliance which only later we were to learn were fundamental constituents in his character.

Yet the innings in 1957 that future events caused me to remember most strongly was his last test innings at the Oval. He faced Trueman and immediately hit him for two uninhibited fours. Gone was the restraint which held him prisoner during all the previous innings against England.

Kanhai, I know now, had made up his mind to have a final fling at the English bowlers. But either he wasn't yet good enough to play such cricket in a Test or he had not shaken off the effects of months of restraint. He was out almost at once. Altogether in 1957 it was the failure of Weekes, Worrell and Walcott to repeat the Victorian cavalry charges of 1950 which threw such burdens on Sobers, Kanhai and Collie Smith. The burden fell most heavily on Kanhai. But the future batsman was there to be discerned.

The next innings that helped to build the Kanhai personality was played as far away as Australia. It was an innings of over two hundred made in one day. Kanhai simply went to the Melbourne wicket and from the first ball hit the Victoria bowlers all over the place until he was tired at the end of the day. It is my firm belief that here again the great Barbados cricket tradition was at work.

In Australia, Frank Worrell made West Indians and the world aware of what West Indians were capable of when their talents had full play. That is Worrell's gift to the West Indian personality. We are much given to individualism (it would be a miracle if we were not). But the West Indians under Worrell could not let themselves go, be their own coruscating selves, knowing that the interest and needs, opportunities and perils of the side as a whole were being observed and calculated by one of the shrewdest minds that the game has known. They could have complete confidence in their captain, go their own way, yet respond immediately to any premonition or request. That the smiting of Victoria was not the kind of brilliant innings which all good batsmen play at some time or other was proved by the fact that Kanhai continued to play that way all through the season. When he made a century in each innings against Australia, he was within an ace of making the second century in even time. Hunte being run out in an effort to help Kanhai towards the century, Kanhai was so upset that it was long minutes before he could make the necessary runs.

Kanhai continued to score, in the West Indies, in India, in Pakistan, but the next great landmark of his career was his innings against England at the Oval in 1963.

All through that season he had never been his new, his Australian self. In Tests he got into the nineties twice, but, while always

showing himself a master batsman, something was wrong somewhere: if something was not wrong, at least everything was not
right. Then at the Oval, with the fate of the match depending to
a substantial degree on his batting (especially after Sobers ran himself out) in this his last test innings in England, Kanhai set off to
do to English bowling what he had done to Australian.

Perhaps I should have seen its national significance, its relation
to our quest for national identity. Here was a West Indian proving
to himself that there was one field in which the West Indian not
only was second to none, but was the creator of his own destiny.
However, swept away by the brilliance and its dramatic circumstances, I floated with the stream.

1964 was a great year, perhaps the most important year in the
steadily growing facts and phenomena I was automatically accumu-
lating about the fascinating Kanhai. High on the list was an opinion
which was the climax of many other opinions. All through the
Tests of 1964 I sat in press-boxes, most often between Sir Learie
Constantine and Sir Frank Worrell. We were reporting England
against Australia; there was a lot of talk about cricket and naturally
about West Indian cricketers. About Kanhai, for quite a while the
only thing notable said was by Worrell. He made a comparison
between Kanhai and Everton Weekes as batsmen who would stand
back and lash the length ball away on the off-side or to the on-
boundary. Then at Leeds, Kanhai himself turned up and came and
sat in the press-box. Learie had a long look at him and then turned
to me and said: 'There is Kanhai. You know at times he goes
crazy.'

I never believe that an intelligent man or a man whom I know
to be well informed about a subject is talking nonsense. I knew
that Learie had something in mind. I waited and before long I
learnt what it was. I shall try as far as I can to put it in his own
words.

'Some batsmen play brilliantly sometimes and at ordinary times
they go ahead as usual. That one,' nodding at Kanhai, 'is different
from all of them. On certain days, before he goes into the wicket
he makes up his mind to let them have it. And once he is that way

nothing on earth can stop him. Some of his colleagues in the pavilion who have played with him for years see strokes that they have never seen before: from him or anybody else. He carries on that way for 60 or 70 or 100 runs and then he comes back with a great innings behind him.'

That was illumination indeed, coming from someone who knew all about batting which aimed at hitting bowlers all over the place. It was obvious that at times Kanhai's audacity at the wicket had earned not the usual perfunctory admiration but the deep and indeed awesome respect of Constantine. We both were thinking of the 1963 innings at the Oval. He had hit the English bowlers all over the place, he gave no chance and never looked like getting out. Yet I knew Learie was aware of something in Kanhai's batting that had escaped me. At off times I wondered what it might be.

Going crazy. That could be Greek Dionysius, the satyric passion for the expression of the natural man, bursting through the acquired restraints of disciplined necessity. I played with that idea for a while. Tentatively, I settled for a West Indian proving to himself that henceforth he was following no established pattern but would create his own.

Certainty came at the end of the 1964 season. Sir Frank Worrell led a team of West Indies players against England elevens at Scarborough and Edgbaston (a third game at Lord's was rained out). I reported both games. Kanhai made a century in each, and what I saw no one has written about: nor have I met anyone who appears to have noticed it.

At Scarborough Kanhai was testing out something new. Anyone could see that he was trying to sweep anything near the leg-stump round to fine-leg to beat both deep square and long-leg. He missed the ball more often than he connected. That was easy enough. But I distinctly remember being vaguely aware that he was feeling his way to something. I attributed it to the fact that he had been playing league cricket all the season and this was his first first-class match. Afterwards, I was to recall his careful defence of immaculate length balls from Trevor Bailey, and, without any warning, or fuss, not even a notable follow-through, he took on the rise

and lifted the ball ten feet over mid-on's head to beat wide long-on
to the boundary; he never budged from his crease, he had barely
swung at the ball. Yet, as far as he was concerned, it was a four
predestined.

We went to Edgbaston. Bailey's side had six bowlers who had
bowled for England that season. If the wicket was not unresponsive to spin, and the atmosphere not unresponsive to swing, the
rise of the ball from the pitch was fairly regular. Kanhai began by
giving notice that he expected Test bowlers to bowl a length; balls
a trifle loose so rapidly and unerringly paid the full penalty that
by the time he had made 30 or 40 everybody was on his best
behaviour.

Kanhai did not go crazy. Exactly the reverse. He discovered,
created a new dimension in batting. The only name I can give to
it is 'cat-and-mouse'. The bowler would bowl a length ball. Kanhai
would play a defensive stroke, preferably off the front foot, pushing the ball for one, quite often for two on the on-side – a most
difficult stroke on an uncertain pitch, demanding precision footwork and clockwork timing. The bowler, after seeing his best
lengths exploited in this manner, would shift, whereupon he was
unfailingly despatched to the boundary. After a time it began to
look as if the whole sequence had been pre-arranged for the benefit
of the spectators. Kanhai did not confine himself too rigidly to
this pre-established harmony.

One bowler, to escape the remorseless billiard-like pushes,
brought the ball untimely up. Kanhai hit him for six to long-on
off the front foot. The bowler shortened a bit. Kanhai in the same
over hit him for six in the same place, off the back foot this time.
Dexter, who made a brilliant, in fact a dazzling century in the
traditional style, hit a ball out of the ground over wide mid-on.
Kanhai hit one out of the ground some forty yards further on than
Dexter. He made over 170 in about three hours.

Next day, Brian Johnston in the *Daily Mail*, Crawford White
in the *Daily Express*, John Woodcock in *The Times* – men who
have watched critically all the great players of the last thirty years
– made no effort to contain themselves: they had never seen such

batting. Here and there some showed that in their minds the Everest conquered by Bradman had been once more scaled.

They were wrong. Kanhai had found his way into regions Bradman never knew. It was not only the technical skill and strategic generalship that made the innings the most noteworthy I have seen. There was more to it, to be seen as well as felt. Bradman was a ruthless executioner of bowlers. All through this demanding innings Kanhai grinned with a grin that could be seen a mile away.

Now to fit his cricket into the history of the West Indies. I saw all his batting against the Australians during their tour of the West Indies in 1965. Some fine play, but nothing in the same category as Edgbaston.

At Melbourne in Australia in 1959, he had experienced a freedom in which his technique could explore roads historically charted, but to him unknown.

He had had to wait until the last Test in England in 1963 to assure himself that his conquest of Australia was not an accident. Now in 1964 at Scarborough and Edgbaston he was again free; to create not only 'a house for Mr Biswas', a house like other houses, but to sail the seas that open out before the East Indian who no longer has to prove himself to anybody or to himself. It was no longer: anything you can do, I can do better. That had been left behind at the Kennington Oval in 1963. Now it was fresh fields and pastures new, not tomorrow but today. At that moment, Edgbaston in 1964, the West Indian could strike from his feet the dust of centuries. The match did not impose any burdensome weight of responsibility. He was free as few West Indians have been free.

Cricket is an art, a means of national expression. Voltaire says that no one is so boring as the man who insists on saying everything. I have said enough. But I believe I owe it to the many who did not see the Edgbaston innings to say that I thought it showed one of the directions that, once freed, the West Indies might take. The West Indies in my view embody more sharply than elsewhere Nietzsche's conflict between the ebullience of Dionysius and the discipline of Apollo. Kanhai's going crazy might seen to be Dionysius in us breaking loose. It was absent from Edgbaston. Instead the phrases which go nearest to expressing what I saw and have reflected upon are those of Lytton Strachey on French Literature: '[the] mingled distinction, gaiety and grace which is one of the unique products of the mature poetical genius of France'.

Distinction, gaiety, grace. Virtues of the ancient Eastern Mediterranean city-states, islands, the sea, and the sun. Long before Edgbaston I had been thinking that way. Maybe I saw only what I was looking for. Maybe.

New World, Guyana
1966

Malcolm Marshall: Joyous Man with the Kick of a Mule

MARK NICHOLAS

He was listening to the radio and did not believe what he had heard. Minutes later, Wesley Hall telephoned to say the same. He trembled, for he had played only one match for his native Barbados – and began to dream.

He dreamt of his hero, Sir Garfield Sobers: the languid, laughing, liquid Sobers whose style entranced a nation. All through his childhood he had mimicked Sobers, collar stiff and turned high, shoulders rolling, hips swaying, and now, suddenly, he had the chance to walk the legend's stage.

Kerry Packer had ripped the heart from the West Indies team and, shorn of their stars, the selectors searched for some young and spirited characters to tour India. One they chose was unknown but was from the most famous island in the cricket empire and destined to capture more Test match wickets than any other West Indian. This week he retired from English cricket.

Malcolm Marshall was born 35 years ago in St Michael, a small parish in the middle of Barbados, to a policeman father and a doting mother who spoiled him rotten. He went to school in the crispest clothes and was, the teachers say, a model pupil and a team man even then.

He did not know his father, who died in a motorcycle accident before the boy's first birthday, but he knew his grandfather, Oscar Welch, because Oscar bowled at him days and nights in the parks and on the beaches.

He loved batting and, in truth, loves it best even now. He took to bowling because he once waited four days for a knock in the school yard. The rules were clear; you batted until dismissed, and one or two could play a bit, so the tiny, frail boy started bowling, as fast as he could. By the end of break-time, he was batting.

Much of Marshall epitomises the calypso cricketer. Much does not. The joyous grin, the incessant chatter, the flailing willow, the stumps flying, the bouncers whizzing, the shiny black face with its gleaming teeth and the wide open laugh, head thrown skywards, that accompanies the simplest of fun.

His youth was conditioned by his environment in the way of Constantine and Kanhai; Ramadhin and Richards; Worrell, Walcott and Weekes. They all, it sometimes seemed, were affected by the sun and the sand and so they performed the most outrageous of deeds and otherwise the most crazy.

The temperament and impulse could run riot in the heat, and thereby came the charm of their brilliant, instinctive cricket that was played without inhibition.

But, today, the West Indian cricketer is not so happy-go-lucky, for he is conditioned by success and salaries, pay cheques and professionalism. Marshall is this, too, a man reared by Clive Lloyd, who played tough, uncompromising cricket in a team that no other could surely have beaten. The rules were for breaking all right, but batting and its beauty suffered as remarkable fast bowlers – collectively the best in the game's history – tore into unprepared and intimidated opposition and laid waste their defences. This was cruel, calculated cricket and Marshall was as impressive in this role as he is when playing the court jester.

He says: 'I am a fast bowler. This is my job. If I bowl dangerously and intimidate, then the umpires are empowered to stop me. I have no problem with that. I love cricket and am a keen professional. I have obligations to meet, mortgages to pay. I am a man who wants to do the best for himself and his team every time I go to work.'

This is the very key to Malcolm Marshall and his incredible success. He has never given less than everything for his team. He is self-interested in the acceptable way of top sportsmen but when it is not his day, and others are wreaking their havoc, he is as pleased as punch.

In fourteen years, I do not remember him once giving short change and, along with Mike Procter and Sir Richard Hadlee, whom Marshall greatly admires, he has been the best overseas cricketer in English cricket. To be so, he has remained supremely fit and his sharp mind has ensured the preservation of those supple, rubbery limbs as the years have taken their toll.

His body, though chubbier now, is absurdly slight for one so powerful. He has small bones and small feet and stands no taller than 5ft 10in, yet at various times he has been the world's greatest, fastest, most skilful, and, more improbably, most lethal bowler.

Around his neck hangs a gold chain and on the pendant glows his nickname, 'Macko.' The word 'Macko' evokes joint emotions of hand-slapping glee and sinister oppression.

When Macko first played for Hampshire in 1979, there was no sign of the hand-slapping glee. The weather was appalling. It snowed and he clung to the radiator, fingers frozen and fearfully homesick. He had an awkward summer, plagued by no-balls and an unsympathetic captain, but he had talent, oodles of it, and we youngsters wanted him back, for we quickly spotted the sinister oppression.

As a boy, he had followed Hampshire from the pages of the Barbados newspapers, initially with an interest in his namesake, Roy Marshall, and then studying the career of another hero, Andy Roberts. It was natural, then, that he should go to Hampshire and he has loved the county ever since that chilly introduction.

In return, we have loved him, too, for he has taught us plenty and won us matches. He has taken 823 wickets for Hampshire, 134 of them in 1982 (1,550 in all first-class cricket and 376 in Test matches).

In the early days, his bowling was based on a whippy, sideways action that caused the ball to skid at its target with deadly out-swing. He bowled a bouncer so evil that even the players with the quickest wit were forced back, thus leaving themselves open to his vicious movement.

As his action became more chest-on, he developed the inswinger and, of course, with age and experience came accuracy.

He is a sprinter to the crease, with light toes that barely scuff the turf. He has based his bowling on a still head, an upright body and a loose wrist which controls his swing. He is revered by umpires, who call it a joy to work with him, and feared by batsmen, who are confused by the whiplash of his fast arm and the intensity of his competition.

He commands a different field for each opponent, and takes some time over setting it, and has a memory so good that no tail-end charlie, let alone top-order optimist, can escape his examination.

At his best, he made fun by nominating dismissals, two outswingers 'watch him leave them, skipper', then an inswinger 'and now watch the off stump disappear.' Bingo! Three balls later, with the job done, he would turn to me, grinning, and make a mock yawn to the heavens.

Those who have seen him only in his twilight years can have no idea of his speed or his genius. Vivian Richards believes him to have been the greatest of all fast bowlers and adds: 'He has the biggest heart and the smartest brain.'

Marshall has memories, like all of us, of Headingley in 1984 when his thumb was double fractured and he took seven wickets in the second innings; of his bowling in India and Pakistan where the odds were against his type: of the Shell Shield and of Test match whitewashes; and of a World Cup winner's medal in 1979, though he played only one match in the tournament and was not selected for the final.

Most fondly he recalls the day when he passed Lance Gibbs's 309 wickets to become the most prolific West Indian bowler of all time.

'I was one short overnight and the radio station played a song written in my honour called "Hit It O Macko O Hit It" over and over again. We were playing India in my home town Bridgetown, and finally after lunch Dujon caught Azharuddin from an outswinger. I was overwhelmed with pride.'

This was the stuff of Boycott's 100th hundred at Headingley . . . the stuff of fiction.

His other favourite triumph came with Hampshire's victory in the Benson and Hedges Cup last summer. 'The county won two trophies while I was away touring and that day at Lord's will be my day of greatest joy in 15 years of top-level cricket.'

He will leave us now for Natal and, next summer, the leagues. With him goes the greatest enthusiasm for cricket I have ever known.

If at times on the field he has appeared cold as an assassin it is because his devotion to the game and his team is so absolute, so whole-hearted. But it is his laughter that counts, and that grin and those dancing eyes. From Sydney to Southampton, in Barbados, Bournemouth and Bangalore, Malcolm Marshall has been a man for all seasons: a devil of a cricketer with the kick of a mule.

Thankfully, for all his modern sophistication there is still the echo of the calypso. May it long be so. He has been my greatest friend and staunchest supporter.

I shall miss him desperately.

Daily Telegraph
1993

Viv Richards

HUGH McILVANNEY

It was a time for going against the tide. While more than 50,000 of the country's most committed football supporters flooded towards one Old Trafford, magnetised by Manchester United's leadership of the First Division, about 1500 of us straggled willingly into the neighbouring premises of the same name to watch Lancashire and Somerset play a bit of cricket.

Our choice, last Monday afternoon, was much less eccentric than it may have appeared. Vivian Richards was due to bat and that is something he is capable of doing better than anyone else on the planet.

The setting – spectators scattered in chilled, huddled handfuls around acres of seating under stubbornly threatening clouds – was scarcely calculated to galvanise the spirit. But greatness does not require a quorum. When he came to the crease, his juices were flowing and the tiny audience was treated to one of the most memorable experiences in the whole of contemporary sport: a bravura (i.e. characteristic) century by Viv Richards.

It is unnecessary to report that many of the shots that took the recently appointed captain of West Indies beyond a hundred for the sixth time this season (he scored a seventh century three days later to strengthen his position at the top of the batting averages) were breathtaking. Some of the 11 fours in his 120 clattered into the boards almost before the bowler's arm had completed its motion and more than one of his five sixes soared away from a swing of the bat so fluid and flawlessly timed, so outrageously relaxed, that the power imparted seemed slightly eerie.

Yet neither the glittering details of a single innings nor the cumulative wonders he has fed into the record books during the long decade of his pre-eminence in cricket can adequately explain the full effect that Richards at his best has on those fortunate enough to be on hand as witnesses.

Of course, a dramatic physical presence is part of it. A man standing an inch under 6 feet and weighing upwards of 13 stone might be expected to look bulkily, perhaps ponderously solid, but in him grace is as basic as breathing. Just watching him walk slowly to the wicket can be more of a thrill than seeing other famous sportsmen at the height of their performances.

His demeanour at such moments has been described as insouciant but regal might be nearer the mark. The downward curve of the fine nose, the level gaze, the wide, expressive mouth within the handsome beard – all combine to indicate that if he ever went after the role of an emperor, the price of the second-favourite at the audition would be 33–1 and drifting.

Still, even when his looks, his sense of theatre and his dazzling technical brilliance are taken into account, the extent to which Richards can electrify his audiences, the way he can stir responses only rarely touched by sport, remains extraordinary. Maybe the best attempt we can make at identifying the extra factor involved is to suggest that he is a remarkable example of a man able to channel a great deal of a large and intense nature into the playing of a game.

All great sportsmen, once in the arena, make statements about themselves but few achieve the eloquence, the vehemence or the depth of declaration that comes from Richards. When he is in action, you have the feeling that you are being addressed by a big spirit and had better pay attention.

The potency of his aura certainly does not diminish at close quarters. One distinguished cricket writer admits to being enfeebled by extreme nervousness at the mere approach of Richards, even when the Antiguan's mood is obviously benign. It's not just that he exudes the kind of challenging strength that makes the contrived machismo of other athletes come across like the currency of a primary school playground. His capacity to make those around him crave his approval is out of all proportion to his own remarkable prowess.

When Ian Botham, with whom he has sustained a long and genuinely deep friendship rooted in mutual affection, admiration and spontaneous rapport, said that he did not seriously consider playing cricket in South Africa because he wouldn't have been able to look Richards in the eye, the chances are that Botham was speaking literally.

Richards does not vociferously condemn those who have been part of compromising expeditions to Mr Botha's *laager*, insisting that each individual must answer to his own conscience. As West Indian captain, he has carefully stayed quiet on the Graham Gooch case and its threat to England's winter tour of the islands, refusing to be drawn when his friend Lester Bird, the Antiguan Foreign Minister, articulated the possibility that Gooch's attitudes would make him unacceptable as a tourist.

The definite impression is that if last week's avowal by Gooch of strong opposition to apartheid clears the way for the Essex man to visit the West Indies, that will please Richards, for it did not take the events of Thursday and Friday at The Oval [Gooch made 196 and David Gower 157 against Australia] to place Gooch and Gower at the head of his personal rankings of outstanding English batsmen. And when he and his team go into battle on their own turf, they don't want any favours in the shape of weakened opposition.

His consistent view is that cricketers who have been drawn from the rest of the world to entertain in South Africa, especially fellow West Indians who have yielded to the blandishments and financial lures, have been systematically 'used'.

'Knowing what the South Africans really think of our people, do you imagine they would offer us that sort of money if everything was right with them?'

His face darkens and he shakes his head in dismissal of the ludicrous thought. Then, suddenly, the frown is swept away by an irresistible smile, the kind that might register on a light metre at a range of 100 yards. 'Of course, our talents are worth more than they could ever pay – but it's not appreciation of our worth that makes them dangle that money in front of us.'

The fact that his century on Monday was followed by a relentless drip of frustration in the field throughout Tuesday as Lancashire progressed to a comfortable victory might have made complications for an interviewer.

But he was as courteous as he was fascinating and the ultimate effect on a scribbler with a fair amount of mileage on the clock was a profound sense of having been privileged to keep such company. Boxing, and a shared respect for the pride and dignity Joe Frazier brought to that rough old pursuit, gave us a good start.

When I first toured India and Pakistan with the West Indies in 1974–75, I remember that in supporting Frazier against Ali I was outnumbered about 17–1 but I didn't mind. Ali was great but Joe, with his big disadvantages in height and reach, had to be very brave and very special to do what he did. I believe in people who put all their heart into what they do and Joe was like that. I used to feel, 'Here's my man, going out to do a job, to give it his best shot.' They might beat him but they could not break him.

The empathy with Frazier, which has combined with a noticeable facial resemblance to give Richards a series of dressing-room nicknames that are variations of Smokin' Joe, has a first-hand basis. In his teens Richards boxed for his neighbourhood in St John's, Antigua, competing with boys from surrounding districts.

'I still spar a lot at the local gym when I go home to Antigua. It gets rid of my frustrations and it helps me to keep fit. I swim too. We have a lot of wonderful beaches. I hate jogging or running for miles, so I like to swim or go to the gym. I believe in burning up the little bit of energy I do possess. Hitting the heavy bag is comforting.'

His aggression has not always found such innocuous outlets. As a young footballer (he actually preferred that game until an ultimatum from a Leeward Islands cricket official abruptly clarified his thinking) his rumbustious activities in the back four caused him to be known as The Bull.

'I was inclined to take things into my own hands, to go for a little bit of physical stuff,' he says, grinning at the memory. Looking across at the relaxed sprawl of his wide-shouldered body, in which what he calls his beef is kept hard and flexible by a daily programme of exercise that includes about 70 sit-ups and 40 press-ups, it was easy to sympathise with The Bull's opponents.

At that moment, dressed in the whites that always heighten his glow of fitness, with an unextravagant glint of gold on one finger of his right hand, at the wrist and at his neck, he was the picture of a successful young athlete at ease with the world. But his fierce pride in himself and his people can release an element in his personality that is positively volcanic.

'I don't stand rubbish from no one,' he said quietly on Tuesday.

A man has to approach me the right way, then I think I can be fair and decent to anybody. But don't come and put rubbish on me, man. I won't stand that shit from no one. I have lost my cool on numerous occasions and I haven't always regretted it. I was not sorry for what I did on the last West Indies tour of Australia.

There was a bad taste about that series. People like Geoff Lawson were behaving like school kids. There were racist remarks and some of our guys were badly hurt. It couldn't go on. Eventually Allan Border was involved and Graeme Wood and Steve Rixon, though Geoff Lawson was at the centre of it. In the last Test at Sydney in January somebody said something to me and I totally went wild. I said, 'No use we talk about it here in the game. After the match we can sort this out.'

I was waving and making a lot of rude gestures and some nasty words came out. I took plenty of stick from the Australian crowd and the Press but I felt better afterwards. I had to make them aware that we are not idiots. The trouble was serious.

We were just waiting for one Australian to get out of hand
again and everything would have turned loose. That's how bad
the guys felt.

His anger then was thoroughly understandable but less explosive
natures are alarmed by the scale of the rage that can be detonated
by the conviction that he has been given out unjustly. It led to
him being banned for two years as a teenager in Antigua and while
on tour in India as vice-captain of West Indies in 1983 what he
did to a dressing room instantly became a legend.

'I didn't get any runs in the first match and I wanted desperately
to do much better in New Delhi,' he recalled. 'I was going really
well until this ridiculous decision put me out. When I got back to
the dressing room all the lunches were laid out and I chucked the
bat and the first pot it hit had curried mutton in it, or something
like that. All hell turned loose.'

In spite of the serious implications that attended the outburst,
he cannot remain solemn when he remembers the curry-splattered
scene. The rich voice breaks into a staccato laugh.

However, there is no doubt that captaincy of his country will
make him more than ever determined to offer the right example
in vital areas.

I always want to behave the way a man should, not to do
anything cheap. It is true that in the West Indies you're
expected to be more than just an exceptional player. You're
expected to present yourself in a particular way, the way you
have known since you were a kid in the islands, with the natural
panache that means so much in a place where the cricket is so
important.

His people, he convinces you, could never settle for any mathe-
matical representation of greatness in a cricketer. True heroes like
Sobers and Worrell had to fill the mind with glorious memories.
The Richards career, brimming though it is with stunning statistics,
will surely survive in the end as a parade of unforgettable images.

He has his own varied pantheon of heroes, from Nelson Mandela to Frank Worrell to Bob Marley, and he is as loyal to the ideals they embody for him as he is to those nearer to his everyday experience who have an affinity with the emotional essence of his nature.

Botham is one, and another was Peter McCombe from Airdrie who befriended Richards in the lonely early days at Somerset and had become as trusted as a brother by the time he died of a heart attack in Antigua last year.

Richards says he would never disown a friend and will certainly never turn his back on the many men who grew up with him and are now Rastafarians. 'These people are a lot cleaner in their hearts than most who criticise them, and they are and always will be part of me. I believe totally in a friend.'

He believes also in his obligations to the mass of ordinary West Indians in this country. 'So many of them work in lowly jobs and when we do well on the field they can walk a little taller, and hold their heads up. Whether I'm batting, bowling or fielding, I cannot feel satisfied unless I give every ounce to try and make them proud of me.'

For some time the wonderful eyes that he reveres as the greatest of his God-given gifts have been susceptible to inflammation from a condition akin to cataracts. He bathes them religiously with an assortment of lotions and balms to keep the problem in check.

Vivian Richards, now 33, long ago realised that he had to do a great deal more than look out for himself and his family.

Observer
1985

Brian Lara: Master of the Universe Must Survive Bonfire of the Vanities

ROBIN MARLAR

At 26, Brian Lara has become the most important figure in world cricket. The game may have provided him with a platform for fame and fortune, but cricket needs assets like Lara and it is no exaggeration to assert that its popularity into the 21st century depends on his continuance as a colossus.

Ironically, there was a greater chance of an orderly progression when that career was motoring along nicely early in 1994. Since the turbo was switched on and Lara gave the world the most exhilarating eight weeks of batsmanship in the history of the game, a return to something more sober has evidently become problematical.

What a record-breaker! Highest individual innings in Test history, highest in first-class history, six centuries in seven innings: all these have to be put in the context of the man's scoring rate, 5.5 runs an over, which by itself propelled Warwickshire to the championship.

Since his childhood in that beautiful Santa Cruz jungle valley behind Port of Spain, where the orchid farm is to be found and where the late lamented Jeffrey Stollmeyer brought up his family, Lara has been recognised as a special talent inside his family and beyond. He had, and hopefully still has, as his own cricketing guru Joey Carew, himself a Test opener and a pillar of the Queen's Park club, Trinidad's version of the MCC. It was after visiting an unwell Carew that Lara had his kit stolen last year.

Lara's main gift is a beautiful pair of feet, so quick and sure, the source of his uncanny balance. His eyes seem to give him a faster printout of the ball's pace, line and length than his peers. That creates its own current of envy. The man is just so good, so unreachably good.

Furthermore, he has brought to the game his own originality, strokes played behind square on the leg side, played with wrist and draw so that the bat lingers longer on the ball, sending it even faster to the boundary. It's almost a century since Ranjitsinhji revolutionised batting by inventing the leg glance. Lara is the latest pioneer of the art of safely using the pace of the ball to make runs in those fertile areas behind the stumps. He is an immaculate steerer through the slips.

Of course, the instinct to compare Lara with left-handers who have gone before is as irresistible as it is irrelevant. Think of all the individual variations. Hitherto, Sobers and Pollock have been inseparable as complete players among the left-handed. When it comes to mighty boomers, Clive Lloyd stands alone. Many southpaws seem either elegant or pugnacious, members of the Woolley–Gower school of creamy batting or durable coves like Leyland and John Edrich, who would never wittingly sell themselves short. The Australians have had a string of highly effective left-handed openers: Morris, Lawry and now Taylor. Lara's own boyhood hero was Roy Fredericks, who can still hook Dennis Lillee in his sleep, and although from a different tradition, Alvin Kallicharran's lightness of foot and touch are reflected in today's star.

Perhaps closest is the Australian Neil Harvey. Like him, Lara seems to display vulnerability at 22 yards, to be giving the bowler a chance precisely because he does not look like a strong character determined to dominate.

For both, any bowler's error, even by a whisker, would mean four runs. No offering is wasted. Like Lara, Harvey's square-cutting turned fielders into statues. With more spin bowling, Harvey chasséd down the wicket a lot but then at Headingley so did Lara. What both these fine players convey is excitement, watchability, the desire for more which leads to the kind of reverence that can turn a head.

Of course there are still batting targets for Lara to hit. That 277 at the SCG in 1992, which so impressed Rohan Kanhai, the West Indies team manager, and confirmed Lara's status as an incipient great, now stands with that record-breaking knock in Antigua. However, Bradman has not two but five entries among the highest Test innings.

There are other cricketing targets. Soon Lara, who has skippered West Indies at youth level as well as Trinidad, is likely to be elevated to the West Indian captaincy. He has to work out for himself how he will knock the Australians off the top perch. He is going to need some new bowlers and batsmen to do that.

All the signs of a glittering future after cricket are in place. It's the lack of that which has driven so many great players to despair, even suicide. The Trinidad government, beset with difficulty in a country riddled with crime, made a shrewd move in providing Lara with a home, even if they did overlook the remnants of the Obeah Man in the corner of the property. Of all the islands in the Caribbean, Trinidad is the most cosmopolitan and, as the home of Carnival, a fun place to be which ought to be more at ease with itself than is the case. Already, through Learie Constantine, the tradition has been established that cricketers and politics can mix. Lord Constantine finished his career in the diplomatic service and there never was a more popular representative in London.

It is a happy accident that the manager of the present team, Wes Hall, has followed that particular path in Barbados and made a success of it. Hall has come a long way from his early start as a messenger boy for Cable and Wireless.

If all this looks imaginative and rosy, then Lara has to be aware that the path is narrow, the sides steep and rocky. He said that his father, who died in 1988, saved him from some teenage troubles. Other great West Indian cricketers have succumbed to the attractions of alcohol, fast women and slow horses. The temptations for Lara are all the greater because he has achieved financial security unimaginable in the days of the three Ws.

Now his temperament is to be tested. At Headingley, Hooper's early dismissal brought Lara to the crease in a state of unreadiness reminiscent of Compton: how wonderful, therefore, that the first steps of a bowler created such a cocoon of concentration, such determination to wrest the initiative by playing strokes. The first sign that he's winning will be how he fares with the bat on this tour. He's averaging 62 in Test cricket, and will, if he's wise, not let that figure slip.

Sunday Times
1995

I Saw the Brisbane Tie

JACK FINGLETON

Let agnostics scoff if they wish, but do not disbelieve that divine providence, with Dr Grace the likely chairman of the advisory committee, did ordain and control those tumultuous last minutes of play at Brisbane last Wednesday. No earthly cricket mind could have thought up such a fantastic finish. If presented in fiction, publishers would have spurned it beyond human credibility.

Wesley Hall had to win or lose the Test in that last over he started at six minutes to six. I saw him walk back slowly to his mark, fingering a cross on a chain he wears around his neck, and I could well imagine him saying a prayer: 'Lord, please, a miracle. Yet not one, but at least three. Please, O Lord.' He stood poised on his mark, giving his sleeve its last roll and taking huge gulps of air into his lungs for the final fling. Hall, with the new ball, was Worrell's final gamble, and what a hopeless one it seems at the last over. Australia three wickets in hand: six runs to win.

With 12 overs straight for four wickets for 38 runs earlier in the day, Hall had broken the Australian batting. Surely spinners on this fifth day could give the *coup-de-grâce*. But they could not, and Worrell sought more of Hall after they had failed. Hall, however, was tired, and Worrell, most wisely, took him off quickly. He kept him for the final gamble with the new ball when Australia would need some 30 or so to win.

Hall came on at 206. His first over did not suggest he could do the job. He bounced one at Davidson, which that noble hero pulled ferociously for four. The game looked over.

Diminutive Joe Solomon who, like Ramadhin, plays with his

sleeves down, set the scene for the final over when he threw David-son out from 12 yards away and side-on. Grout blundered when he scurried for a single from Sobers' seventh ball, because this left him ripe for execution at Hall's end in the final over of the day and match.

That was provided Benaud did not get a single from the final ball of Sobers' over. Benaud meant to: Sobers never pounded a ball harder on a length than he did and some seven fielders galloped in on Benaud to cut off the single. It is history now how Hall hit Grout in the midriff and doubled him up, and how Benaud, with-out calling, charged to take a single from the unsuspecting West Indies with the ball in the very block-hole. And how Benaud got the strike. And how Hall got him very next ball with a thunderbolt that shot from the pitch and tempted Benaud's bat up with it for the tickle to Alexander. And how Grout, with a dazzling flash of genius, called Meckiff for a run when the ball went through to the keeper.

And how Grout, attempting the winning boundary, spooned it some 50 yards into the air and how Kanhai, with his all under the catch, saw Hall go over his head in Australian Rules football fashion, and muff the catch.

Negligently, the grass in Brisbane had not been cut for some days. An important point, because Meckiff's soaring hit to leg – Grout got a single from the missed catch – would have gone into the fence. As it was Hunte gained on it like an Olympic sprinter. From a full 100 yards away he wheeled and sent a low throw – a superlative throw – straight to Alexander who took it and hurled himself at the stumps as Grout dived for the line like a wing-threequarter at Twickenham.

This would have been the winning run. The two tied the game.

With a tremulous Kline to bat, Hall poised himself again, gulp-ing and gulping in the air before he began his flying intimidatory run. Meckiff ran full tilt and Solomon, with only one stump show-ing from square-leg, hit it from 10 yards. Nobody could get up for the throw-in. Solomon had to hit the stumps.

Worrell was the ideal skipper. He kept his men cool when some looked like boiling under the pressure. This game, of course, has set an impossible standard. It has created, too, some insufferable bores – I am one – who will prate as long as they live 'I saw the Brisbane tie.'

The Oblivion of Eddie Gilbert

DAVID FRITH

The Queensland Aboriginal cricketer Eddie Gilbert, famed for his bursts of express bowling during the 1930s, had not been heard of for so long that I took it upon myself when in Brisbane to track him down.

An old-timer in the suburb of Red Hill, where Eddie was last seen, thought he had died about five years before. We checked in the general store run by a cricket fan of some 60 summers: 'I'd just about swear to it. Old Eddie went right out of circulation and we never heard nothin' of him for ages. I reckon he must've died 10 years back at least. They had him in Goodna for a while.'

I drove out to the psychiatric hospital along the Ipswich Road in the hope of establishing the truth of the matter. The superintendent, barely concealing his surprise at my questions, led me through to the records office, where he produced Eddie Gilbert's hospital history card. 'Eddie was admitted on 8 December 1949. His age was shown as 37.'

I thought he would have been slightly older than that; perhaps the paperwork was completed hastily that sad day. 'If you're writing about him,' the superintendent volunteered, 'I can tell you a few things. He took six wickets in his last game for Queensland. Terrific bowler – only ran half a dozen steps. He got the knack from boomerang throwing. Some reckoned he chucked, but I never thought so. It was just his funny wrist action. Wish we had somebody like him right now.'

Some weeks earlier Bill Hunt, the prewar New South Wales player, had been in no doubt about it: 'Eddie threw *me* out! By cripes, yeah! And later on I deliberately did the same to him. And d'you know what he said? I'll tell you, he put his arm round my shoulder and said, "Well bowled, Bill. That was a beauty!" So you see, the little fellah couldn't tell a bowl from a chuck anyway! Nice chap, but . . .'

It was Hunt's contention that Stan McCabe, whose name will live for his three classic Test innings, considered his best hand to have been a 229 not out against Queensland at Brisbane in 1931 after Eddie Gilbert had served Don Bradman with the 'luckiest duck I ever made'. Bowling with horrifying hostility on an under-prepared pitch, Gilbert had New South Wales in ribbons at 3 for 31, with Alan Kippax in hospital after a dreadful blow on the temple from a mistimed hook off Thurlow. At that point McCabe took command.

So long ago. Now here was I seeking to trace the conclusion of a life story. The superintendent glanced up from the history card. 'He was married at the time he came here. Nobody's visited him for ages. He used to be violent occasionally, but he's all right now – no trouble. But he's bottled right up within himself. You won't get him to talk. We've tried everything. He'll never change. Just as well perhaps. If he went out again he'd be back among the plonkies down at the Adelaide in no time.'

'You're telling me he's here – alive?' He nodded. 'As I say, he's completely withdrawn. It's impossible to get through to him. He walks the grounds all day – he's content in his own private world. We've tried to interest him in some kind of recreation. His reflexes are still sharp. But when we put a cricket ball in his hand he just stared at it.'

It came as a shock. Eddie – still ticking after all. Even the locals had seemed so certain. I had fallen into line with them and quietly and briefly mourned their popular hero of long ago, the fast bowler to whom they had bellowed encouragement to 'give Jardine a taste of his own bodyline medicine'.

In *That Barambah Mob*, David Forrest's amusing blend of fact and fantasy, Eddie has already been immortalised: on the top of Henry Stulpnagel's head was imprinted in reverse 'nufactured in

Austra', a living souvenir of a Gilbert bumper. 'When the ball hit the concrete,' he exclaimed, 'she'd smoke!' Mr Stulpnagel also knew why Eddie never became a Test cricketer: 'He made an ape of Bradman, and he was black, and he was born in Queensland, and they didn't like the look o' that whippy wrist of his.'

I made my reverent plea to the superintendent: 'I'd like to see Eddie.'

'It's no use. He won't talk.'

I pressed him. I had to see the historic cricketer. He picked up the phone and asked the attendant at the appropriate wing to 'find Eddie'. We walked across the sunlit lawns, past slumbering patients, small-talk lost in the insistent buzz of insects. The coolness in the outer block was a relief.

Eddie was some time in coming. Sitting in the office, I scanned the grounds through the open window. Suddenly a male nurse was standing at the door and behind him, reluctant to advance, was a thin man in a maroon T-shirt and black shorts. His hair was white and close-cropped, his skin glistening ebony. It was unmistakably Gilbert.

He shuffled into the room, head to one side, eyes averted, impossible to meet. His physique would have been insignificant beside Tom Richardson, Miller or Trueman, yet he was not the midget legend has depicted. Five feet eight, with long arms: the devastating catapult machine he must once have been was apparent.

'Shake hands, Eddie,' his attendant urged kindly. The hand that had propelled the ball that had smashed so many stumps was raised slowly; it was as limp as a dislodged bail. He was muttering huskily and incoherently, gently rocking his head side to side.

'Want a fag, Eddie?' the nurse asked softly. Eddie grunted, watched the cigarette begin to smoulder and puffed at it. His legs, typical of his race, were thin. He turned on them restlessly. He was an outdoor man; a room was a cage. When I asked the nurse if Eddie could write his name for me he coaxed him to pick up a pen. At the end of an agonising minute Eddie backed away, leaving only a tortured 'E' on the paper. His squinting eyes, deep-set and bloodshot, flashed briefly across all of us.

I thought then of what Archie Jackson, Australia's batting genius, had written about Eddie Gilbert in 1933: 'The adulation he has received has not affected his mental equilibrium. Such a player is an ornament to the game; may he continue to prosper!'

Eddie walked off, still breathing his wheezy monotone; he wandered through the meal hall and the last I saw of him was as he drifted, a desolate individual, across the parched grass.

The Cricketer
1972

A Colonial View of the Sward

PAUL SHEAHAN

'Come on' is what I have learned the refined Englishman says in preference to a raucous 'Yeah'. However refined it may be, it almost brought about my downfall in the first game of this season. I had taken what is euphemistically called a 'plunger' in my initial sortie into the world of English social cricket last season and was desperate to get off the mark in 1978.

A colleague here at Winchester took me aside to ask whether I would play for the Common Room in their annual clash with the Winchester Doctors. I readily agreed but was rather taken aback when told that the toss would take place at 6.25 pm! The great day arrived, we won the toss and batted; fortunately we did bat first because by the time the doctors batted it was a case of 'Deep into the darkness peering, long I stood there, wondering, fearing . . .' After a short while I found myself at the crease – 'Come one' as I pushed to mid-on. To my horror, the doctor at mid-wicket appeared like a bolt from the blue and threw down the stumps at my end. A sonorous appeal; a studied rejection; none-too-mild surprise in the opposition camp, as it was a 'needle' game. At the conclusion of the over, one of the doctors said to the umpire, a certain Arthur Kingsbury, a man of fine mettle, 'That must have been close'. With a fairly familiar statement Arthur replied, 'Close! He was out by a mile but I'd come to see him bat!'

The same Arthur Kingsbury exacted his revenge later in the season when the Common Room played the Winchester Staff. I found myself batting with carefree abandon against an attack that was not likely to force the England selectors to reconsider the touring party, on a pitch, let me hasten to add, that was very close to the road and, therefore, within range of a terrace of the staff houses. Circumstances allowed some indiscriminate hitting. Slog number one caused dismay in some quarters: it went through the upstairs bedroom window of the end house. The owner's wife returned home a minute or so later, quite fortuitously, to find a score of grimy little faces – you must pardon the Dickensian allusion, they really do wash well at Winchester College – peering over the fence, shrieking with laughter. She was not amused, understandably, as she had to clear up a myriad of glass slivers in the room.

On the other hand, it brought innumerable benefits to her husband: the recounting of the story has been worth many a pint in the Queen Inn! Slog number two broke a couple of tiles on the roof of the house next door. Next ball brought a stifled appeal lbw to a bat-pad. To the bowler's amazement, Arthur upheld the appeal. As I departed, the bowler made noises to Arthur which cast doubt upon his interpretation of Law 38 (I *think* it is 38) but there was method in his supposed madness. 'My house was next in line!' he confided.

My naivety as a captain was exposed by a certain man whose name was not unfamiliar in these parts. The fixture was with the Broadhalfpenny Brigands and I was to learn that they were very aptly named. The mantle of captain of this erudite gathering of Winchester dons for the game rested on my shoulders and it weighed heavily. Of course I was anxious, a little nervous even. My opposite number suggested that his troops were not overpowering in batting strength and that perhaps we could ease back if wickets fell quickly. I won the toss and, in my innocence, failing to bear in mind numerous Test match disasters and heedless of the fiendish grin on their captain's face, I inserted the visitors. The pre-match advice came wafting back at 28 for 5 so I took heed and the score duly mounted. At 100 for 5, I thought that we ought to put the brakes on but, as invariably happens in these situations, was powerless in the face of two firmly entrenched veterans, one of whom was the Brigands' skipper. As time slipped by and the score neared 150 for 5, I suggested that we had fulfilled our part of the bargain. I was completely floored when he said, 'Oh, I forgot to tell you that Learie Constantine always said, "If you're silly enough to put us in, you get us out"!'

This delightful world of cricket has no parallel in Australia: the social game that is competitive, but never descends to the level of surrogate war, and that is played, apart from this season, in the pastel, filtered light of an English June evening rather than the harsh, uncompromising atmosphere of a burning Australian summer when it is more a feat of endurance than a pleasure to play a game of cricket. Where in the Southern Hemisphere could one play cricket while the spectators partook of strawberries and cream and the strains of a military brass band playing something marvellously melodic carried across the playing field?

Cricket played on pitches that remain relatively docile in the rain – unless 'Deadly' Underwood is playing – rather than the sleeping vipers in the Antipodes that subdue even the stoutest heart in the batting fraternity at the mention of moisture. Cricket played for the 'squire' of Longparish, Johnny Woodcock, followed by a country church service. Cricket played on a south lawn at Blenheim Palace. Is it true that the cricket must cease when the Duke's mallet is seen to wave above the hedge of the croquet lawn? Visits to Arundel Park whose wooded groves surround one of the loveliest grounds imaginable. And so *ad infinitum*.

Perhaps the greatest pleasure that I experienced was the vicarious one of looking after a school team. I had not realised previously that cricket-watching could be such a nerve-racking business. Possibly despite, rather than because of, my coaching, the boys played some very good cricket! How rewarding it would be to see one of them touring Australia in MCC colours or is it now England ones?

One of the really enjoyable games in which I played was the one organised by Vince Broderick, the professional coach at the college and formerly a Northants player of great distinction. Vince rallied many of the past Winchester captains to honour the retirement of the much-loved Podge Broadhurst who *was* Winchester cricket for quite some time. During proceedings I learned that one can rarely get the better of an English pro. At one stage runs were particularly hard to come by in our quest for their total so I caustically remarked to Vince, 'Are you trying to destroy Podge's afternoon by making a draw of it?' Vince's instantaneous retort, 'Looks like it by the way you're playing!' set one smug Australian back firmly on his heels.

They say that you should learn something every time you undertake any activity. If there is one thing that I have learned during the summer it is, to borrow the phrase of a friend, that I could be quite happily laid to rest facing my own bowling!

The Natwest Boundary Book
A Lord's Taverners Australia Miscellany of Cricket
1978

Message from Oz

MARTIN JOHNSON

There were injuries, tantrums, even a Test match win, but in the end, from Brisbane to Perth, there were Aussies with a bigger will to win. Martin Johnson reflects on a tour that left England searching for 'empathy'.

There was an airport scene in Casablanca when Humphrey Bogart, recalling a fond memory in a poignant parting with Ingrid Bergman, said: 'We'll always have Paris'. As Michael Atherton clambered on board today's flight from Perth to London, it is doubtful whether he put his arm around Graham Gooch and said: 'We'll always have Adelaide'. The England cricket captain is no romantic, and is beginning to get the nasty feeling Australia will always have the Ashes.

Losing the final Test match in Perth was, ironically, a good result for England, in that now they can remember their win in Adelaide for what it was. A blip. As Atherton himself said: 'We won in Adelaide after playing moderate cricket for the first four days.' His end-of-term report to Lord's will not dwell on excuses, even for a side so consumed by injury and illness that they consulted every medic in Australia bar the Flying Doctor.

Instead, Atherton believes that English cricket will remain in an international second division until the domestic fixture list and a few yellowing birth certificates are set fire to, placed inside an urn, and stuck on display inside the Lord's museum.

Modern-day Test cricket is not only played virtually around the clock, but with an intensity that means it requires regulation by the equivalent of international policemen. As preparation for a Test match, however, the domestic game is the equivalent of training for the Olympic marathon by taking the dog for a walk. The county championship, despite getting a little closer to Test cricket by being played over a longer distance recently, remains a breeding ground for mediocrity, with too many ordinary players and too many treadmill matches. Compared to his Australian counterpart, the English professional is soft, and never more delighted than when a convenient cloudburst drives him off the field and back to the card table.

England have just completed a 13-month, near non-stop international cycle, while Australia prefaced this series with a two-month tour of Pakistan, and before flying off for a four-Test series in the West Indies next month they are off to New Zealand for a fortnight of one-day internationals.

Yet while England's cricketers were talking yesterday, not surprisingly, about badly needing a rest, the Australians reacted in an entirely different manner. 'Are you playing too much high-pressure cricket?' Mark Taylor, the Australian captain, was asked. 'Certainly not,' Taylor replied. 'I love Test cricket and the fact that England rallied in this series when they were apparently down-and-out after two matches gave us just the kind of hard preparation we need for a much tougher series against the West Indies.'

Likewise, man of the series Craig McDermott, who has bowled for longer spells than any Englishman, mostly on oppressively hot days, was asked what he would be doing during the three weeks he is taking off before the Caribbean tour. The answer was: 'Swimming, cycling, and weight training'. 'Every day?' 'Every day.'

It is an education to watch the way these two teams prepare for a Test match. Australia come close to organising commando drills, while England's practice sessions would not cause a sumo wrestler any great discomfort in the wind and limb department. This has been most apparent in two areas: Australia's batsmen turn singles into twos, while England's turn twos into singles; and Australia's fielders save about 30 runs per day, while England's leak the same amount.

England have a bowling coach whose most obvious contribution is to wander around with a baseball glove on, and to hit balls high into the air for people to catch. They have a team manager who organises practice sessions about as intense as a game of hopscotch, a tour manager who organises the baggage, a chairman of selectors who watched most of the series at home on satellite TV, and a physiotherapist who believes that non-stop county cricket is the reason he has spent most of this tour administering potions and plasters.

At one stage of the tour, the physiotherapist, Dave Roberts, even got a place as an emergency fielder, and England eventually ended up using 22 players after leaving home with 16. In fact, a large chunk of the original party – five of them came home – could well make it to Heathrow to meet them off the plane tomorrow.

If anyone else is planning to greet them, the one you won't recognise is Joey Benjamin, who has been Australia's lowest-profile tourist since Ronnie Biggs popped over to Melbourne after robbing a train. In a team that has been almost impossible not to get into at some stage, Benjamin's tour record is nil Tests, 88 first-class match overs for four wickets, and 11 runs at an average of 2.2. Since the first week of November, he has bowled 80 overs in all cricket on tour, which works out at an over a day.

Test cricket, Atherton said yesterday, is now a young man's game, so much so that he predicted nobody would ever again remain at the top for as long as Gooch. Gooch himself finally recognised on this tour that he was mentally and physically off the pace, and it was his fielding, rather than batting, which ultimately persuaded him to retire.

Atherton himself has had a personally satisfying tour, despite failing in both innings in the final Test match, and only Graham Thorpe scored more runs in the series – 444 to Atherton's 407. Thorpe has also been an outstanding slip fielder, although the second of his two dropped catches in the last Test actually earned

Australia two extra runs when Thorpe, exasperated, booted the fallen leather through extra cover.

Perhaps the most significant role Atherton has played out here, apart from stoically holding the batting together, is the extra steel he has attempted to inject into England's cricket. It is Atherton who has sailed closer to the wind of etiquette than his opposite number, and when he breached convention in Sydney by stealing a single off a ball that had rebounded off his body at the non-striker's end, it was a deliberate, and successful, attempt to wind up the Australian bowlers. McDermott and Co were needled into bowling badly, and Atherton and John Crawley repaired such a hopeless looking situation that England not only got back into the match, but eventually almost won it.

He has been a tough captain, which is a good trait, and is an even more stubborn character than his predecessor Gooch, which is both good and bad. He will not, for example, easily backtrack on personal judgements, possibly as a consequence of being talked out of playing the younger Crawley in favour of Gatting (whom he did not want on the tour in the first place) for the first Test in Brisbane. As a result, the player he regards as his trusty lieutenant, Steve Rhodes, continued to bat up the order despite the fact that he could barely score a run. Rhodes' 39 in his final Test innings more than doubled his runs in nine previous visits to the crease, and as England were 27 for six when he arrived, it hardly counts as delivering when it matters.

Atherton also decided to trade over-rate fines for slowing down the game tactically when he needed to, which all captains do, but he is generally a chivalrous and fair-minded opponent, as he demonstrated when walking off the field on the fourth evening in Perth with his team 27 for five. He suddenly turned around and walked back several yards to shake hands with Australia's young century-maker Greg Blewett, and it was an indication of how much less animosity there is between the sides since Allan Border's departure from the captaincy.

The current Australian captain, Taylor, is a breath of fresh air after Border, who was an essentially nice bloke but decided – after years of Australia losing – that he would turn nasty in order to win. If the volatile Shane Warne had not inherited Taylor as captain, a large chunk of his sizeable spin-off earnings would now be sitting in the International Cricket Council's fines account. Under Taylor, even Ian Healy and Steve Waugh, who under Border had legendary reputations for the brand of verbal intimidation known as sledging, have cleaned up their act. 'I can't remember anyone sledging me at all in this series,' Atherton said. 'Australia are a good side, and under Mark Taylor, they play the game in the right spirit.'

Atherton's ambition now is to be able to captain a team as competitive as Taylor's, and that, he believes, will take more than changing the county system and kicking out a few grey hairs. He spoke yesterday about a 'lack of empathy and unity' in the squad, which was Gooch's lament on the previous Ashes tour here in 1991.

What we can glean from this is that one or two players will not be receiving glowing tour reports. Australia keep on winning because they are proud to represent their country. Sadly, some of our lot play for their country because they get paid for it. Until that attitude changes, whatever cricket's authorities do – revamp the county championship, disqualify everyone old enough to need a shave or zip around the field on roller skates – won't matter a hoot.

Independent
1995

Shane Warne

CHRISTOPHER MARTIN-JENKINS

People tend to forget prophecies which fail to come to pass but for spot-on prediction Bobby Simpson's assessment of Shane Warne, made at Worcester well in advance of his matchwinning performance in the first Test at Old Trafford, was almost biblical: 'He'll turn the ball from the first ball of every Test. He's the best leg-spinner of twenty-three I've ever seen.' It was because Warne turned the first ball he bowled at Manchester two feet to bowl a dumbfounded Mike Gatting that England got into a mental as well as technical tizzy against him. If David Gower, not Gatting, had received it, it might have given him a nasty shock, but it would have been very unlikely to have bowled him. Facing Warne out of the rough in the second innings would not have been easy, but neither would Warne have enjoyed having to switch his line, aware that a left-hander pushing well forward would be unlucky to be given lbw, but that to anything pitched straight far more shots would be available than for right-handers.

That England's selectors, well briefed about Warne's prodigious power of spin, should have seen all this in advance does not concern me here. The potential for Warne to lead a wholesale revival of the art of wrist-spin round the world over the next ten years certainly does. When Ian Salisbury becomes a regular member of the England attack, which, with luck, he should and will, four of the nine Test-playing countries will be including young leg-spinners. Sri Lanka should be able to find one with the ease that England once whistled up fast bowlers from the mines, and South Africa, New Zealand, Zimbabwe and even the West Indies will be earnestly on the look-out for themselves. For batsmen from all these countries, the wrist-spinner, as in England, causes chronic unease borne simply of complete unfamiliarity with the art. We all fear the unknown.

Warne and Salisbury are both twenty-three, Anil Kumble and Mushtaq Ahmed both only twenty-two. Each has different qualities but none gives the ball such a vicious rip as Warne does, and with his blond hair ('not so much of the peroxide, mate, it's natural', he says) and diamond-studded ear, he should attract the young. He may look a playboy, and off the field he has certainly enjoyed himself on the way to being a national hero, but he is intelligent, as his sparing use of the googly and the other variations – top-spinner and flipper – shows. Against Graeme Hick at Worcester he refused to bowl anything but leg-breaks, preferring, apparently certain of his Test place, to plant doubt in Hick's mind about the major matches even as Hick was cracking him to all parts of the ground on the way to 187.

For sheer ability to turn the ball, Warne has probably had no equal since 'Chuck' Fleetwood-Smith, who started life as a fast right-armer but became famous as a left-arm googly bowler. The England leg-spinner Ian Peebles wrote of him: 'Fleetwood-Smith spun the ball tremendously, more than anyone else I can think of, and bowled a very good "boosie". His trouble was, not unnaturally, lack of control, but on his day he could be all but unplayable to all but the highest class.' Peebles recalled how in the match against Victoria in 1923–33, Wally Hammond was commissioned to go out and destroy him. He did so and Fleetwood-Smith was not picked for another three years. A pity for England that Hick's onslaught did not have a similar effect.

One reason is that Warne does not lose control as often as Fleetwood-Smith, or give the batsman respite with a frequent bad ball as Salisbury is still inclined to do. The West Indians noticed a big improvement in this respect during last winter's series in Australia and Carl Hooper says he has 'come on in leaps and bounds' even since the end of the Australian season. 'The tours of New Zealand and now of England are obviously doing him good,'

Hooper says. 'When we played him in an early match before the Tests he lacked control and gave us a few too many loose ones. But he bowled very well in Melbourne (1–65 and 7–52) and I was very impressed with what I saw on the television from Old Trafford. I don't think I've ever seen anyone turn the ball more, but he's not too difficult to read. We were lucky to have a couple of left-handers against him; especially Brian Lara who never let him settle – down the pitch to drive or back to pull or cut. I think England's batsmen are lacking a little bit of confidence at the moment.'

Just a little. They were warned – no pun for once intended – by no less a batsman than Martin Crowe, following Australia's tour of New Zealand in which Warne took 17 wickets in three Tests – that he was something special. Crowe's advice, conveyed via Dennis Amiss to Keith Fletcher before Old Trafford, was that he is unusual in that he makes the ball turn across the right-handed batsman, often from outside leg stump, rather than pitching middle-and-off or off stump like most of his kind. Forewarned or not, Gatting was taken aback by the first ball he bowled – who would not have been? – and although by the second innings the England batsmen had worked out that they could safely put their pads to anything pitched in the same area, Warne was already varying his line better and a ball pitched outside the off stump was not necessarily the googly. Graham Gooch played him with the greatest confidence, but even he did not always get it right and it was worrying that Hick played him better in the first innings than he did in the second.

Warne was brought up in an expensive Melbourne suburb on the sea and says that although he preferred Aussie Rules football at first, 'by the age of sixteen my ambition was to play cricket for Australia'. He won a scholarship to the Adelaide Cricket Academy (government financed) and prepared for life there by playing league cricket in Bristol, acquiring such a taste for English pub fare that he put on two stone. The Academy coaches thought he was a spoilt boy and sacked him but he played his first match for Victoria in 1991 and spent the following summer at Accrington in the Lancashire League.

He had played only five first-class matches and taken only fifteen wickets when the Australian selectors picked him to play against India in the Sydney Test of January 1992. Shades of the England selectors choosing Douglas Carr, the mystery googly bowler, at the age of thirty-seven in his first season in first-class cricket, to play against Australia in 1909. Carr took three prime Australian wickets in his first seven overs and seven in the match but did not play for England again. Warne, after chastening figures of 1 for 150 against India, was given a second chance at the Academy by Rod Marsh, gave up the beer, started early morning running, swimming, gym-work and boxing and lost 28 lb. He also spent the winter practising his bowling art with another ex-larrikin leg-spinner, Terry Jenner.

Picked to go to Sri Lanka last August, Warne took 3 for 0 with his last eleven balls to win a match Australia had looked certain to lose. In all three of the games his country has won since – against the West Indies at Melbourne, New Zealand at Christchurch and England at Old Trafford – he has been outstanding. As Simpson says: 'He is proving to youngsters that leg-spin isn't old fashioned.'

Leg-spinners often become less effective once they become familiar but the England batsmen need to sort him out soon if the beaming face of 'Hollywood' Warne is not to be the very symbol of Australian success this season.

Daily Telegraph
1993

Brearley v Thomson

MIKE BREARLEY

The first thing most cricket followers ask me is what it is like to bat against such out-and-out fast bowlers as Holding, Roberts, Daniel, Lillee, Pascoe and Thomson. My short answer is 'exciting'. The adrenalin is pumping, you are alert and, as Dr Johnson said about the man who faces hanging 'it concentrates his mind wonderfully'.

Thomson was bowling with more hostility that second innings at Old Trafford then he did all summer – angrily, as if expressing all the frustration of a side about to lose in England for the first time in fourteen Tests.

He looked hostile, too. He's known as 'Two-Up' among the Australian players, because at times he has given two fingers to the crowd.

Coming in only a few minutes before close of play both hinders and helps a batsman. The most dangerous part of an innings is when you start and, over two days, you obviously start twice. On the other hand, you can see the end, you know how long you have to stick out. I don't mind going to the crease after a long time in the field, however, because I'm relaxed and play a bit more freely because of it. If I could trust my body more, let it go more, I often think, I might do better.

I took middle-stump guard, as I do every innings. I then looked round the field. Thomson, whom I didn't face until the last five balls of the evening, had brought up everybody except fine leg. With that attacking field, if he did pitch it up, which he would have to do every now and again, I knew if I came into the ball firmly there would be some ones and twos to be had.

I looked especially for the short leg because for a certain ball, one about middle-and-leg that bounces high, there is a danger of being caught at short leg. It is important to know that if short leg is just in front of square, you can get out of trouble at the last moment by turning the ball behind square, which I had just done to a delivery from Max Walker.

I then tick off a few check-points of my stance, though rather less meticulously than some golfers such as Jack Nicklaus or, I'm told, Graham Marsh, whose brother, incidentally, was a full sixty feet behind me. Is my head upright? 'Keep your head still.' Are my hands holding the bat easily?

I hum to ease the tension. I like to let musical themes run through my head and my favourite is the cello passage from the opening of the first Rasoumoffsky Quartet. I use the music like a talisman: how can I ever be out with this tune running through my head? I was comfortable. It was cool that evening and my helmet wasn't sweaty and my chest-protector, a pad nine inches square, felt snug.

Thomson reached his mark: he glared. I stopped humming. I replaced it with a different theme – 'take it easy, you'll see him soon enough' – and he started in. I have never seen him come in from such a long run-up, about fifty yards. I don't like to concentrate on a fast bowler until he is well into his run-up, perhaps half-way, because you get over-impressed by his power and speed and become mesmerised. As he approaches the wicket, I stand up and lift my bat high.

Thomson's unusual catapult-like action makes it sometimes hard to pick up the ball early. At Old Trafford the screens are better than on any other Test ground, and I cannot remember having difficulty seeing the ball. As he delivers the ball, I move a little on to the back foot. This movement gives me a fraction of a second longer to react, and it does not prevent me from coming forward into the ball if it is pitched up.

One thing that gives me pleasure is playing a fast bowler straight back down the pitch. Thomson bowled one to me that was just slightly leg-side, fairly well up, and I played it perfectly balanced,

coming into the ball and it went to mid-on for two. I hit another
ball to cover for two. When play ended that day I had six runs on
the board. I was satisfied.

Sunday Times
Adapted from The Return of the Ashes
1978

Mike Brearley

SAM MENDES

As a boy, between the ages of about 12 and 15, the walls of my bedroom in North Oxford were plastered with pictures of cricketers. Any image I could find, from a multitude of publications, was carefully cut out and glued (yes, glued) in a vast and permanent collage – such was my certainty that I should never want them removed. Over the bookcase, Derek Randall hooked Dennis Lillee in the Centenary Test; on the wardrobe Geoffrey Boycott on-drove Greg Chappell to reach his hundredth hundred; and Viv Richards flicked imperiously through mid-wicket, above my sink. All these and many others were frozen in poses effortlessly gladiatorial.

With my bat – an over-large size 6, which my mother had promised me I'd grow into (she didn't understand) – I would do my best to mimic my heroes, flailing awkwardly in front of a full-length mirror in the tiny hall. But there was one figure who featured most prominently in my bizarre personal Test Matches – played against the wall of the bedroom with a table-tennis ball – and that was Mike Brearley. It may seem an odd choice, with such a plethora of batting talent at my disposal, but while others chose the pantomime heroics of Ian Botham, or the balletic grace of David Gower, it was the Chekhovian complexities of Brearley that, for some reason, fascinated.

I had first noticed him scratching around for England in the 1976 series against the West Indies, and then scoring a quietly determined 91 for Tony Greig's team in India during that winter's tour. Each innings, however short, was carefully notated in my

Frindall's Score Book, with a red pencil for fours, a blue for sixes and a special 'details of dismissals' section. And when Tony Greig defected to the floodlit arenas of Kerry Packer's cricket 'circus', it was Brearley, to my delight, who was made captain and led England to a famous victory in the 1977 Ashes series.

I loved him for his absurdities: his precarious straight-backed stance, bat held aloft; his tentative footwork and ginger forward prod, and the way he twisted his head round following the flight of the ball from his outside edge into the slips; and for the ridiculous skull-cap he wore while facing Jeff Thompson, which, if one squinted, made him seem totally bald. He was a bag of eccentricities, a non-conformist, and, most importantly, excellent to imitate.

But it was when he led the team out as England captain that shivers were sent down my young spine. From his position at first slip, he pointed, cajoled, chivvied, applauded. He arranged the field like a visual artist or a film director. Sometimes, in the middle of an over, he would jog to the bowler's end, and the field seemed to hold its breath as he imparted some doubtless revelatory piece of advice – it might have been 'keep him tucked up', for instance, or 'look to make him drive'. The mystery merely increased his potency.

He had, I learned, taken some years off professional cricket to do something which involved philosophy or psychology, which further increased his glamour. When interviewed on telly, he talked with an edgy eloquence, like a young don or a political commentator. In my eyes, he could do no wrong. I had even encountered him at a charity match at Westminster School to which my Dad had dutifully taken me. But when my time came to bowl at him in the nets – legs shaking – all I could come up with was a double bouncer which, although it nearly yorked him on the second bounce, didn't elicit the 'well-bowled' that my friend had achieved and I so coveted. Later, I posed next to him for a £2.50 polaroid photograph, standing awkwardly, and holding my bat so that the maker's name was visible. But the camera wasn't held steady and all that emerged was a small blue-anoraked blur next to a rather large whiter one. I blushed as my father complained about the cost.

Looking back now, I flatter myself that I understand more clearly what Brearley's attraction was, and can put it down to more than the star-struck fantasies of an adolescent, would-be England captain. I suppose it was the combination of the natural talent of a sportsman with an unashamed intellectual vigour. And the way he took and moulded a team of wayward lads, explosive talents, and sulky egoists (Botham, Randall, Boycott et al) made him one of the great English team leaders. This, of course, is the sort of job that, subsequently, has been most dreadfully and publicly mishandled. Observe Graham Taylor's handling of Chris Waddle and Paul Gascoigne, or Graham Gooch's of David Gower. or Micky Stewart's of everyone.

One hopes Mike Atherton has it in him, too, but one doubts whether even he would have the courage to grow a bushy philosopher's beard for a tour of Australia, or to have the chutzpah to admit that in order to concentrate whilst facing Jeff Thomson he used to hum a passage from the Rasoumoffsky Quartets, or indeed to describe Botham's great 149 in the Headingley test of '81 as having 'made village cricket respectable'. In the increasingly humourless and cliché-ridden world of professional sport, Brearley really was the best. And in 39 test matches he never scored a century. Now *that* was cool.

'A Life in the Day Of'
Sunday Times Magazine
1994

Michael Atherton: A Monument to Heart and Craft

PETER ROEBUCK

Through the teeming streets of Calcutta we drove, weaving and hooting, waiting for a prang and, instead, surviving a thousand scrapes. England had played four fast bowlers at Eden Gardens, and Ted Dexter was talking about the stars. Respite was needed. Michael Atherton was among the travellers, and the city's most famous film studio was our destination. Not being in the England team, or much in its thoughts, time lay heavy on his hands. A quiet, determined career that had promised so much was in danger of disappointing. Somehow he had been left behind as English cricket lurched between the extremes. Not quite forgotten, not quite remembered, Atherton was in a cricketing purgatory.

It wasn't so long ago. Atherton was not considered bold enough for the 50-over matches either, though as he pointed out (was it wryly or dryly?), he'd been man of the match in his last two. He was somewhat discombobulated. 'There's a lot more inside me – I hope it comes out,' he said. (He'd have been good on the Magic Roundabout – he 'says' rather than growls or barks or whines or screeches, and this anonymity of emotion is the most frustrating part of his captaincy, even to himself.) He felt he had much more to offer.

No longer was this judgment widely shared. They'd put 'God' on his locker at Old Trafford and begun to wonder if the word had been written back to front. There was no outcry against his absence from the national team. Certainly his omission on India's turning pitches surprised those who'd seen him play the spinners in Sydney, waiting for the ball, every ball (he has a constancy about him), never groping, never lurching, never losing patience, a minister calmly answering every question thrown by rabid back-benchers.

But to imagine him as a batsman to set beside John Edrich and Boycott, craftsmen at the top of the order taking the spirit from the new ball with their formidable resources of courage and technique, required a leap of the imagination. He didn't seem a definite enough person. He seemed too detached. Boycott, everybody knew, was impossible, an emperor from a coalfield. Edrich was pragmatism writ large, stylish off the field and punchy on it. Both had heard the call of their natures and responded to it with a stubbornness so absolute that it wore the clothes of charisma. Atherton, in contrast, seemed to flirt with life: a little of this, a little of that. It was hard to get to grips with him.

Hard, too, to imagine such a player leaving his mark on the game. We underestimated him because we yearned for something more – a drama, a colour, a conquest of the humdrum. No longer can Atherton's prowess be disregarded. And now, perhaps, comes the time for readers in Yorkshire to sit down in a comfortable chair with a lighted pipe and a stiff drink. I doubt if Boycott could have matched Atherton's effort at The Oval nine days ago. I doubt if he could have batted as Atherton did in Guyana two winters past, driving Walsh on the rise through cover. He would never have let himself.

Boycott was the superior craftsman, superb against spin, but he was not, dare it be said, a better batsman. He was tough, mean, ruthless, more powerful of stroke and personality yet not much more likely to score runs in good company. Neither was Boycott quite so talented. It had been Atherton's gifts as much as his mind that we misread.

He is England's best technician since Boycott. He is more aggressive than Boycott, and lighter on his feet. He hooks with greater willingness, though the shot is sometimes lifted. Nor is he as haunted; mediocre left-arm seamers could never disturb his equanimity. His sense of the collective, too, is somewhat superior.

To compare Atherton with players of yesteryear is fair because he is, in so many ways, himself a batsman of yesteryear. He might have studied on the rain-affected pitches of the 1960s, surfaces on which position, placement and patience were everything. His feet move further forward or back than most contemporaries, and he plays the ball under his chin in time-honoured fashion. He is, though, more confident than were most batsmen of his sort 30 years ago, and it shows.

Perhaps it is the age. Cricketers of the 1960s were raised in a time of rationing in which every knob of butter mattered. They were not inclined to take risks or bowl half-volleys. Cricket is more entertaining these days, and more aggressive; it is a game of power as much as craft. Atherton manages to be both past and present. To watch him bat is not to know the age.

He is England's best batsman, and his is the wicket West Indies most need to take at Headingley this week. His batting has sprung to life in a manner only sporadically evident in his captaincy. And if England are to prevail, he must lead with the same confident gusto.

As he plans his campaign, Atherton could do much worse than consider the tactics adopted by the Australians in the Caribbean. Last week, an Australian selector listed the characteristics needed if the West Indies are to be beaten. 'Teams must,' he said, 'catch everything, bowl nothing at their legs, refuse to be intimidated and appoint a captain with flair who will not let the game just flow along.'

It is to this fourth requirement that Atherton must turn his mind. His captaincy can be commonplace; he can bring a run-of-the-mill approach to a task demanding distinction, if not distinctiveness. Doubtless he has felt, at times, a callow youth in a hostile world. But he is hardening, and is over the worst. The ball-tampering business always was a lot of rot.

Atherton must bring humility and patience to his leadership, must leave his opinions at the selectorial table. Chairman Illingworth was right about that. Most particularly, he must bring a sense of moment to his captaincy, must see the possibilities in every situation rather than guarding against what might be lost. Fear is England's chief enemy.

Much good has come from Atherton's period in office, and his team seems stronger than it was a year ago. Provided he does not portray himself as a superman and returns to being an honest, capable if occasionally boneheaded fellow, this good work can continue and England will have a chance of beating a team that, if checked, may fade.

Sunday Times
1995

Brave New World for Cricket

TONY LEWIS

The Test and County Cricket Board, which administers first-class cricket in this country, has stretched its pants to ripping point. One foot is cemented in the old order trying to preserve the game's pristine skills in the only full-time professional circuit in the world; the other has been edging forward into the less familiar world of hard entertainment ever since the first one-day competition was sponsored by Gillette in 1963. Lack of income from the game and rising costs is the repeating tale. So just as stately homes have been jazzed up with safari parks and adventure playgrounds which would torment old Capability Brown if he could see them, so county cricket is doing its best to keep smiling even though some fancy cosmetics have been slapped on its face.

Life for the counties is crammed with fund-raising schemes. Last year only three clubs – Leicestershire, Kent and Essex – made profits, and modest ones at that. At this moment the Test and County Cricket Board's chairman, Doug Insole, and its Finance Committee chairman, Edmund King, are completing a report on the financial state of every county club, and will reveal the grisly news during the summer. In 1975 the first-class game will cost £2 million to run, but hopefully, this being an Australian year with four lucrative Test matches ahead, income will exceed that by a little. Yet it is sponsorship which accounts for almost half of the game's income, and overshadowing all the deliberations at Lord's must be the fear of losing some of the extensive television coverage. Unfortunately, the form of cricket devised for a result in one day is a bastardised version of the true art. It places much emphasis on defensive skills – keeping a batsman tied down and waiting for his mistakes. In Test matches played over five days the bowler has to muster the wit and talent to penetrate and take wickets. Only in the three-day County Championship can he work at those skills. Yet even that game has been fitted with a bonus points system to produce an instant climax at the conclusion of the first innings, which comes compulsorily after 100 overs. Experimental laws have been heaped on, many of them intelligently conceived and beneficial, but everyone in the game agrees that too much short-cut cricket is suicidal. Young batsmen develop chancy techniques, and spectators are often ignorant of the game's complexities. The symphonic structure of the old game played by Hobbs and Hammond long ago is disappearing. It has disintegrated into a series of crash-bang overtures. The true intent of cricket needs restating – that one side shall bowl out the other, then go in to bat and try to score more runs. Simplicity itself.

In 1966 a sub-committee was set up under the chairmanship of former MCC tour manager, David Clark. Its terms of reference were 'To examine the future of county cricket in the widest possible terms and, if thought fit, to recommend alternatives in the structure and playing conditions of the County Championship'. The committee faced a choice. Either it was satisfied that a wholly professional game was best for British cricket, or it could turn back and seek salvation in the amateur game. It chose to strengthen the professional set-up, and who is to say it was wrong? Professionals nearly always beat part-timers. The exceptions I recall are Yorkshire and Glamorgan being beaten in Gillette Cup ties by Durham and Lincolnshire, and Northamptonshire losing a Benson & Hedges regional game to Oxford University. The Clark Committee concluded that too much cricket is played by full-timers, and that the game might be missing potentially good players. For career reasons some outstanding cricketers have retired prematurely to commit themselves to more lasting work. Edward Craig, the prolific Charterhouse schoolboy who scored more runs at school than Peter May, his famed predecessor, opted for the academic life at Churchill College, Cambridge, after only six matches for Lancashire. The remainder of his first-class cricket was as an undergraduate at Cambridge, 1961–63, and from 93 innings he scored 3,103 runs at an average of 36.08. The large amount of cricket played excludes the part-timer altogether.

In fact, if that committee was to report now, it would also draw attention to the virtual disappearance of players who are professional footballers in the winter and cricketers in the summer. There used always to be about thirty of them. Now the football season has spread, and first loyalties go to the larger pay-packet. The one man I know who has made a stand for cricket by declaring himself unavailable for football until the cricket season is finished is Chris Balderstone, who plays football for Carlisle and cricket for Leicestershire. The show plods on, sometimes with a limp, nine years after that report.

I could argue that there is humour in the game which does not change; if only it could be communicated to audiences on the boundary's edge! Not all players get the message over like Fred Trueman, who once yelled to me before a full Scarborough Festival crowd after I had mis-fielded off his bowling (Fred knowing that my wife and I ran a new-style boutique in those days): 'Ayup! Pick your bluddy feet up, Mary Quant!' But is there a perfect answer for cricket . . . A Utopia in which everyone can play first-class cricket, as indeed they do through a longer season in other countries, club and Test player shoulder to shoulder; where pitches are good; where money problems are under control? Did the 'Dave Clark Five', as the Clark Committee was cynically called by us professionals, take the right turning? What would happen if we turned to amateurism for a solution?

In the crystal ball I see *town* cricket being as important as *county* cricket. Each weekend, Saturday and Sunday, with a national inter-town league, say in three divisions, two of them on a North and South basis to cut down excessive travel. The professional cricketers would play for their town sides in these two-day matches, not more than four professionals to a club. The remainder would be amateurs. This would break down the exclusion of the part-timer, who would have a chance to prove, by bowling out Geoff Boycott, the Sheffield opener, that his standards could be raised by high-quality opposition. One innings per team over two days would be ideal for restoring proper techniques and nurturing further County and Test players. The County Championship I see as consisting of three-day or four-day matches, on Tuesdays, Wednesdays and Thursdays; 16 matches per team, one against each county. This would be much fairer than the current 20 games, which may afford you the luxury of playing against a weak county twice or, if luck is against you, of facing Andy Roberts of Hampshire in two games instead of one! However, when I look more closely at my crystal, I see no-one playing the county game who would not be free to play for England if chosen! Less cricket, Mr Clark wanted. This way he would have it. Monday and Friday would become free days for the professional, so ending the present chaos of weekend travel. Chaos is hardly too strong a word. The ultimate absurdity was reached by Glamorgan in 1974 when we travelled from South Wales to Buxton, in Derbyshire, for the Sunday match. At two o'clock on the Sunday morning we roused the night porter in the chosen hotel. His first remark – 'You lot ain't booked in 'ere' – we put down to the tetchiness of the insomniac. But within a minute we found ourselves, surrounded by kit-bags and cases, on the public benches in the town centre. An hour later we found beds in another hotel; later that day we threw away a match we were winning. Lack of sleep was no excuse, but neither was it any great help. How the hotel had managed to lose our booking remains a mystery, but it was on that Buxton bench that I determined to campaign to win cricketers a breathing space from the motorway treadmill.

It is a brave revolution that puts one-day cricket in its place irrespective of sponsorship, but just consider the good of cricket and cricketers. If the town and county competitions take place over sixteen weeks, then four whole weeks (not in succession of course) are left for one-day sport. The quarter-finals, semi-finals and final could even be played on Saturdays.

What of the schools, where so much is changing? There is a crying need for better pitches. Former Test selector Jack Bond believes that 'future Test cricketers in this country will come only from public schools, because no-one else has the proper facilities these days and very few care enough.'

Two schools I have visited recently bear this out. Colin Cowdrey took me round his old school, Tonbridge, last summer. The wide expanse of mown grass was inviting; the pitch, plumb and carefully manicured, had the feel of runs and good strokes. Neath Grammar School, now (unpronounceable to most) Dwr-y-Felin Comprehensive School, was where I played my teenage cricket. The school field looked poorly tended. It had been opened up to join the local playing fields. The pitch itself was scarred with white blotches apparently from a wrong dressing administered by someone who did not quite understand. Most people I have met who are connected with comprehensive education agree that team sports decline in such schools if no master interests himself. Off the boys go to the nearest sports centre and practise their archery, table-tennis, swimming and so on. It is a soft option for pupils and staff. Without denigrating those sports, cricket administrators must see the problems clearly and shift the emphasis from schools to local clubs. So they have in part. Four hundred Under-13 teams from clubs have entered this summer's National Cricket Association Competition. Money must go into the clubs and they must care for the schoolboys.

So let us dream that hard cash will rush into the new world of amateur cricket from sports councils, local sponsorship, club contributions and other schemes, and into the professional game from television, major commercial sponsorship, football pools and Test-match games. (Let's dream, too, of Test-match cricketers bowling 18 overs an hour. I can hear Tony Greig splutter: 'Is this the Welsh wizard who pleaded with me to slow it down to 12 in Calcutta?')

The game of cricket makes so many people happy. If only those who followed it avidly in the newspapers paid their county club subscription; and if only those who never missed an action-replay on television tossed 10p through the screen, visionaries like I could sit back in deck-chairs and enjoy it all.

Sunday Telegraph
1975

The Shambles of Things to Come

DENNIS CASTLE

The Brits v Poobasha, first Test at the People's Oval yesterday. By a show of hands in the crowd the Brits batted first. Poobasha had 'blacked' several Brits selected in the original XI for playing against a Dutch team. Going 'dutch' was contrary to union rules. No worker should ever pay for anything. However, the Brits mustered a useful second team which contained the required quota of shopfloor representatives. Art Mule, Battery Hens Controller, North Hove, was, after a recount, elected shop steward for the match. 'There's gotter be money on the table,' he averred, 'otherwise we'll all be out.'

From the pool of umpires at his disposal Ali Money, the Poobasha captain, selected his brother and grandfather, who learned the game by braille. Bill Bard, of Avon, and Blaydon Keel-Rowe, a product of Eton Comprehensive who plays for Tyneside, opened for the Brits, both prolific scorers in the Gripe Water County Championship. They were greeted by a magnificent reception of well-organised aggro, a credit to the sponsors. Empty beer-cans containing pebbles were on sale, as were hooters, cymbals, drums and alpenhorns. Spectators who brought their own whistles and trumpets had them confiscated by the Karate Security Corps on behalf of Boo It Yourself Ltd, who hold the sole UK rights for democratic din in sport. High See High Ltd had provided a giant computerised scoreboard upon which could be illuminated likenesses of both batsmen and bowlers for the edification of citizens who cannot read.

British Steel Co-operative saw to it that the batsmen were helmeted, breastplated and even spurred to tread back on wicketkeepers daring to stand up to the stumps. As the batsmen were wearing red pads, the umpires settled for a green ball. Poobasha objected. In their religion green denoted a yellow streak, so a mauve ball was chosen. The first delivery from Hup Andover, the Poobasha paceman and Kangaroo Court convenor, was predictably a bumper, as befitted a bruise-coloured ball. Bard hooked it into long leg's hand. He dropped it, to be immediately ordered off, given his airline ticket home, while his personal substitute took his place. As the Poobasha manager, Pinta Dude, said afterwards: 'We cannot condone trouble-makers. Our fellows have their mortgages to think of.'

After the first over, in which three runs, two wides and eight appeals had been made, drinks were brought out. Bard and Keel-Rowe at first refused, but, as the managing director of Lime-Panni-Substitute Ltd threatened to withdraw sponsorship, the two Brits reluctantly quaffed their ration. Then, much to the delight of the TV cameramen who enjoy recording such incidents, they spat it out.

An over later play was again held up when the chairman of Notbest Bank announced over the tannoy that the raffle prize of £1 million had been increased to £2 million owing to a sit-in by keepers of the computerised turnstiles in protest at the derisive prizemoney. Their action had now spread to dredgermen at Scapa Flow, who had come out in sympathy. The crowd reacted sullenly. 'It's still peanuts,' said Ken Knuckles, MP for Birmingham Bullring, 'but a victory for our right common sense.'

Poobasha's slow bowler, Pinky Djinn, who used six different coloured balls an over, appealed against Bard for lbw. While the umpire's coat was still being tugged, Bard's probation officer rushed on the field. A fierce argument ensued over the unconstitutional nature of the appeal, which had included the word 'bastard'. On Djinn rephrasing it to 'For . . .'s sake, 'ow's that?' Bard had to go, but warned that he would appeal to the European Court of Human Rights. Poobasha's captain laughed at this. As he said, in his country no European had any rights at all . . . indeed they were not even considered human.

With this success, Poobasha supporters invaded the field to embrace and garland Pinky Djinn. When the field was finally cleared and the stolen stumps replaced, a retired judge in the pavilion said benignly, 'Just their high spirits . . .'

After the next over the Fair Trading Commission held up play again. Complaints had reached them from the advertising agents of Seven-Countries-a-Day Coach Tours, the Yorkshire Pee Bank, Alec Smart – Your Local Cat Mart, Jerry Building Society, The Daily Striker, Fly Zipp Airways and other clients who had noticed that the crowd now spilled over the boundary line and masked their posters from the TV cameras. After a midfield consultation with the ground staff, identifiable by their T-shirts labelled Growmore Seeds, the hoardings were placed in front of the squatters. Even so, it was not long before letters O and D had been split to frame laughing cavalier skinheads.

The graffiti-covered screen caused further delays. 'I like a wheel to sit on when I'm on a trip,' said one mazed youth. He was marched off between two policemen while the crowd sang *You'll Never Walk Alone*. Again, over the tannoy the secretary had to inform spectators of the true purpose of a sightscreen. 'That's utter rubbish,' snorted Dyer Liberty, a full-time strike convenor. 'He's selling us down the river . . . that screen is a whitewash, a cover-up . . .'

Bart Att, East Riding Sidesaddle CC, replaced Bard and now faced Mustapha Snifta, the Poobashian quick bowler. He had been included because the original selection, Kevin O'Nana, professional for Cork in the Potheen League and son of a Dublin barmaid and a Poobashian minaret electrician, was no longer available. In the previous match he had complained about the shape of the new ball, which then exploded in the Eire-born bowler's hand. The IRA, while claiming responsibility, admitted that never in their wildest dreams did they think O'Nana would be given the new ball, at all, at all.

Att and Keel-Rowe continued to suffer from both seam attack and seamier comments from the slips, together with gully's transistor, tuned into high-decibel reggae. Both batsmen knew that they would have to get a hundred apiece if they were to pay for their Rolls and swimming pools in their council estate mansions. If they failed, they would be dropped into penurious obscurity, the fate of many ex-Test players now reduced to lowly village games at a mere thousand quid per half-day match. Sadly Bart Att got a touch outside the off stump. The wicketkeeper dived far to his right to take the catch. At first Bart refused to leave on demarcation grounds. That catch was really first slip's; the wicketkeeper had poached that area. This was an indisputable fact and it looked as if Bart's right of reply (TUC Cricket by-law 12547(d)) would be upheld. However, someone remembered that Bart had an aunt in Cape Town. He was given out.

Back in the pavilion Bart was greeted with cries of 'Scab' and 'This'll cost yer!' He was sent to Coventry and, unable to face that prospect, shot himself in the toilet under the Euthenasia (Firearms) Act. A charity match was immediately organised for the widow, and many stars agreed to turn out if the money was right and free petrol was provided from the takings.

Herd Instinck, Piston Ltd, whose sole job was to turn the scores for the conductor of their brass band, now faced the attack. He played back to an outswinger and got a nick. The wicketkeeper dived and held aloft an orange ball although the bowler had delivered a blue one. Being colour blind, as Poobasha well knew from Herd's many motoring offences, he walked and the fielders hugged and kissed in delight.

The afternoon was heightened by an invasion of the pitch by topless libbers with banners proclaiming 'No More Maiden Overs' and 'Third Man OUT – Third Person IN'. Keel-Rowe, then on 99, had been denied his hundred for an hour by the umpires signalling his every run a leg-bye. The sight of the topless space invaders caused him to retire immediately with cramp. He left the field with a blonde who told him she was a masseuse whose name and phone number were in the flyleaf of every Gideon Bible in Newcastle hotels.

The Brits battled on. Pop singer Des Demona, part-time superstar and lower-order performer for Soho, in the Middlesex Porn

League, was taking guard when the TV producer saw that the player's mouth was firmly set. *He was not chewing!* A cricketer whose mouth was not moving constantly made terrible TV. A temporary-fault card was whisked on the screens while a frantic phone call was made to the pavilion balcony allotted to Lord Molar of Munch, chairman of Goo-Gum Inc. A steward scampered onto the pitch and forced a tablet into Demona's mouth. He choked, fell against his stumps and was given out.

The Brit numbers 7 and 8, Dai A'Deth and Trumbril Black, both of the Coffinmakers Co-operative, got dug in. The Poobasha team had found great difficulty in losing their sun-hats and caps when fielding. The fear of seeming big-headed was such that a fresh supply of much larger headgear was brought out to ensure the convention was complied with.

After tea the Poobasha fielders grew tired and began using rain-making prayer mats. By now only four of the original team were left. The others had conscripted their personal substitutes, leaving themselves free to use the secretary's office phone to place bets on the match. Television commentators had already informed the world the odds against the Brits. This generous act caused each to receive from the bookmakers the gift of a bungalow in North Wales. However, these were burned down during the night by Welshers who hated bookies.

Poobasha's second-string seam bowlers now chose fresh umpires and the two Brits struggled against this four-pronged attack. When Djinn was recalled, both batsmen were so tightly ringed by close fielders that they appealed against the light. This was turned down and almost at once Tumbril was bowled. His complaint that forward short leg had made a flapping shadowgraph butterfly with his hands right on a length was turned down as 'devisive and uncomradely'.

The incident, however, caused conservationists to rush on the field shouting 'Red Admirals and Cabbage Whites for the people, not the killing bottle'.

This statement was misinterpreted by confused brewery barons who now rolled on to the pitch in a protest demonstration. Beer, they slurred, was the bread and butter of cricket. Citizens had a democratic right to get stoned out of their minds at Test matches, sing in their neighbour's ear, or even fall down and vomit. It was their heritage. The chairman of Badbreff's Lager shouted over the tannoy: 'Drink creates employment not only within our hallowed industry but also gives the indolent police something to do.'

This diversion, however, was not heard by radio listeners. This medium's commentators immediately shut their box windows, drew the chintz curtains and, taking time out from Lower Fourth jape anecdotes, informed the listening millions who of their team was going to be mother at the tea table. 'Ah,' ejaculated Pylon Boners, 'chocolate cake! Yummy, yummy.' Unfortunately this remark caused a diplomatic incident at the Poobasha Embassy as, when translated into their language, it meant 'I desire your wife next Tuesday'.

At 5.45 the Poobasha team demanded overtime for working unsocial hours. So, on the instructions from their captain, the umpires consulted their light-meters. One recorded a moving glacier in Greenland, the other an earth tremor in Yugoslavia. It was enough. The players scurried from the field. Stumps were pulled up and hurled to the baying spectators, thus saving the umpires' lives. The ball, hit to the boundary, was pocketed by a young boy who later used it as a cosh knob which, as his counsel told the magistrate, he had to use in self-defence against the 80-year-old lady plaintiff.

Itchy Bondai, the Australian TV commentator, in his late-night round-up, summed up the day's play thus: 'If advertising is the name of the game and is needed to keep the wolf from the door, I've news for you, sport. It's got in and had pups . . .'

Wisden Cricket Monthly
1982